D0358101

Meeting Needs

Meeting Needs

NGO Coordination in Practice

Jon Bennett

with
Mark Duffield
Monika Kathina Juma
John Borton
Alun Burge
Charlotte Benson

EARTHSCAN
Earthscan Publications Ltd, London

The views expressed in the various chapters of this book are solely
those of the authors.

First published in 1995 by
Earthscan Publications Limited
120 Pentonville Road, London N1 9JN

Copyright © Jon Bennett, 1995

All rights reserved

A catalogue record for this book is available from the British Library

ISBN: 1 85383 235 9

Typesetting and figures by PCS Mapping & DTP,
   Newcastle upon Tyne
Printed and bound in Great Britain by Biddles Ltd, Guildford
   and Kings Lynn

Earthscan Publications Limited is an editorially independent
subsidiary of Kogan Page Limited and publishes in association with
the International Institute for Environment and Development and the
World Wide Fund for Nature.

CONTENTS

About the Contributors

Jon Bennett was Executive Director of ACBAR in Pakistan/ Afghanistan from 1990–92, then Director of ICVA's NGO Coordination Programme from 1992–94. Prior to this, he spent 10 years working for a number of NGOs in the Horn of Africa, including Oxfam (where he was Regional Representative in South Sudan and earlier in Tigray, Ethiopia), CAFOD and ACORD. He has published widely on aspects of aid to Ethiopia, Sudan and Afghanistan and was author of *The Hunger Machine* (Polity Press, 1987) and *NGO Coordination at Field Level: A Handbook* (ICVA, 1994). He is now a Research Associate at the Refugee Studies Programme, Oxford University, and an independent consultant.

Monica Kathina Juma is a postgraduate student and lecturer at the Department of Government and Public Administration, Moi University, Kenya. She has previously been a Management Analyst for the Office of the President in Kenya and from 1992–93 was a Visiting Research Fellow at the Refugee Studies Programme, University of Oxford, during which time she undertook the research for the chapter contained in this book.

Mark Duffield has a background in anthropology and political economy. From 1985–89 he was Oxfam's Country Representative in Sudan. He now works for the School of Public Policy at the University of Birmingham. He has published widely and completed a number of major consultancies in the field of complex political emergencies, including recent work for UNICEF. His interests include the nature of war economics, the development and impact of international relief safety nets, and helping forge new directions for agencies working in conflict situations.

Alun Burge is currently undertaking an MPhil in Development Studies, specialising in issues of development in Central America. He has worked for CIIR, War on Want and Christian Aid, where he was Programme Officer for Central America. He is now a freelance consultant while completing his academic work.

John Borton is Research Fellow at the Overseas Development Institute, London, where he has been lead researcher on a two-year study of NGOs and relief operations. He is also Coordinator of the Relief and

Rehabilitation Network which has a memebrship of 190 NGOs and is funded by EuronAid. He is a member of the editorial board of *Disasters* journal and has conducted a number of external evaluations of relief programmes in Africa and Asia. He has published widely on aspects of disaster relief and is currently involved in a multi-donor evaluation of the international response to the Rwanda crisis.

Charlotte Benson is a Research Fellow at the Overseas Development Institute, London. Her interests include economic aspects of natural disasters and relief, food aid and food policy. She is currently working on two studies on the economic impact of drought in sub-Saharan Africa and natural disasters in South-East Asia and the Pacific.

FOREWORD

The 1980s saw the coming of age of non-governmental organisations (NGOs). The increasing size and scope of their work brought them into much closer collaboration with each other than ever before. Yet NGO coordination, particularly in emergencies, has often been regarded as peripheral to the main task of delivering assistance to needy populations. Collaboration would, so the argument runs, arise spontaneously if required. In many quarters this perception persists and, with notable exceptions, professionally run field-based NGO coordination structures are still relatively new additions to the growing institutions of international relief and development.

Increasingly, however, it is recognised that the coordination of large scale aid programmes is a specific and often little understood skill requiring more than simply the ability to hold a meeting. This book is perhaps the first attempt to bring together the experiences of professional NGO coordination bodies worldwide. It has its own intrinsic worth as a comment on some of the major international disasters of the last decade. But it is more than that. It points to the critical role that cooperative umbrella organisations can play in enhancing the visibility and efficiency of the NGO sector.

Jon Bennett and his team have done an excellent job in pulling together the common elements found in coordination experiences around the world. At a time when the UN and other international agencies are in a state of crisis as they confront ever more complex issues, this volume is a timely reminder of the responsibilities of the NGOs themselves to rationalise their own approaches to relief and development work in the years ahead.

One of the main goals of the International Council of Voluntary Agencies (ICVA) is to encourage and facilitate NGO collaboration and cooperation, among NGOs and between NGO and other actors in the field of Humanitarian Affairs. We hope this book will contribute to that end.

Trygve Nordby
ICVA President

PREFACE

In 1993, the International Council of Voluntary Agencies (ICVA) initiated a new programme, Non-Governmental Organisation (NGO) Coordination in Humanitarian Assistance. This was an attempt to distil and disseminate information about the many NGO umbrella organisations around the world. The programme – extended to include training and management advice to these structures – was directed by Jon Bennett, in consultation with ICVA's President, Trygve Nordby, and the Executive Director, Delmar Blasco. Funding has come mainly from the Ford Foundation, with additional assistance from five Norwegian agencies (members of the Norwegian Refugee Council), the British Government Overseas Development Administration (ODA), Commonwealth Foundation, World Bank and Christian Aid. Jon Bennett has 17 years' experience working for NGOs in emergency situations and from 1990–92 was the Executive Director of the Agency Coordinating Body for Afghan Relief (ACBAR), one of the largest NGO coordination bodies in Asia.

To date, the programme has included:

- the evaluation of eight NGO coordination modalities worldwide;
- the ongoing establishment of a directory of NGO coordination bodies worldwide;
- the production of a handbook, *NGO Coordination at Field Level: A Handbook* (ICVA, June 1994);
- the convening of a three-day seminar in April 1994 attended by 55 individuals from coordination bodies worldwide and from Northern NGOs and intergovernmental organisations.

ICVA wishes to generate a more active 'coordination culture' by identifying where coordination has been most successful, how such models can be replicated, and how the NGO community should respond to the articulated needs of coordination structures if and where they exist. Although the emphasis is on field-level coordination, ICVA will further explore how these modalities can be strengthened regionally and internationally, particularly in relation to multilateral agencies such as the United Nations (UN).

ICVA already has a particularly close working relationship with the UN Department of Humanitarian Affairs (UN-DHA) and with the United Nations High Commissioner for Refugees (UNHCR), notably through the 1993–94 PARinAC (Partnership in Action) process. NGO coordination is high on the agenda of these and other related initiatives. Through this publication and future activities of the programme, ICVA hopes to build up the capacities and profile of NGO coordination mechanisms worldwide.

International Council of Voluntary Agencies (ICVA)
Case Postale 216
1211 Geneva 21
Switzerland
Tel: +41 22 732 66 00   Fax: +41 22 738 99 04

INTRODUCTION

RECENT TRENDS IN RELIEF AID: STRUCTURAL CRISIS AND THE QUEST FOR A NEW CONSENSUS

Jon Bennett

In international aid circles, coordination is a value-laden concept. For some it has overtones of 'control' while others fear being swamped by interminable layers of bureaucracy. Long-established institutions such as the UN have always accepted, at least in principle, that a multi-faceted approach to relief and development requires a degree of regulation – a 'coordinator' – to oversee its entirety. By contrast, the smaller, independent and relatively younger non-governmental organisations (NGOs) have traditionally resisted centralism. For them, working together might at best entail a loose consensus, a tacit agreement not to tread on each other's toes.

This may be changing. The last decade has seen a discernable shift in favour of closer, more routine cooperation among those who deal with the ever increasing demands of humanitarian assistance. In part, this is a necessary response to the sheer scale of the operations. NGOs collectively spend an estimated US\$9–10 billion annually, reaching some 250 million people living in absolute poverty.[1] Bilateral govern-

---

1. The Organisation for Economic Cooperation and Development (OECD), representing the 'rich' countries of the north, counted 2542 NGOs in its 24 member countries in 1990 compared with 1603 in 1980

ment donors increasingly channel resources, especially for emergencies, through their favoured NGOs rather than through allegedly less accountable governments of the South. In several emergencies of the late 1980s and early 1990s, short-term money available to NGOs – albeit mostly to Northern NGOs – exceeded even that of the UN. This was the case in a number of countries covered in this volume.

NGOs now move more funds to the South than the World Bank group *(Clark, 1991)*. They are the frontline forces of 'neutral' intervention and are linked more than ever before to the wider aid community – the UN, other multilateral bodies and international governments – in a manner that could not have been foreseen in the days when NGOs simply filled the gaps at a grassroots level.

It is not simply the number and size of NGOs that has changed. Freed from the Cold War straitjacket, NGOs in strategically unimportant countries have become political actors with their mandates expanded to encompass human rights, conflict resolution and public advocacy through the media. Their role in determining the parameters and scale of international response to human disasters has never been greater. Yet, in the wake of the 1994 Rwanda crisis, which highlighted the dangers of 'humanitarianism unbound' *(African Rights, 1994)*, it is necessary to recognise the potential damage NGOs can do in the name of neutrality. If there is to be a useful debate about the impact and mandates of NGOs, this must take place at all levels, not least at the field level where day to day decisions are being made. The modalities of coordination do not point simply to organisational principles; consensus of any kind implies an agreed agenda and mutually reinforced concepts. A critique of relief mechanisms will at least inform that consensus and, hopefully, allow for a critical appraisal of why, for whom, and in what circumstances, we undertake humanitarian work.

The phenomenal increase in the number, size and financial status of NGOs in the 1980s and 1990s has to a large extent happened without close inspection of their actual performance. For all their laudable success, some NGOs have been guilty of poor practice, wastage and a lack of professionalism, which to a large extent has gone unchecked. They tend to throw a veil of secrecy over actions that would not stand up to public scrutiny and rarely are NGO programmes evaluated from the standpoint of a broader analysis of their political as well as humanitarian impact. Critics of NGOs have pointed to lack of accountability, mutual competitiveness and poor coordination as perhaps the three most serious charges levelled at the so-called 'Third Sector'. Concern has also been expressed about the fact that some NGOs have crowded out governments by offering better resources and salaries and, in some cases, have made little secret of their wish to replace government structures. Another serious charge is that Northern NGOs have singularly failed to transfer skills to any significant degree to their Southern counterparts *(Elliot, 1993)*.

This volume looks at the specific ways coordination has developed at field level and how these have related to various emergencies over the last decade. Eight case studies have been selected, each for their unique, though comparable, approach to NGO coordination at field level. Where there is a predominance of Northern NGOs, we ask to what extent this was necessary and how much attention was paid to building local capacities. During emergencies, the tendency is to bypass developmental principles in favour of rapid responses dominated by Northern capital and Northern agencies. Where indigenous NGOs have initiated and led various coordination structures, we examine their relative strengths as catalysts for civil society. Firstly, however, I shall briefly examine the wider context in which NGO coordination takes place and highlight the major trends that have shaped the international relief system as a whole.

My contention, backed by the evidence contained in some of the following case studies, is that the shift in favour of using NGOs as implementors of humanitarian assistance is symptomatic of a profound crisis facing the international relief system. The crisis is located in three inter-related themes:

- the scale of needs;
- the underlying policies of donor states;
- the increasing use of the relief model as a device for disengaging from a wider political responsibility towards chronically traumatised societies.[2]

COMPLEX EMERGENCIES, DONOR POLICIES AND DISENGAGEMENT

The number of so-called complex emergencies – the interwoven results of war, politics, economics, famine and often refugees – in the 1990s has increased beyond the capacity of existing response systems.[3] The human toll has been immense: 100 million people were affected by major disasters in 1980, rising to over 310 million by 1991 (IFRC, 1993). Refugee numbers in the same decade more than doubled to 17.5 million and in 1992 the number of internally displaced people stood at 24 million in 31 countries. In the 1960s, there were about ten ongoing wars around the world. Today there are about 50. These are now mostly internal wars rather than wars between nations, and their duration and

2. The notion that the promotion of relief systems underscores a more general disengagement from the South is here borrowed extensively from Duffield, 1994a.

3. To designate complex emergencies multicausal implies that natural disasters – earthquakes, floods, etc – are monocausal. This is clearly not the case since complex social and political, as well as environmental factors, determine the severity of the outcome.

intensity are also increasing *(SIPRI, 1992)*. The resulting implosion of states has created a simultaneous spread of political fundamentalisms, autonomous war economies and an ever widening gap between rich and poor.[4] One result has been the growing number of international economic migrants, now estimated at 60 million worldwide *(Pellerin, 1993)*. The end of the Cold War may have hastened the end of some disputes but it exacerbated others. It broke the log-jam in the Security Council (created usually by the eastern bloc veto) and resulted in increased UN activity. It also, however, lifted the lid off underlying tensions in parts of Africa, Eastern Europe, the Caucasus and Central Asia.

Complex emergencies have a singular ability to erode cultural, political, economic and civil structures of a society. This is the very reason why humanitarian agencies have become embroiled in the local politics of warring parties and why, from the Horn of Africa to Bosnia, food aid has assumed such strategic significance *(Loescher, 1993)*. Yet I would argue that the crisis facing the international relief system is not merely the failure to respond adequately to the overwhelming need; it is also a structural issue. The growth in humanitarian relief lies at the very centre of policies reflecting a profound change in North–South relations: relief, as a policy model, is a form of disengagement from the South.

This disengagement reflects the declining strategic and economic importance of countries outside spheres of post-Cold War interest. It allows for a critical review of aid policy that has generally resulted in a decline in overall development assistance. Countries deemed too complex, too distant or too impenetrable for conventional aid have received the lion's share of relief assistance, much of which has been implemented by NGOs. In 1988, 2.26 per cent of Development Assistance Committee (DAC) members' bilateral aid was spent on emergencies and relief. This had risen to over 7 per cent by 1991 with some stark increases in certain Northern countries.[5]

Some analysts have suggested that the concept of developmentalism, which still dominates relief thinking, is itself outmoded (for example, *Duffield, 1994a* and *Gronemeyer, 1992*). Clearly, concepts and definitions inform the mandates employed by relief agencies in this increasingly specialised field. Centred on the delivery of basic survival items, the relief apparatus helps to define, and thus limit, our approaches. If Ethiopia was a short-term 'famine', normal linear development could be resumed at a later date. Scant attention is paid to the long-term decline and fragmentation of states where formal economics and civil structures are undergoing chronic upheaval.

4. The implosion of states would suggest the prevalence of internal 'resource' wars, often without political ideology or a clear social programme. Economic and political survival depend increasingly upon violence which leads to state disintegration (see, for example, *Duffield, 1991* and *Keen, 1992*).
5. The figures for individual countries are even more revealing: the Netherlands spent 2 per cent of its bilateral aid on emergencies in 1988 and 10 per cent in 1992; and European Community spending on emergencies leapt from 3 per cent in 1988 to a staggering 26 per cent in 1991 (*ICVA/Actionaid/Eurostep, 1994*).

In Chapter 4 of this volume, for example, I explore the negative as well as positive aspects of Mozambique's absorption of massive quantities of foreign relief aid. Some contend that Mozambique was simply a hostage to foreign intervention *(Hanlon, 1991)*, others that relief aid played a central role in weakening the capacity of the state to pursue progressive development policies *(Kanji,1990)*. NGOs were undoubtedly used as part of a ploy that avoided channelling money through the national government. A two-tier support system, evident also in other African countries, was put in place: institutional government support through the UN and more flexible and conditional support through the NGOs.

Monika Kathina in Chapter 5 explores emerging tensions between the state and NGOs in Kenya. The Kenyan Government's recent NGO Coordination Act met vehement resistance from NGOs backed by powerful international donors at a time when 'good governance' conditionality resulted in serious declines of bilateral assistance to the country. Aid channelled through NGOs in Kenya amounts to about US$35 million per year, some 18 per cent of all official aid to the country *(NGO Task Force, 1991)*. The government's wish to regulate its disbursement, particularly in the face of the Somali refugee crisis, was perhaps understandable. Of wider significance here is the extent to which any government caught in a downward economic and social spiral finds itself at odds with NGOs claiming to uphold the structures of civil society. Participatory structures present a potential political threat to an embattled government.

The role played by NGOs in the process of disengagement from the South may, paradoxically, encourage an actual increase in overall aid figures in the short term. In Chapter 1, I explore how, with the newly negotiated legitimacy of a UN cross-border operation from Pakistan, donors were able to pour huge quantities of money into Afghanistan for the first two years of the peace process. Yet by 1994 the collapse of US and other interests in the region meant a dramatic decline in the aid budget in spite of the increasing demands of refugees and displaced people. Again, NGOs, especially those contracted by the United States Agency for International Development (USAID), were buoyant with funds one year and struggling to stay open the next year. A tentative redirection of funds in favour of local Afghan NGOs in no way offset the dramatic collapse of overall NGO funds.

Significantly, though, prevailing ideology, reinforced by the media, continues to portray relief as a form of positive intervention, doubtless suiting politicians with an eye to public opinion. It would be absurd to suggest that relief programmes are inherently conspiratorial or that the relief needs of millions can be ignored. Rather, the contention here is that the increasingly sophisticated relief apparatus, coupled with the array of policy instruments now available to donors, has contributed to a weakening of the principle of collective responsibility towards the South. If this points to a long-term strategy of disengagement by donors, then NGOs play a role in this strategy as the acceptable face of a regrettable trend.

Cross-border programmes: a new paradigm

The late 1970s and early 1980s saw the growth of NGO cross-border operations, where sovereignty was violated in favour of reaching people in need. Constrained by sovereignty, the UN was unable to deal with internal wars. Only a handful of NGOs and the International Committee of the Red Cross (ICRC) were able to deliver relief items into rebel-held areas of Afghanistan, Ethiopia, Sudan and elsewhere. Two important principles were established: first, relief aid, externally managed and short-term, was neutral; second, in the absence of alternative policy instruments, relief aid became the only viable approach to conflict or political crisis. These two key concepts – neutrality and working in conflict – came to maturity in the mid 1980s. Ethiopia was one of the testing grounds for both concepts.

Mark Duffield in Chapter 3 explores how NGOs were able to develop a sophisticated cross-border operation into Ethiopia from Sudan at a time when the implementing agencies – two well-organised indigenous structures in Eritrea and Tigray – were known to be closely related to anti-government rebel forces. Providing externally monitored basic relief items and thus avoiding the political connotations that longer-term development assistance might have carried, NGOs were able to maintain their neutral stance. Although solidarity was the name of the game for many NGOs delivering assistance across the Sudanese border, neutrality was underlined by referring to the local implementing agencies as 'NGO partners'. If this was a confused approach, its corollary was perhaps predictable. As Duffield explains, a unique opportunity for an NGO–government relationship was missed in the 1990s when most NGOs preferred to resort to their traditional neutral stance vis-à-vis the incoming government in Ethiopia.

John Borton in Chapter 2 focuses on an issue closely related to this. He sees the onset of the Ethiopia famine as a key moment in the major shift of donor policy as resources were diverted from states to NGOs. The rapid growth of NGOs saw the development of donor–NGO subcontracting arrangements. Changing donor policy meant that previously illicit cross-border operations gained *de facto* recognition. In the closing years of the Ethiopian war, donors eschewed the strict rules of sovereignty for a cross-line, cross-mandate approach that allowed relief goods to be delivered into both sides of Ethiopia's contested territory. In doing so, they found a flexible tool in NGOs, a tool which could be applied with an element of discretion depending on their shifting interests.

By contrast, withholding relief aid in certain regions in the 1980s allowed donors discriminately to pursue certain foreign policy objectives. In Chapter 8, Charlotte Benson and I point to how donor political interests determined the hugely disproportionate amount of relief assistance received by Cambodian refugees in Thailand while Cambodia itself was politically isolated. In per capita terms, total western assistance to Cambodia was a mere US$4 per annum, compared to financial assistance on the Thai border amounting to some US$327. Meanwhile, a handful of NGOs in Cambodia acted as torch-bearers for a nascent aid policy that could only begin to take shape in the 1990s.

New policy instruments

It was not long before the UN was itself able to become a broker of aid. The late 1980s saw the emergence of 'corridors of peace' in South Sudan, Ethiopia and Angola, to be followed by 'zones of tranquillity' in Afghanistan. In a complete departure from its Cold War position, the UN negotiated with warring parties and accepted for the first time the principle of working in conflict. Its lack of implementing capacity meant that NGOs were increasingly sub-contracted. There was an interesting sub-text that arose out of post-Cold War optimism: the notion that negotiated access between warring factions for humanitarian aid could itself promote peace. The notion failed spectacularly in Afghanistan, Somalia and Bosnia.

Negotiated access programmes also saw the beginnings of the UN's integrated approach to complex emergencies. UN specialised agencies retained their traditional roles under a formal division of labour while a coordinating lead agency oversaw the humanitarian workload. This was underpinned by the 1991 UN General Assembly Resolution 46/182 which created the Department of Humanitarian Affairs (DHA). Negotiated access programmes also created the outline for a new NGO/UN relationship. The increase in the humanitarian workload exposed the lack of implementation capacity within the UN specialised agencies. NGOs were thus thrust to the fore as agencies who, under a new set of contractual agreements, would carry out the actual relief programmes.

The DHA restated the centrality of the NGO/UN relationship by inviting NGOs to sit on the Inter-Agency Standing Committee (IASC) alongside heads of UN operational agencies and the ICRC. The IASC provides a consultative forum for determining, among other things, ways to enhance the international community's relief capacity in general, and specifically in complex emergencies. Through the Consolidated Appeal Process, the DHA has also attempted to put emergency funding on a more secure basis.

The development of these policy instruments changed the operational equation for NGOs and donors alike. Some NGOs have chosen to remain outside the UN integrated programme, not least because of frustration with the apparent ineffectiveness and lack of political weight being given to the DHA. Donor governments now have a broad choice of policy instruments available to them. They can either work through the ICRC with its unique mandate, through independent NGOs or NGO consortia or through integrated UN operations. Yet another alternative lies in the increased interest donors have in becoming operational agents themselves.

The European Union (EU) is an important case in point. In 1993, European Currency Unit (ECU) 630 million was spent from the EU budget on humanitarian assistance, 93 per cent of which was allocated to relief in conflict situations *(ICVA/EUROSTEP/Actionaid, 1994)*. Significantly, 6 per cent of this relief money was spent directly through the European Community Humanitarian Office (ECHO), established in March 1992. NGOs are increasingly concerned with ECHO's apparent ambitions to assume responsibility for all humanitarian activities of the EU. Various proposals have been mooted, including the idea that ECHO should be responsible for disbursement of food aid (already the case in Central and Eastern Europe) and NGO co-financing (currently within the Directorate General structure). By 1994, some 80 NGOs already had framework agreements with ECHO which were based on a sub-contractor approach. Nevertheless, ECHO's approach had been dominated by short-term thinking and NGOs fear that the long-term focus on sustainable poverty reduction will be lost in the confusion between public and political profile and effective relief *(ICVA/EUROSTEP/Actionaid, 1994)*.

If the international relief apparatus system is beginning to accommodate NGOs to serve its own needs, then ultimately NGOs may be financed globally to do what they do nationally – welfare *(Fowler, 1992b)*. This throws up certain contradictions, for not only might NGOs represent the interests of an externally managed aid establishment but also aid delivered to the poor by NGOs might just be sufficient to avert or blunt social protest caused either by government neglect or international paralysis *(Porter et al, 1991)*. For example, much Northern NGO activity in refugee Collective Centres in Slovenia was of this palliative kind and has been criticised for creating imbalances in power relations with local authorities and local NGOs (see, for example, *Elliot, 1993*).

In summary, donors have found significant political and operational flexibility in NGOs at a time when total aid budgets are declining. *Duffield (1994b)* pinpoints the resulting dilemma:

> 'Tragically, as Bosnia has shown, donor flexibility has
> contributed to the erosion of ideas of collective
> international responsibility for the Southern predica-
> ment. The UN Charter and Geneva Conventions have
> been weakened... In their place narrow perceptions of
> national interest, or calculations based on media

exposure or domestic political advantage, have become
the arbiters of engagement... [This flexibility] has been
helped by the emergence of a private and competitive
NGO sector... NGO financial and media dependency,
plus their ability to work in a variety of situations, has
been important in allowing donor governments to shape
humanitarian programmes around national interests – a
major charge that many NGOs appear unable to
contemplate, let alone accept.'

Increasingly, NGOs are being sucked into a foreign policy vacuum
with which they are ill-equipped to deal. The use of humanitarian aid
as a tool to encourage stability in political volatile situations has disturbing consequences (see, for example, *Fennell, 1994*). This was no
more apparent than in Rwanda in 1994. The unprecedented carnage in
that country, in which an estimated one million people were systematically murdered between April and July 1994, sent shock waves across
the world, not least because the international community had been
given ample warning and yet spectacularly failed to intervene and
prevent the genocide. Rwanda was unique in that the human rights
violations were already underway before any sizable humanitarian
operations began. Operational agencies could not, therefore, claim that
their pre-existing programme was threatened by taking politically
controversial positions.

Several larger NGOs struggled with the issue of human rights and
publicly condemned the actions of the former Rwanda government
and *interahamwe* – the government-sponsored militia. The condemna-
tion of genocide should, in turn, have meant denying legitimacy or
impunity to those responsible for horrendous crimes. In the event,
international isolation and systematic purging of those responsible for
these crimes was compromised by the priority given to the international humanitarian response. When nearly two million refugees poured
across the borders of Tanzania, Burundi and, most dramatically, Zaire,
the humanitarian imperative set by a handful of NGOs and the UN to
some extent overshadowed the relatively greater horror that happened
before. The extremists who mounted the genocide knew that material
assistance from the international relief community would help them to
reassert authority over a traumatised and dislocated population in
refugee camps. The familiar synergy between an abusive authority and
humanitarian relief was established *(African Rights, 1994).*

The Rwanda crisis throws up difficult questions and no easy
answers. It does, however, highlight the mutual incompatibility of
pursuing 'neutral' humanitarianism, human rights and political objectives under the roof of one agency. Perhaps in a sense we have come
full circle and must re-examine the developmental roots that launched
many NGOs in the 1960s and 1970s. Conflict prevention, for instance,

implies a renewed effort to engage in the institutions of civil society in a profound manner. It points to developmentalism rather than reliefism, to solidarity rather than neutrality.

Coordination and participation

The focus of activity for many NGOs – particularly those engaged in relief and rehabilitation work – rests on the assumption that the appropriate unit of intervention is the organisation itself and the 'project' is its vehicle. Yet a central tenet of sustainable development is that the performance of any project – government or private - is critically dependent on the functioning of institutions. An institution is broader than an organisation – though some organisations become institutions – for it implies a stable pattern of behaviour recognised and valued by society. Institutions exert themselves through the rules, norms and values that influence people's lives *(Fowler, 1992a)*.

The distinction between an organisation and an institution is not merely convenient semantics. We have seen how, at an international level, Northern NGOs in particular are more and more engaged in macro-policy: a level of action that is often institutional in its nature. By contrast, Southern NGOs have little space to evolve a development agenda of their own. In many countries they lack institutional identity. Their role is increasingly as part of an imposed aid system rather than as an autonomous sector within the larger society with a self-determined contribution to make towards national development. Also, as competitors for external aid, they have occasionally felt the brunt of government legislation in an attempt to curtail their activities.

To invest in institutional development, therefore, is to accept the need for a community of viable organisations and a change in the pattern of interactions between the NGO community and other development actors. Such an investment requires more than short-term funds for predetermined projects. It demands an awareness of the distinction between change in social structures – the institutional dimension – and change at an individual organisational level. An institutional development perspective regards NGOs as a sector promoting values associated with self-reliance, social justice, countervailing power, etc: values that need to be protected and extended. Governments or, indeed, individual NGOs cannot by themselves champion such values. At best, the state can provide a conducive political, social and economic environment in which development takes place though a mixture of private and public endeavours. Where freedom of association, participation and empowerment are valued, it is civil society that creates the necessary normative framework.

It is within civil society that we locate the need for collective, coordinated and policy-oriented action by the NGO sector as a whole. This is precisely the unique role that a strong national association, council or collaborative network of NGOs can play. Power relations can be addressed by endeavouring to transfer decision-making to the field, to the recipients as well as to the givers of aid. Much has been said about involving refugees, for instance, in the decisions that affect their lives, yet very few lasting structures have been created to ensure that this is not simply rhetorical good sense. Field-based NGO coordination structures are potentially a way forward for they can be 'owned' not only by the multitude of small local NGOs rarely seen on our television screens but also, with careful nurturing, by at least some of the voiceless majority they serve. The level of genuine participation will depend on how such structures are set up and who controls them.

The case studies in the following chapters are necessarily eclectic. Some coordination bodies were born of a particular emergency; others emerge from a general desire to bring together a disparate NGO community under one umbrella. They each share the goal of improving information exchange, representation and advocacy. Where emergency programming is beginning to be seen as a long-term issue, contractual relations, codes of conduct and the like are dealt with by the coordination body in an increasingly professionalised relief context. The relationship between Northern and Southern NGOs is touched upon in each of the studies presented here.

Crucially, some NGO coordination structures are beginning to address aspects of the systemic crisis we have outlined above. They reinforce a sense of collective responsibility while championing the specific advantages of the voluntary sector in dealing with the political, social and economic roots of what has become a state of permanent emergency in the South. NGO relations with government, the UN and international donors require a new political consensus and a realignment of respective roles. This may at least ensure that original and still valid notions of partnership and solidarity are upheld.

ACRONYMS AND ABBREVIATIONS

NGOs   Non-Governmental Organisations
OECD   Organisation for Economic Cooperation and Development
DAC   Development Assistance Committee (of OECD)
USAID   United States Agency for International Development
ICRC   International Committee of the Red Cross
UN-DHA   United Nations Department of Humanitarian Affairs
IASC   Inter-Agency Standing Committee
EU   European Union
ECHO   European Community Humanitarian Office
ECU   European Currency Unit

REFERENCES

African Rights (1994) 'Humanitarianism Unbound? Current Dilemmas Facing Multi-Mandate Relief Operations in Political Emergencies', *African Rights Discussion Paper No 5*, November 1994

Clark, J (1991) *Democratising Development; the Role of Voluntary Organisations*, Earthscan, London

Duffield, M (1991) 'War and famine in Africa', *Oxfam research paper no 5*, Oxfam Publications, Oxford

Duffield, M (1994a) 'Complex Political Emergencies, with reference to Angola and Bosnia: An Exploratory Report for UNICEF' School of Public Policy, University of Birmingham, March 1994

Duffield, M (1994b) 'Complex Emergencies and the Crisis of Developmentalism' *IDS Bulletin: Linking Relief and Development* vol 25, no 3, October 1994

Elliot, S (1993) 'The Impact of Humanitarian Aid on Local NGOs: The Slovenian Case' MA thesis, Oxford Brookes University, unpublished

Fennell, J (1994) 'A Conspiracy of Ignorance' *The Health Exchange*, 12 December 1994

Fowler, A (1992a) *Institutional Development and NGOs in Africa: Policy Perspectives for European Development Agencies* INTRAC, Oxford

Fowler, A (1992b) *Prioritising Institutional Development: A New Role for NGO Centres for Study and Development*, IIED Gatekeeper Series no 35, London

Gronemeyer, M (1992) 'Helping' in Sachs, W (ed) *The Development Dictionary: A Guide to Knowledge and Power* Zed Books, London, 1992

Hanlon, J (1991) *Mozambique: who calls the shots?* James Curry, London

ICVA/EUROSTEP/ActionAid (1994) *The Reality of Aid, An Independendent Review of International Aid* Geneva/Belgium/London, May 1994

IFRC (1993) *World Disaster Report, 1993* International Federation of Red Cross and Red Crescent Societies, Geneva

Kanji, N (1990) 'War and Children in Mozambique: is international aid strengthening or eroding community-based policies?' *Community Development Journal, 25 (2)*

Keen, D (1992) *Refugees: Rationing the Right to Life – The Crisis in Emergency Relief* Zed Press, London

Loescher, G (1993) *Beyond Charity: International Cooperation and the Global Refugee Crisis*, Oxford University Press, Oxford

NGO Task Force (1991) 'Towards A New Vision for Non-Governmental Organisations in Development', NGO Task Force, Nairobi, Kenya, May 1991

Pellerin, H (1993) 'Global Restructuring in the World Economy and Migration: The Globalization of Migration Dynamics' *International Journal XLVII* pp 240–254, March 1993.

Porter, D, Bryant, A and Gaye, T (1991) *Development in Practice: Paved With Good Intentions*, Routledge, London

SIPRI (1992) *Year Book, 1992: World Armament and Disarmament*, Oxford University Press, Oxford

1

AFGHANISTAN:
CROSS-BORDER NGO COORDINATION, 1985–93

Jon Bennett

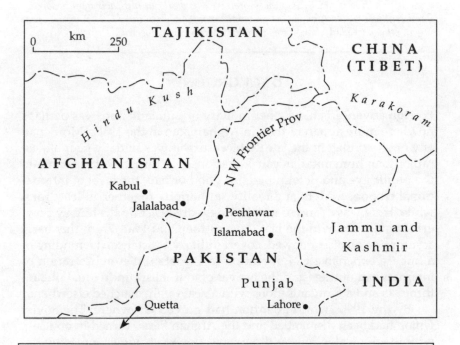

The People: Population: 16.5 million. The Pushtus account for about 60 per cent of the population, the Tajiks for 30 per cent and Uzbeks 5 per cent. The remainder are Hazaras and nomads of Mongol origin.

The Government: following ten years of Soviet occupation and a further three years of a Soviet-backed regime, the Mujahideen resistance entered Kabul and proclaimed an Islamic Republic in April 1992 headed now by President Rabbani. Fighting has again resumed between the various Afghan factions, further exacerbating the refugee problem and internal displacement in neighbouring countries.

Development Aid: US$143 million in 1990 but now much reduced. Additional assistance across the Pakistan and Iran borders.

After the signing of the Geneva Accords in 1988 that brought to an end the surrogate war in Afghanistan, a large amount of money was made available to the UN and NGOs alike. The world's largest refugee population did not return when expected, though the majority had repatriated by 1993. War, however, continued and further displacement occurred. The Agency Coordinating Body for Afghan Relief (ACBAR), with its offices in the border town of Peshawar, Pakistan, was one of the largest and best resourced NGO coordinating bodies in the world. A high level of participation in regional and sectoral coordination activities was perhaps in part due to the large, yet closely knit NGO community in Peshawar. As inter-ethnic fighting in Afghanistan intensified, NGOs found also that security concerns made close cooperation imperative. ACBAR was service oriented, producing guidelines, maps, province profiles and position papers. It also housed an impressive resource centre. The UN system and bilateral donors increasingly used ACBAR as a point of contact for the NGO community. Afghan NGOs, though numerous, were still relatively new. The more established ones were active in ACBAR, others preferred to work within their own umbrella. Persistent war inside Afghanistan prevented many NGOs – and ACBAR – from opening an office in Kabul, though this remained a long term objective.

BACKGROUND

Foreign adventurism, whether military or humanitarian, was perhaps nowhere more apparent than in Afghanistan in the 1980s. More than any other conflict in the late 20th century, it was initially geopolitical rather than humanitarian considerations that thrust Afghanistan into the public eye and determined, for good or bad, the level of international response. Myth and reality sat happily together, at least for a while. Here was a land of heroes, doggedly resisting the hugely powerful Soviet army in the last days of the Cold War. From this basic assumption all else followed: covert military assistance, the funding of a hugely expensive UN operation in Pakistan, the orchestration of international outrage and the arrival of journalists, individual philanthropists and aid organisations with a zeal rarely matched elsewhere.

By the 1990s world attention had moved elsewhere. The Soviet Union had been dismantled and the Afghan *'jihad'* turned in on itself, with ideological, ethnic and personal power struggles replacing the 'common enemy'. Some would claim that this was historically inevitable, for Afghanistan's contemporary crisis is above all a reflection of the struggle between the 'traditional' Islamist and the 'progressive' socialist movements in Afghanistan, overlaid by complex tribal and ethnic loyalties. Modern borders drawn up in the late 19th century cut across some of the principle ethnic groups; thus there are as many Pushtus living in Pakistan as there are in Afghanistan.

The 'aid story' begins with the country's greatest modern upheaval, the invasion of Soviet troops who took control of Kabul in December 1979. A sense of unity against a common enemy appeared to overshadow ethnic division and the United States began its covert assistance to what appeared to be a fairly cohesive resistance, the

Mujahideen. The scene was set for one of the most bitter, protracted guerrilla wars of the century. From 1980–1985 Central Intelligence Agency (CIA) military assistance to the Mujahideen rose from US$30 million to US$285 million. In 1984–1985, Saudi Arabia matched these funds with contributions of over US$500 million (*Arney, 1990*).

After President Reagan's re-election, US assistance increased and funds were approved for a programme of humanitarian assistance inside Afghanistan. For the first time, large sums of money were made available to US and European NGOs working across the border. The Mujahideen were supplied with US hand-held Stinger anti-aircraft missiles and their renewed confidence contrasted starkly with the con- current slow demise of the Soviet Union. The Soviet-backed Kabul regime no longer bombed the countryside with impunity and as the Mujahideen consolidated its hold, ever larger areas were now open for NGOs to supply cash for food and medical supplies of a more sub- stantial nature.

International peace efforts brokered by the UN were largely unsuc- cessful for the first decade of the war, although a UN Special Envoy was appointed as early as 1981. Real change came about with the suc- cession to the Kremlin of Mikhail Gorbachev in 1985. Soviet intentions to withdraw from Afghanistan were mooted in 1986. Two further years of UN-sponsored negotiations successfully ended with the sign- ing of the Geneva Accords in April 1988 and the withdrawal of all Soviet troops by mid-February 1989.

Understandably, the Mujahideen claimed victory and a significant role in the final dismembering of the Soviet Union, though this is open to question.[1] Whatever the case, the war was by no means over. Immediately after signing the Accords the US and Soviet military authorities announced their intention to pursue 'positive symmetry' – the matching of levels of arms provided to each side in the conflict. Soviet support to the Najibullah regime in 1989 rose to between US$220 million and US$300 million a month, while US and Saudi Arabia each contributed over US$500 million of military hardware in the same year (*Arney, 1990*).

The collapse of the Soviet Union in 1991 brought assistance to Kabul to an abrupt halt. This in turn gave extra impetus to the UN peace process and succeeded in replacing 'positive symmetry' with 'negative symmetry' wherein the supply of military hardware from both the US and Soviet Union was stopped. Deprived of support, the Najibullah regime finally crumbled and in April 1992 an interim Council made up of six of the eleven Mujahideen rebel groups entered Kabul.

---

1. Although the war in Afghanistan had reached a stalemate by the mid 1980s with the Mujahideen firmly entrenched, some claim that the final withdrawal of Soviet troops had as much to do with the strain on the Soviety economy and the increasing rapprochement between Presidents Reagan and Gorbachev, the latter recognising that Afghanistan remained an obstacle to his reform policies.

Celebrations were short lived. The years of exile and resistance had produced a generation of warlords whose power base depended on the continuous demonstration of military might. Various well-equipped Mujahideen parties – with an impressive stock of arms needing no replenishment for many years – had entrenched themselves in key positions around Kabul. Their claims to political ascendancy were irreconcilable. Bitter fighting flared up between various ethnic factions, with eastern Pushtus contesting the recent ascendancy of northern Tajiks, and Uzbecs and Hazaras each bidding for a share of power. With little apparent ideological basis, allegiances shifted frequently and opportunism was rife. Uprooted civilians caught in the cross-fire were again the innocent victims and a new wave of refugees hit Pakistan. From August 1992 to March 1994, more damage was done to Afghanistan's major towns than in the entire Soviet occupation. Viewed as a purely internal feud, the world turned its back as the heroes of yesteryear became the villains of ethnic squabbles likely again to be consigned to the footnotes of history.

FORCED MIGRATION

The Afghan crisis from 1979 onwards led to a forced migration of more than one-third of the population. The consequent changes in demographic balance, ethnic and linguistic distribution, and the inevitable political and economic instability that followed, raised the question of the very survival of the Afghan nation. In addition to the massive refugee exodus in Pakistan and Iran, the consequence of internal displacement was acutely felt. The population of Kabul, for instance, doubled in ten years. The sociological and economic impact of urbanisation was further heightened by the loss of farming skills among refugees in neighbouring countries; a whole generation grew up retaining little traditional attachment to the land.

For many years the civilian population was subjected to 'scorched earth' tactics involving blanket bombing and the deliberate destruction of villages, irrigation systems and farming lands. Whole areas were laid to waste, precipitating the largest displacement of human population in modern times. Between 1979 and 1984, some 2.5 million people fled to neighbouring Pakistan and a further 1.5 million to Iran. In the next five years the number of refugees in Pakistan rose to 3.5 million and in Iran to nearly 3 million. This was by far the largest refugee population in the world.

Shortly after the signing of the Geneva Accords in March 1988, an Afghan Interim Government (AIG) was formed in Peshawar, Pakistan, from a somewhat shaky Mujahideen alliance of seven parties. With the ending of Soviet hostilities and the anticipated imminent collapse of the Kabul government, the AIG was expected soon to form a government in Kabul. The international community began rapidly preparing for the return of the majority of refugees from neighbouring countries. Donors were more willing than ever to release funds for cross-border rehabilitation programmes.

The mass return did not happen. The Mujahideen had warned that until the last remnants of communist government were removed the 'jihad' would continue. In spite of United Nations High Commissioner for Refugees (UNHCR) and Government of Pakistan mechanisms being in place from 1990, the continuation of the war meant that very few refugees returned. They would have to wait a further two years before any significant movement took place.[2] The Geneva Accords had, however, opened the coffers for a new generation of NGOs and contractors backed by increased donor interest in Afghanistan.

LEVELS OF ASSISTANCE

Although figures are notoriously difficult to verify, it has been estimated that assistance to refugees in Pakistan, alone, cost the international community an average of US$300 million annually throughout the 1980s. Of this, perhaps US$230 million was provided by bilateral donors, the UN and NGOs and US$70 million by the Government of Pakistan. From their own resources, NGOs contributed about US$10–15 million annually, though, like many other areas of the world, it is impossible to determine how much of this was actually spent at field level. By mid-1987 the number of so-called Refugee Tented Villages (RTV) in Pakistan totalled 62 in Baluchistan, 248 in the North West Frontier Province (NWFP) and 15 in Punjab *(Dupree,1988)*. The relatively much larger influx into NWFP and Peshawar District is due to the proximity, both geographical and ethnic, to the areas where the refugees originated. Not surprisingly, it also resulted in a large and concentrated NGO community in the border town of Peshawar. By 1987 over 50 were cooperating with UNHCR and the Chief Commission for Afghan Refugees (CCAR) *(Magnus, 1987)*.

Covert and modest cross-border operations in the early 1980s were mostly done by a handful of small NGOs. Only after 1986 did other organisations such as International Committee of the Red Cross (ICRC) and United Nations Children's Fund (UNICEF) become involved, yet neither were able to support significant programmes. The handful of NGOs – the so-called 'solidarity' organisations who often combined journalistic work with the placing of short term (main-

---

2. The Kabul government had, in 1987, launched a National Reconciliation programme that included the building of some Peace Guest Houses for returnees. In January 1992 the Ministry for Repatriation announced that 374,438 Afghans from 22 countries had taken advantage of the scheme. The UNHCR contributed not only with food aid from Pakistan but also with a high-cost airlift from Herat of refugees returning from Iran. The figures are still very much contested *(Centlivres, 1994)*.

ly medical) personnel in Mujahideen areas – may have commanded resources totalling US$5–10 million.

When the US government launched its humanitarian support programme in 1986, the scale of refugee and cross-border programmes increased significantly, particularly with regard to 'contractors' – commercial US-based agricultural and medical organisations funded through the United States Agency for International Development (USAID) programme. The extent to which NGOs at this time were 'political pawns' of a CIA strategy in Afghanistan may never be known, but the paucity of concise information on their activities from 1980–87 has led to some interesting speculation (see, for example, *Baitenmann, 1990*).

The most dramatic increase in international assistance followed the signing of the Geneva Accords and the creation of the UN's Operation Salam programme. The scale of cross-border programmes reached an estimated US$300 million in 1989 and US$400 million in 1990.[3] Substantial sums were made available to NGOs, either directly from bilateral donors or as implementing partners of the various UN agencies. The Office of the United Nations Coordinator for Humanitarian and Economic Assistance Programmes Relating to Afghanistan (UNOCA) dealt with the coordination of the UN programme as a whole and the allocation of a special Trust Fund for projects not covered by the specialised agencies. In addition, individual UN agencies raised money through their own separate appeals from time to time.

It is instructive to look not only at amounts of money released after 1989, but also at the relative allocation between the Pakistan (refugee) programme and the Afghanistan (cross-border) programme. In a sample of 58 Pakistan-based NGOs studied in 1991, a three-fold increase in money allocated to cross-border projects was noted since 1989 *(Bennett et al, 1992)*. This combined with the unique cross-border operational mandate given to Operation Salam as part of the Geneva Accords, meant that in-country rehabilitation programmes attained a new respectability. Crossing the Afghanistan border from Pakistan was no longer the sole province of small adventurous NGOs; it was now a rationale for expediting the return of thousands while simultaneously repairing the damage of war. Indeed, with the addition of the cross-line – ie from government to non-government held areas – route, some UN officials ambitiously proclaimed the programme a major inducement to a lasting peace in Afghanistan. They were to be proven very wrong, though the UN Secretary General's special envoy presided over both UNOCA and the political peace process with equal enthusiasm until 1992.

---

3. A recent comprehensive report is careful to point out that information on assistance flows was extremely sparse until 1990–92 when Operation Salam (for the UN) and ACBAR (for the NGOs) were able to sort out, at least in part, some of the funding sources and channels. They were not, however, ever able to obtain figures on support from the Gulf states *(Nicholds & Borton, 1993)*.

The period from 1993 onwards saw a dramatic decline in external assistance to Afghanistan. The USAID programme was cut by more than 50 per cent, a trend followed by almost all major donors. Short-term funds were made available to NGOs dealing with thousands of newly displaced people from Kabul, many of whom settled in the Jalalabad area and were thus easily accessible to NGOs operating across the Pakistan border. The United Nations Development Programme (UNDP) office and most of the staff remained outside the country in Islamabad as the fighting around Kabul intensified.

By 1994 the largest single donor to Afghanistan was the European Union (EU) with a budget of some ECU 35 million, now far surpassing that of the USA. The EU was able to fund emergency inputs into Kabul, especially through the Médecins Sans Frontières consortium, as well as an increasing number of vocational training initiatives through local NGOs. We shall return to the issue of Afghan NGOs later, but it is worth noting here that as the budgets and international staff of foreign NGOs decreased, the number of local NGOs increased, a trend which was significantly to alter funding priorities in the future.

EVOLUTION OF NGO ROLE

Broadly speaking, there are four distinct phases of NGO entry into the aid programme for Afghans. The first, from 1979 onwards, was pre-dominantly a relief phase when NGOs played a comparatively modest role compared to the UN and Government of Pakistan. Only a handful of international NGOs were present, mostly those long established in Pakistan, for example, Save the Children Fund (UK) (SCF), Catholic Relief Services, Oxfam and Cooperative of American Relief Everywhere (CARE). They began opening health and income generating programmes in the new refugee camps along the border. The Pakistan government, reluctant at first, gradually accepted the comparative advantage of more specialised NGOs. By 1983, 17 NGOs were cooperating with UNHCR and CCAR (*Magnus, 1987*).

The second phase began with limited cross-border work from 1980–85. It was then that, in addition to the more established NGOs, the Afghan-specific agencies began working in the refugee camps and across the border. It is a unique aspect of the Afghan crisis that so many of these organisations emerged during the 1980s and in several cases had budgets exceeding those of the more 'usual' NGOs. Recent NGO directories listed no fewer than 20 such organisations that started life as political lobby groups and were soon to become operational agencies with, in some cases, multi-million dollar programmes (*ACBAR, 1991a*). Following the creation of UNOCA an even greater number of international NGOs became involved on both sides of the border.

A characteristic of this second phase was the lack of concise reporting which makes it extremely difficult to research the quantitative impact of the NGOs concerned. Yet the active role of the 'solidarity' NGOs in Europe and the USA – notably the Austrian Relief Committee, the Swedish Committee for Afghanistan, the Norwegian Refugee Council and a number of smaller US-based agencies – meant that they were virtually the only source of information on Afghanistan for journalists and academics for many years.

With some obvious overlap, the third phase was characterised by the increasing importance of Islamic NGOs funded by governments and private sources in the Gulf States and elsewhere who were keen to reflect Muslim *umma* concern for the plight of the Afghan people. The Peshawar-based Islamic Coordinating Council (ICC) comprised 16 such agencies by 1992 whose combined budgets could only be guessed at since figures were rarely given. Estimates, however, ranged between US$25–75 million. In 1991 some of these organisations came under close scrutiny by the Pakistan government. Evidence had pointed to a close relationship between some Islamic organisations and the radical Arab *jihad* mercenaries, young men trained in Afghanistan who allegedly 'exported' terrorism across the world. It was precisely the secretive nature of some of the Islamic aid agencies that raised such suspicions, though it is unlikely that many were guilty of harbouring or encouraging these activities.

The fourth phase saw the advent of indigenous Afghan NGOs, extremely rare in pre-war Afghanistan. Some were already well established and well-funded, others were encouraged through partnerships with international NGOs, and a third group were funded almost exclusively by various UN agencies. Afghan NGOs became increasingly important players after 1991 and we shall look more closely at this phenomenon below.

By the end of 1993, ACBAR identified 242 NGOs with offices in Pakistan (usually Peshawar), though the figure may have been larger if one takes into account the non-operational funding agencies. Of these, only 43 worked exclusively with refugees, 144 worked exclusively cross border, and 55 worked cross border and in the refugee sector *(ACBAR, 1993)*. Budget allocations by sector are shown in Figure 1.1.

We should be cautious in assigning too much importance to the notion of 'phases' of NGO development as such, for there was an important, and dominant, caucus of NGOs who remained throughout all the periods outlined above. Their work continued to be influenced more by internal political events in Afghanistan than by trends in the wider aid community. Inevitably, however, their funding base was equally susceptible to 'donor fatigue' and, by 1994, even these NGOs were forced drastically to cut their programmes.

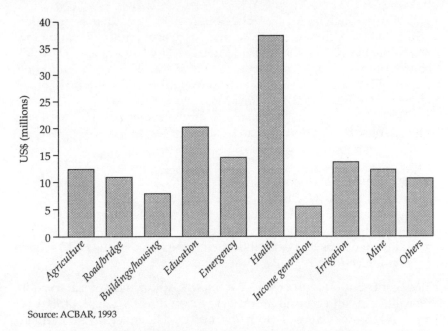

Source: ACBAR, 1993

Figure 1.1 *1993 ACBAR member budget allocation by different sector*

COORDINATION OF THE UN

Through its unique mandate and accessibility to all areas of Afghanistan, Operation Salam heralded the arrival of UN agencies in a manner hitherto reserved almost exclusively for NGOs.[4] NGOs in turn had to adapt themselves to a new order of funding and a new hierarchy within the aid community. Established NGOs found new funds as partners of executing UN agencies and, as we shall see, this new UN factor was itself to create a flood of Afghan NGOs, in particular, wishing to benefit from the funding bonanza.

UNOCA's role was to assist in the mobilisation and coordination of the resources to be provided by the international community. The first Consolidated Appeal for Operation Salam was launched in June 1988. It envisaged a hugely ambitious two-phase programme. The first – 'relief and rehabilitation'– was budgeted at US$1.6 billion and was to cover the period until the end of 1989. The second – 'rehabilitation and recovery' – was budgeted at US$0.8 billion and was to take the programme to the end of 1993.

In the event, repatriation was slow, with only 300,000 spontaneous returnees leaving Pakistan's refugee camps by the end of 1990. The US$430 million allocated from the Appeal for voluntary repatriation

---

4. Until 1989, only UNICEF had funded NGO programmes in Mujahideen-held Afghanistan.

was hardly touched. Meanwhile, donors held back their support for rehabilitation activities inside Afghanistan, arguing that it should be conditional upon a major return of refugees. By September 1990, total contributions pledged and received were just over US$1 billion of which US$694 million (67 per cent) were contributions in kind – mostly food aid – and US$337 million were in cash.[5]

Yet UNOCA's actual control over funds was surprisingly limited. The reasons are complex, but can be summarised in terms of three constraining factors:

- the reluctance of donors to invest too much authority and financial strength in UNOCA itself;
- the extent to which individual UN agencies failed to cooperate among themselves and with UNOCA;
- and the tensions that existed between UNOCA and the NGO community.

How contributions from the Consolidated Appeal were earmarked is revealing. In-kind contributions were given directly to executing UN agencies, as was agreed from the outset. However, to strengthen UNOCA's coordinating role and operational flexibility, the Afghanistan Emergency Trust Fund (AETF) was established. It was hoped that all cash contributions would be channelled through this. In the event, only US$232 million (69 per cent) of the US$337 million was actually under UNOCA management, the remainder being given directly to executing UN agencies or NGOs. Moreover, a large proportion of the AETF money was itself earmarked for use by UN agencies rather than UNOCA itself, and most of the remaining funds were 'frozen' pending a discernable increase in repatriation. In summary, if in-kind contributions are taken out of the equation, UNOCA's sole allocative control extended to just 3.3 per cent of total contributions by the donor community (for further breakdown of figures, see *Nicholds & Borton, 1993*).

The following two UNOCA Appeals saw a continuation of this trend. Donor 'fatigue', the continuing war, the fall off in geopolitical interest and demands from elsewhere in the world meant that actual sums raised fell dramatically between 1990 and 1992. Through the Trust Fund, UNOCA struggled to maintain its only remaining programme in the field, the demining operation. Donors increasingly channelled limited resources through NGOs and individual UN agencies, particularly the UNHCR which launched its own appeal in 1992 when substantial repatriation began at last.

---

5. These figures are drawn from various sources: UNOCA's First Second and Third Consolidated Reports (1988, 1989 and 1990); intermediary reports from UNOCA, Islamabad; and ACBAR news summaries drawing from figures given by UNOCA at the ACBAR Forum.

Most importantly, 1991–93 saw a major shift in emphasis away from UNOCA and the cross-border programme towards an in-country programme now spearheaded by the UNDP office in Kabul. The UN's regular Indicative Planning Figure (IPF) funds had accumulated over the years and senior officials began preparing a country-wide reconstruction programme. With the collapse of the communist government and its replacement by a Mujahideen alliance in April 1992, UNDP began courting NGOs in Pakistan who, they hoped, would become important partners in a newly unified nation. Their hopes were dashed when, in 1992 and again in 1993, UN offices in Kabul were forced to close in the wake of heavy fighting as the battle for Kabul intensified.

Nevertheless, UNDP had successfully asserted its leading role in the reconstruction programme and negotiated a more modest role for UNOCA. This may in part be due to the establishment of the UN Department of Humanitarian Assistance (UN-DHA) under UN Resolution 46/182 that was to reassign the coordinator's role to the UNDP Resident Representative. UNOCA's special status was an anachronism in the new arrangement, a point often expressed openly by other UN heads in Islamabad. At the end of 1992, UNOCA was renamed UNOCHA – the United Nations Office for the Coordination of Humanitarian Assistance. Its brief was to be restricted to humanitarian emergency programmes only, with the now well-funded demining activities as its major field programme. UNDP Kabul had become the focus for reconstruction programmes as a whole.

A thorough evaluation of UNOCA's programme has yet to be undertaken. In its first two years it became the focus of barely disguised hostility on the part of NGOs who felt that the level of consultation had been poor and that past and present NGO inputs into Afghanistan had been understated in UNOCA's bid for ascendancy. Style of leadership was perhaps as important as content. By the time a closer working relationship was established with NGOs with the arrival of a new Coordinator in 1991, total NGO funds already exceeded UN's by a factor of approximately 3:1 *(Bennett et al, 1992)*. Funding sources are given in Figure 1.2

Yet UNOCA had been an important catalyst for other parallel developments. The changing circumstances brought about by its creation in 1988 – and a perceived need to temper the increasing dominance of the UN system – spurred NGOs into creating their own collective lobby and coordinated group later in the same year. Thus, ACBAR was formed in August 1988.

AFGHAN NGOS

In the highly charged political atmosphere of Afghanistan in the early

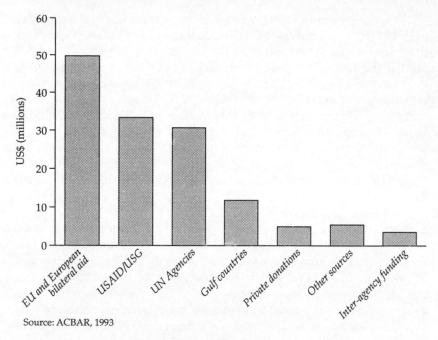

Source: ACBAR, 1993

Figure 1.2 *NGO funding sources, 1993*

1990s, it was perhaps inevitable that Afghan NGOs would to some extent reflect party and ethnic alliances. A comprehensive categorisation cannot be attempted here, but four broad groups are discernable *(Rahim, 1991)*:

- The so-called 'independent' Afghan NGOs – generally the longer established – were formed from non-affiliated professional groups of doctors and engineers;
- The 'field-based' NGOs were those backed by local *shuras* (councils) and/or commanders;
- The NGOs established by political parties present in Peshawar;
- The NGOs established by international organisations were the fourth and by far the largest group by 1992.

By 1992, ACBAR had identified no fewer than 82 Afghan NGOs employing more than 25,000 people *(ACBAR, 1992a)*. This increased to 148 by the end of 1993 *(ACBAR, 1993)*. Their collective budget was probably in excess of US$7 million, about 80 per cent of which came from the various UN agencies *(Bennett et al, 1992)*. Other international funders and trainers included the Norwegian Refugee Council (NRC), the International Rescue Committee (IRC) and USAID. A few international NGOs turned over their programmes to self-created Afghan NGOs, the most notable examples being the Dutch Committee for Afghanistan and the Salvation Army *(Bruce, 1993)*.

After 1990 UNOCA rapidly increased the number of Afghan NGOs participating in its reconstruction programme. Critics accused the UN of 'creating ' these agencies as purely delivery agents without supporting their institutional capacities. The FAO, for example, through UNOCA contracted some 45 Afghan NGOs for agricultural projects in Afghanistan, but many simply ceased to function once their particular contract had elapsed.

The Afghan NGO Coordination Body (ANCB) was created in 1991 to bring together an initial gathering of 32 Afghan NGOs. Membership expanded to 52 by the end of 1993 *(ACBAR, 1993)*. In spite of political and personality differences within its membership, especially at the outset, its formation was regarded as a signal to donors and local politicians alike that Afghan NGOs were to become important players in Afghanistan's future. When the new interim government in Kabul was announced in April 1992 following the collapse of the communist regime, no fewer than eight of the 19 ministers had been Afghan NGO senior staff members. If this caused some amusement in Peshawar circles, it above all indicated that the new government, unlike the old, were no strangers to the role of NGOs.

COORDINATION MECHANISMS PRIOR TO ACBAR

Prior to the formation of ACBAR, a number of NGO coordination mechanisms existed, some informal, others with a particular sectoral emphasis. The Cooperative Committee, formed in 1985, was an informal group interested primarily in exchanging information on cash-for-food (CFF) programmes. Its 12 members appear to have continued meeting for about 18 months. No formal voting structure or constitution was enacted and coordination in terms of sharing resources was on a purely *ad hoc* basis.

The Voluntary Agencies Group (VAG) was established in 1986 in Peshawar. It was set up by those NGOs working with UNHCR on refugee assistance programmes, though later the work of VAG also extended into repatriation and cross-border activities. There were initially 14 NGO members, though there was no formal constitution or voting structure.

The first officially constituted coordination body was the Committee of Medical Coordination (CMC), set up in 1986 to deal with cross-border work in the health sector. Funded by USAID and the Swedish Committee for Afghanistan (SCA), its prime activity was an attempt to standardise medicines and medical practice in training courses for Afghans and in support of health facilities in Afghanistan. Interestingly, it was the only coordination body that ever attempted an independent monitoring of member's activities. CMC had a Board, statutes regulating elections of board officials, systematic collection of minutes and data, and a Secretariat of paid officers, including a medical coordinator and three to four local staff. It closed in 1991.

CONTEMPORARY COORDINATION MECHANISMS OTHER THAN ACBAR

The Southern and Western Afghanistan and Baluchistan Association for Coordination (SWABAC) was formed in Quetta shortly after the creation of ACBAR in Peshawar. Several members of the ACBAR Steering Committee, including the first Chairman, were instrumental in setting up SWABAC. Its activities and mandate were similar to ACBAR's, though its staff and capacity was very much smaller. It had two full-time staff and an operating budget in 1992–93 of US$28,000. Although the distance between Quetta and Peshawar mitigated against daily contact, SWABAC was usually referred to as ACBAR's sister agency and shared the same database, guidelines, etc.

Other Pakistan-based coordination structures included the above mentioned ANCB and the ICC. The ICC membership comprised 18 Muslim organisations, most of whom did not disclose their budgets (nor, indeed, did the ICC), though it was understood to be a substantial amount *(ICC, undated)*. Outside of Pakistan, a small number of coordination bodies were set up in Europe and North America in the 1980s to facilitate regular exchange of information. These included La Coordination Humanitaire Européenne pour l'Afghanistan (CHEA) with a membership of 20 NGOs (closed 1991) and the British Agencies Afghanistan Group (BAAG) with a membership of 15 NGOs (still open in 1994).

The Government of the Islamic Republic of Iran convened a Seminar in July 1992 at which it invited NGOs to assist in meeting the needs of refugees in Iran and in facilitating their repatriation. To this end, the International Consortium for Refugees in Iran (ICRI) was formed in October 1992 with a small secretariat in Tehran. Members included Islamic, Scandinavian and British NGOs. ICRI facilitated a number of missions into Herat which led to a number of NGOs opening programmes in Herat, western Afghanistan. Although Pakistan was to remain the centre for NGO cross-border activities, the initiative in Tehran highlighted the fact that Iran had the largest numbers of refugees in the world – mainly Afghans, Iraqis and Kurds – for which it received little assistance.

ACBAR

As we have seen, the huge increase in international flow of funds after the Geneva Accords was to rapidly expand the activities of existing NGOs as well as trigger the arrival of new NGOs in Peshawar and elsewhere. More important, it was to change the nature of NGOs' programmes and the level of 'professionalism' expected by donors. It is no accident that exact figures on NGO aid inputs prior to 1987 are rela-

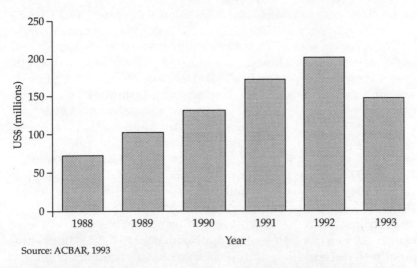

Source: ACBAR, 1993

Figure 1.3 *Total ACBAR member budget expenditure, 1988–93*

tively difficult to find. Quick and flexible response, personal commitment and a sense of solidarity within a small community were in those days more important than close financial inspection, monitoring or evaluation. The change came after 1988 when there was a discernable shift in the kind of senior managers employed by NGOs. Broadly speaking, the community now entered a period of consolidation with far greater importance given to policy formulation, strategic planning and diplomacy with the newly arrived inter-governmental bodies.

In creating ACBAR, NGOs sent a clear message to donors and the UN alike: that they recognised the importance of collective information sharing and advocacy on behalf of the NGO sector and were keen to assert the sector's comparative strengths and experience. Several NGOs took a lead in formulating the first term of reference for ACBAR, not least the SCA and the IRC. Indeed, the IRC's senior managers had themselves been closely involved in the Committee for Coordination of Services to Displaced Persons in Thailand (CCSDPT), set up 12 years previously. The first ACBAR constitution was closely modelled on CCSDPT.

ESTABLISHING A MODUS OPERANDI

Debates concerning the mandate and operational limits of ACBAR took place in the second half of 1988 prior to its first formal constitution published in November of that year. Views were divided over whether ACBAR should become a recipient of funds on behalf of others – ie a consortium that would channel funds for joint NGO ventures. Debate also centred on whether ACBAR could act as a clearing house for donors wishing to vet NGO performance. Both approaches were ultimately rejected, though the extent of ACBAR's influence over policy and funding was to become a perennial issue.

The Charter was built around a fairly standard 'international' model which allowed for one-organisation, one-vote and was built upon a three-tier structure: General Assembly (comprising all members who met every two months), Steering Committee (12 elected members) and Secretariat. Unlike many comparative field coordination bodies, ACBAR had a large secretariat comprising 12 professional and 23 support staff. A Coordinator and Deputy Coordinator were appointed in the first year, responsible for a budget in excess of US$600,000. Donors, flush with new funds for NGOs, were keen to support the new initiative and the UN and eight foreign missions in Islamabad contributed to the annual budget.[6]

Participation in the General Assembly – meetings often attended by over 100 persons representing approximately 15 nationalities – was initially characterised by European/North American dominance in discussions. Afghans, though numerous, were more reticent. Language was an issue, though ACBAR later instituted a system of translation in meetings and in minutes. More significant, perhaps, was the reluctance of Afghans to be seen to speak or vote against their compatriots on even minor issues. The more thorough Afghan *jirga* method of debate – in which all parties would be expected to have the floor at least once in a meeting, and in which decisions were eventually reached by consensus – would have been impracticable in a two hour General Assembly. Although Afghans soon adapted themselves, the stigma of 'western domination' was periodically to raise its head.[7]

The Charter itself was the source of some frustration in later years. It was drawn up at a time when several dominant NGOs – SCA, IRC and the Arms Control Research Centre (ARC), for example – were concerned with using ACBAR as a platform for lobbying activities. Indeed, ACBAR's agenda was more or less set by a handful of influential individuals with an acceptable 'track record' in the NGO community. Bureaucratic intricacies, loopholes in the text and ambiguities were not recognised until later. Many NGOs – not least the Afghan NGOs and the smaller 'solidarity' international NGOs – were not familiar with the general rubric of international constitutions and, on occasions, simply ignored them.

---

6. At no stage in ACBAR's development was 'donor dominance' an issue. Contributions were received in roughly equal amounts from the bilateral aid programmes of Norway, Denmark, Australia, Holland, USA, United Kingdom, Sweden and Canada. Additional funds for specific programmes were received from the Ford Foundation, Koenraad Adenauer Foundation, UNICEF, UNDP, UNHCR and UNOCA. Membership fees accounted for about 15 per cent of ACBAR income.

7. With notable exceptions, it was raised not by Afghans but by those more zealous expatriates belonging to 'fringe' organisations set up to champion Afghan rights. This is not to say the charge was unfounded; the complex question was how realistically to address it.

This relaxed approach to ACBAR affairs was not to last. When a series of reviews were undertaken early in 1991 to determine the parameters of ACBAR's role, the organisation became embroiled in a time-consuming, though arguably necessary, review of mandate and objectives. A new and more experienced Executive Director had been appointed the previous year and staff roles became more clearly delineated. It was recognised that if ACBAR was to compete for sparse and decreasing funds for Afghanistan – already apparent by 1990 – it must raise its head above the parapet of internal squabbles and provide a quantifiable service to its members and the wider aid community.

At a secretarial level, the review resulted in a pared-down annual budget for the next two years.[8] The most visible effect at General Assembly level was the increasing attendance by UN and donors that created a feeling of unity of purpose, previously missing. External relations were high on the agenda and ACBAR became a clearing house for information and briefing to journalists, researchers and donor delegations.

One should not under-estimate the influence of the Steering Committee and Director in determining not only the activities of ACBAR, but also the general approach of NGOs towards the UN and bilateral donors. From 1990–93, the Steering Committee comprised, at one time or another, the directors of SCA, SCF-US, Islamic Relief Association (ISRA), IRC, NRC, Norwegian Afghanistan Committee (NAC), Salvation Army, Volunteers in Technical Assistance (VITA), CARE International, Afghanistan Vaccination and Immunization Centre (AVICEN), and several Afghan NGOs. Collectively, their agencies represented up to 75 per cent of the total NGO budget for Afghanistan and many of the individuals had direct access to donors and policy makers. The extent to which they represented a cross-section of NGO opinion was perhaps debatable; their influence in the community as a whole, however, was undeniable.

ACBAR activities

By 1991, ACBAR had become one of the most sophisticated NGO coordinations in Asia and had become comparable in size and scope to the longer established mechanisms such as CCSDPT (Thailand) and Christian Relief and Development Association (CRDA) (Ethiopia). Yet it was to remain strictly non-operational with an emphasis on information gathering and dissemination and a particular emphasis on NGO policy formulation. Strictly speaking, ACBAR's membership remained at about 62 NGOs able to pay dues, but participation in meetings and joint ventures was open to all NGO and UN agencies. There were four core activities:

---

8. ACBAR's 1990/91 budget was $465,000, including $142,000 for the ACBAR Resource and Information Centre – ARIC – then housed separately. By bringing ARIC into the main building and further reducing costs, the total budget for 1991/92 was $379,000.

Regional and sectoral coordination

The 14 regional coordination groups covered NGO activities in 20 provinces of Afghanistan. Some were more regularly attended than others, particularly those covering provinces along the Pakistan border where a relatively large number of NGOs had projects. Kunar and Nangarhar provinces, for instance, were reported in great depth, with ACBAR's Afghan programme manager able to produce province profiles that facilitated needs identification and avoided duplication. On several occasions, coordination meetings took place inside the provinces with commanders and local people (see, for example, *Shakir, 1992*).

In the summer of 1990, NGOs and UNOCA were faced with an urgent security review of programmes in Paktika province where vehicles and equipment had been stolen. A special task force was created to forward recommendations for an inter-agency response. The final report recommended withdrawal until goods were recovered, a ploy which achieved only limited response from those responsible. More significantly, strong criticism was made of both the UN and NGOs of their lack of local knowledge of the area and of the complex politics they had encountered (*ACBAR/UNOCA, 1990*).[9] The exercise was proclaimed a 'success' in so far as security improved, though it was notable that one major international NGO did not uphold the recommendations and again raised the issue of 'control' versus 'coordination'.[10]

A further notable coordination exercise undertaken by ACBAR was the Eastern Paktia Task Force, created in September 1991. The town of Khost had recently been rid of government forces by the Mujahideen and NGOs were anxious to open a number of integrated programmes in the area. UNDP funded and actively participated in the task force which involved about 60 NGOs. ACBAR for the first time effectively 'vetted' applications for funding and UNDP were reluctant to grant contracts to any group who had not participated in the coordination meetings. Although strictly ACBAR's mandate had been superseded, the task force was often cited as one of the organisation's most successful endeavours (*ACBAR, 1991*).

ACBAR's six sectoral sub-groups were able to produce published guidelines from 1990–93 in health, agricultural training, veterinary skills and a directory of programmes for the disabled (*ACBAR & GTZ, 1990; ACBAR, 1991b; ACBAR, 1991c; Meier, 1992; ACBAR, 1992b*). With a UNHCR grant, a Repatriation sub-group was formed in January

---

9. The French NGO, AVICEN, for instance, continued to work successfully in the area, undertaking an Expanded Programme of Immunization and claiming 'unique' socio-political knowledge of Afghanistan (*Van Brabant, 1992*).
10. The NGO in question, CARE International, remained an active member of ACBAR's various committees, though it was later again to clash with other NGOs over the issue of food aid deliveries in Afghanistan. It would be unfair to suggest that CARE was 'wrong' in each instance: it merely highlights the difficulty of reaching consensus in a heterogeneous NGO community and a volatile war situation.

1992 at the beginning of the massive repatriation of some 1.5 million people that took place in the following 12 months. Additional activities included training surveys, transport surveys and a USAID-funded salary survey undertaken in 1992 *(Meier, 1992)*.

ACBAR Resource and Information Centre (ARIC)
Set up in April 1989, ARIC rapidly attained a prodigious reputation in the Peshawar aid community. Its main services included a library, map copying facilities, press cuttings, special events (lectures and presentations) and a monthly bulletin covering all publications relating to Afghanistan. Above all, it constituted ACBAR's permanent collection of materials that were, ultimately, to be transferred to Afghanistan as possibly the most complete collection of written materials on the war years.

Women's Coordination Unit
When the notoriously conservative Afghan rural community was uprooted by war many observers noted the manner in which women in particular were marginalised within the refugee community. Village elders, community leaders and commanders – the intermediaries for most aid deliveries – were always men and international NGOs were perhaps unnecessarily reticent to engage in any programmes specifically for women that might ignite local prejudice. Such fears were ostensibly confirmed when, in April 1990, 5000 Afghan men looted and destroyed the property of the Australian NGO, Shelter Now International, which ran a widows' programme in Nasir Bagh refugee camp *(Shelter Now International, 1990)*.

ACBAR's women's programme helped to provide a counterbalance to prevailing opinion. Using Afghan female staff (unusual in itself), a Women's Forum and a series of three seminars were held from 1990–93. Within a 'safe' environment, they attracted hundreds of women able to discuss their own problems and perspectives on repatriation and reintegration in a post-war society. Progress was slow, however, and frustrations were often expressed over the lack of quantifiable improvements brought by such fora. Donors – many of whom had insisted on a 'women's clause' in their grants – nevertheless relied heavily on initiatives such as these for raw data on activities among Afghan women.

ACBAR database
It was a condition of membership that NGOs submit details of their programmes to ACBAR for the annual published database. The first two editions (1990 and 1991) covered only the 65 or so ACBAR members with details of their inputs at district level. In 1992, however, the net was widened to all NGOs able to provide data. It was now possible to map NGO activities throughout Afghanistan down to

sub-district level. Other databases were maintained in Peshawar – notably by the World Health Organisation (WHO) and USAID – but few were as regularly updated or available for critical inspection in the field. Information was provided by the NGOs and could not be independently checked by ACBAR, a constant source of sceptical amusement by NGO field staff who claimed that the database was unlikely ever to be more than 60 per cent correct.[11]

Donor and UN relations

Relations between ACBAR and UNOCA had been rather poor in 1990 following the publication of a critical report commissioned by ACBAR on the disarray within the UN system *(Lawrence, 1990)*. Perhaps unfairly, UNOCA was singled out for its performance since the Geneva Accords and when ACBAR called a conference in Islamabad for NGOs, donors and the UN, Pakistan's UNDP Resident Representative refused to attend. However, by 1991 there was a marked improvement in relations, not least because security concerns inside Afghanistan had made interdependency between UN agencies and NGOs all the more critical. UN field staff from all the executing agencies began regularly attending ACBAR coordination meetings; in several instances, UN officers themselves chaired sessions on a regular basis. ACBAR soon became an indispensable forum for joint planning and debriefing and was open to all interested parties, whether members or not.

For their part, UNOCA officials often claimed that ACBAR represented only one part of the NGO community and to give it undue influence would go against the UN's stringent impartiality. However, with the exception of the much smaller SWABAC in Baluchistan, it was well known that ACBAR was the only NGO coordination body able systematically to gather information and represent the views of the vast majority of operational NGOs in Afghanistan and the refugee sector.

Early invitations to NGOs to attend the UN's inter-agency meetings in Islamabad (chaired by UNOCA) were not followed up in any formal manner and by 1990 NGOs in Pakistan were no longer invited. Neither was it possible to have NGO representation on the Trust Fund Approval Committee responsible for allocating unearmarked funds. The first Consolidated Appeal process in 1989 paid scant attention to the role of NGOs, though this was to improve in subsequent years. However, it was not until the launch of UNDP's Afghanistan Rehabilitation Strategy (UNORSA) in 1992 that NGOs were invited to be fully involved at all stages of planning.

By contrast, ACBAR's relations with the UN specialised agencies improved over the years, not least exemplified by funding contracts signed with UNICEF, UNDP, Food and Agricultural Organisation

---

11. There was often also a confusion over terminology. A 'clinic,' for instance, might be anything from a large medical centre to a single barefoot doctor under a tree.

(FAO), UNHCR and UN International Drugs Control Programme (UNDCP). In addition, grants from seven bilateral donors with offices in the country ensured that ACBAR kept regular contact with foreign missions in the capital. This was particularly important since ACBAR was one of the few organisations able to present regular briefings and an overview of NGO sector trends to visiting officials. All were sent ACBAR publications and newsletters and several officials regularly attended ACBAR Forum meetings. Notably, however, USAID maintained a uniquely independent voice on Afghan matters that led to several policy decisions at odds with the wider donor community.[12]

Recent developments

In June 1992, an ACBAR delegation, with the logistical assistance of UNOCA, flew to Kabul. It was the first official joint NGO delegation to the new government. An NGO Protocol was negotiated and it was expected that ACBAR would play a leading role in facilitating the arrival of NGOs in Kabul in the near future. Sadly, infighting between the various Mujahideen factions intensified and not only did ACBAR remain in Pakistan, but also the UN and all other agencies were eventually forced to evacuate Kabul. One key event of 1993 was the murder of one UN expatriate, a Dutch engineer, and two UN Afghan staff in February. This tragedy overshadowed many aid decisions in the first six months of 1993. It effectively pre-empted the notion that ACBAR might open an office in Jalalabad to coordinate relief supplies being delivered to the estimated 350,000 people now pouring out of Kabul and surrounding areas. In mid-1994 the situation remained volatile and Peshawar, against all predictions, was still essentially the centre of the aid operation.

CONCLUSION

The intriguing mix of political and military interest, humanitarian concern and plain adventurism in Afghanistan was bound to make the quest for coordination an uphill task. For many years, NGOs with little experience elsewhere in the world had enjoyed a relatively free

---

12. From July-October, 1991, for instance, two USA nationals working for an NGO called Global Partners were kidnapped in Ghazni Province. This and related incidences provoked USAID to impose a total embargo on aid to Afghanistan for six months. A subsequent internal evaluation pointed out that such an embargo had little, if any, effect on the behaviour of Afghans towards aid organisations; indeed, it was unlikely that such a heterogeneous population would have had the slightest notion of the intended impact of this embargo. In another instance, following a US Congress decision in 1991 to refuse funding programmes in drug-producing areas, USAID's drug prevention programme was drastically reduced. The above events were undoubtedly part of an overall strategy of total US withdrawal from Afghanistan which was almost complete by 1994.

hand with little or no interference from the Pakistan or Afghan governments. The arrival of UN executing agencies in the cross-border aid programme after 1988 changed both power relations and expectations of donors; NGOs were now part of a much larger endeavour to put Afghanistan back on its feet. Closer inspection and monitoring of their work soon followed and a call for greater coordination came from all quarters, not least the NGOs themselves.

The task for ACBAR was initially onerous. Members were often unclear of what they should expect of a coordinating body. Either it pursued the goals of a small number of influential members or it was rendered virtually impotent by the lowest common denominator of NGO concensus. In reality, the answer lay in responding to needs as they arose and consciously avoiding too close an inspection of its mandate. ACBAR's most successful coordination projects were those arising out of urgent needs – the Paktika security incidents, the 1991 Hindu Kush earthquake, the 'liberation' of Eastern Paktia, the 1992 exodus from Kabul. The constant refinement of information systems helped bolster its reputation among donors and researchers.

From 1989 onwards, a distinct change of 'mood' within the NGO community was due in part to demands for greater professionalism and a corresponding de-emphasis on solidarity with the Mujahideen. While this involved a more rigorous approach to funding and setting priorities, it also implied a disengagement from Afghanistan as a whole. Pragmatism, flexibility and the utilisation of 'local knowledge' were replaced by technical proficiency. The demand for, and ways of, NGO coordination were bound to reflect this change.

Despite early setbacks with UNOCA, ACBAR played a critical role in encouraging the participation of NGOs as part of a community with broadly similar aims. The UN, donors and others, for the most part aware of the pivotal role NGOs played in Pakistan and Afghanistan, increasingly used ACBAR as a discussion forum and information platform. Indeed, there was no other such open forum in Pakistan.

Between 1989 and 1993, an average day would see more than 60 persons participating in ACBAR meetings. Though virtually impossible to quantify, savings in terms of avoiding duplication of projects, exchanging security information and providing assistance priorities would have been incontestable. It should be remembered, however, that Peshawar was unique in being a small town where NGOs operated in a close knit community. ACBAR simply facilitated and improved upon an already high level of communication between agencies.

ACRONYMS AND ABBREVIATIONS

ACBAR	Agency Co-ordinating Body for Afghan Relief
AETF	Afghanistan Emergency Trust Fund
AIG	Afghan Interim Government
ANCB	Afghan NGO Coordinating Body
ARC	Arms Control Research Centre
AVICEN	Afghanistan Vaccination and Immunization Centre
BAAG	British Agencies Afghanistan Group
CCAR	Chief Commission for Afghan Refugees
CCSDPT	Committee for Coordination of Services to Displaced Persons in Thailand
CFF	Cash-For-Food
CHEA	La Coordination Humanitaire Européenne pour l'Afghanistan
CIA	Central Intelligence Agency
CMC	Committee of Medical Coordination
CRDA	Christian Relief and Development Association
ECU	European Currency Unit
EU	European Union
FAO	Food and Agriculture Organisation
ICC	Islamic Coordinating Council
ICRC	International Committee of the Red Cross/Crescent
ICRI	International Consortium for Refugees in Iran
IPF	Indicative Planning Figure
IRC	International Refugee Council
ISRA	Islamic Relief Association
NAC	Norwegian Afghanistan Committee
NRC	Norwegian Refugee Council
NWFP	North West Frontier Province
RTV	Refugee Tented Village
SCA	Swedish Committee for Afghanistan
SCF-UK	Save the Children Fund (UK)
SWABAC	Southern and Western Afghanistan and Baluchistan Association for Coordination
UNDCP	United Nations International Drugs Control Programme
UNDP	United Nations Development Programme
UNHCR	United Nations High Commissioner for Refugees
UNICEF	United Nations Children's Fund
UNOCA	United Nations Coordinator for Humanitarian and Economic Assistance Programmes Relating to Afghanistan
UNORSA	United Nations Office for the Rehabilitation Strategy of Afghanistan
USAID	United States Agency for International Development
UN-DHA	United Nations Department of Humanitarian Affairs
UNOCHA	United Nations Office for the Coordination of Humanitarian Assistance
VAG	Voluntary Agencies Group
VITA	Volunteers in Technical Assistance
WHO	World Health Organisation

REFERENCES

ACBAR (1991a) *ACBAR Directory of Members, 1991-92* ACBAR, Peshawar

ACBAR (1991b) *Health Standards and Guidelines* ACBAR, Peshawar.

ACBAR (1991c) *Agricultural Guidelines* (translated into Dari in 1992), ACBAR, Peshawar

ACBAR (1991d) Various 'Eastern Paktia Task Force reports', ACBAR, Peshawar

ACBAR (1992a) and ACBAR (1993) *Directory of Humanitarian Agencies Working for Afghans* ACBAR, Peshawar

ACBAR (1992b) *Register of programmes for Disabled Afghans*, ACBAR, Peshawar

ACBAR (1993) *Summary of the Database of NGO Activities*, ACBAR, Peshawar

ACBAR & GTZ (1990) *Coordination of Management Training for Afghans*, ACBAR, Peshawar

ACBAR/UNOCA (1990) *The Paktika Report* ACBAR, Peshawar

Arney, George (1990) *Afghanistan*, Mandarin, London

Baitenmann, H (1990) 'NGOs and the Afghan war: the politicisation of humanitarian aid' *Third World Quarterly*, vol 12, no 1, pp 62–83

Bennett, J et al (1992) *Overview of NGO Assistance to Afghanistan* ACBAR, Pakistan

Bruce, A (1992) *Developing an NGO: An Afghan Example*, Politics Dissertation, Edinburgh University, unpublished

Centlivres, P (1994) '*A "State of the Art" review of research on internally displaced refugees and returnees from and in Afghanistan*', paper presented at the 4th International Research and Advisory Panel Conference on Forced Migration (IRAP), Oxford

Dupree, N H (1988) 'Demographic Reporting on Afghan Refugees in Pakistan' *Modern Asian Studies*, vol 22, no 4, pp 845–865

ICC (undated) *Islamic Coordination Council* a briefing paper, ICC

Lawrence, F (1990) *The United Nations in Pakistan and Afghanistan: a critical assessment* ACBAR, Peshawar

Magnus, R (1987) 'Humanitarian Response to an Inhuman Strategy', in G Farr and J Merriam, eds, *Afghan Resistance: the politics of survival*, Westview, Boulder, Co

Meier, D (1992) *Salary Standardization for National Staff of NGOs in Afghanistan*, ACBAR, Peshawar

Nicholds, N and Borton, J (1993) '*The Changing Role of NGOs in the Provision of Relief and Rehabilitation Assistance: Afghanistan/Pakistan*' Working Paper 74, Overseas Development Institute, London

Rahim, A (1991) 'The Role of Afghan NGOs in Relief and Reconstruction of Afganistan', ANCB, Pakistan, unpublished

Shakir, M (1992) *NGO Programs in Kunar (1990-92)* ACBAR, Peshawar

Shelter Now International (1990), 'Press Package', 29 April, Peshawar

Van Brabant, K (1992) 'Childhood immunisation in rural Afghanistan: the EPI programme, 1987–91' *Disasters*, vol 16, no 4

2

ETHIOPIA:
NGO CONSORTIA AND COORDINATION
ARRANGEMENTS, 1984–91[1]

John Borton

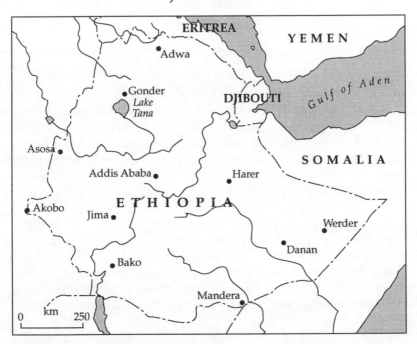

The People: Population: 47 million approx. Two-thirds are of Amhara or Oromo (Galla) descent. Other large ethnic groups include Tigre, Gurage, Niloti, Somali and Afar.

Religion: Majority are Coptic Christian, though a significant percentage (perhaps as much as 20 per cent) are Muslim.

The Government: Interim government headed by Ata Meles Zenawi since June 1991 following the overthrow of the communist regime by the Ethiopian People's Revolutionary Democratic Front (EPRDF).

Development Aid: US$888 million (1990); US$17 per capita; 14.6 per cent of GNP.

---

1. This paper draws upon research on the role of NGOs in relief operations funded by the UK Overseas Development Administration. The Ethiopia/Eritrea material from the research is published by the Overseas Development Institute (ODI) *(Borton, 1994)*. The views contained here are the author's own and do not reflect those of the ODI.

A number of coordination arrangements were developed by NGOs during the massive relief operations undertaken in northern Ethiopia and Eritrea between 1984–91 on both the government side and in areas controlled by the Eritrean and Tigrayan Front organisations. Those examined briefly here are the Christian Relief and Development Agency (CRDA), the Joint Relief Partnership (JRP) and the Emergency Relief Desk (ERD). Many of the arrangements were, in fact, NGO consortia with multiple objectives of increasing access to resources and sharing the costs involved in the provision of relief assistance as well as to ensure that it was properly coordinated.

A conclusion that can be drawn from the widely acclaimed effectiveness of CRDA, and also the coordination difficulties experienced in early 1985 on the government side, is that effective coordination requires the body concerned to have allocative control over a proportion of the total resource flows. Such control gives the coordination body the ability to enable and encourage NGOs to respond promptly to needs not met by the prevalent donor policy of allocating relief resources on the basis of project proposals prepared by individual NGOs working in defined geographical areas.

BACKGROUND

The success of the Ethiopian People's Revolutionary Democratic Front (EPRDF)[2] and the consequent fall of the Mengistu regime in May 1991 marked the end of the 'complex emergency' which had persisted for much of the previous decade. The 'complex emergency' was the product of a number of factors. Principly these were: the effects of the Government of Ethiopia's (GOE) social and economic policies which aimed at collective ownership and centralised direction; the conflict between the GOE and the Fronts which disrupted trade and resulted in the deaths of tens of thousands of non-combatants as well as combatants; and droughts which affected all areas of the north in 1984 and parts of the north variously during the second half of the decade. These factors interacted to produce a significant deterioration in food security, massive population displacements and substantially increased morbidity and mortality, including those casualties directly caused by the conflict throughout the period. The 1984/85 famine marked the period of greatest mortality. Estimates of the overall excess mortality during the period from the early 1980s to 1991 vary widely, but would appear to be in the region of 800,000 to 1,100,000.

In response to this situation, large-scale relief and rehabilitation operations were undertaken in northern Ethiopia and Eritrea by NGOs, the Red Cross Movement, UN agencies and agencies of the GOE and the Fronts. (Figure 2.1) Information on the total value of assistance provided during the period is not readily available but as a measure of the scale of the overall operations, a total of 4.8 million tonnes of food aid was distributed in GOE controlled areas between 1984 and 1990 and during the same period approximately 900,000 tonnes was distributed in areas under the control of the Fronts. Figures

2. The EPRDF was formed in January 1989 by the merger of the Tigray People's Liberation Front (TPFL) and the smaller Ethiopian People's Democratic Movement (EPDM),

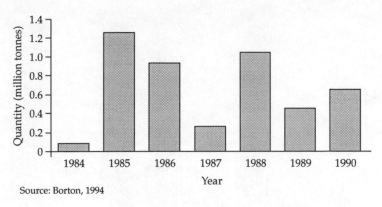

Source: Borton, 1994

Figure 2.1 *Food aid deliveries*

2.1, 2.2 and 2.3 show the scale and trends in the amounts of food aid distributed in the GOE controlled areas and in the areas controlled by the EPLF and TPLF.

These relief operations relied upon NGOs to an unprecedented degree and several consortia and coordination mechanisms developed among NGOs involved in the provision of relief and rehabilitation assistance in both the GOE controlled areas and in those areas controlled by the EPLF and TPLF. We shall here provide an overview of the role of NGOs on both sides of the conflict and examine the coordination arrangements that developed. As another contribution to this volume focuses upon the ERD – the principal NGO coordination mechanism for assistance to the areas controlled by the Fronts – we shall restrict ourselves to a discussion of the principal NGO coordination mechanisms in the GOE controlled areas, ie the CRDA and the JRP.

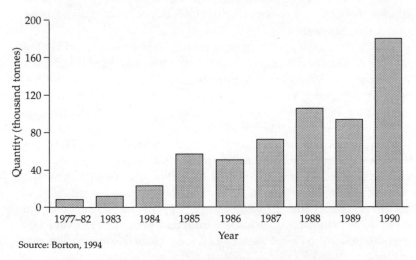

Source: Borton, 1994

Figure 2.2 *Food aid distributions by ERA*

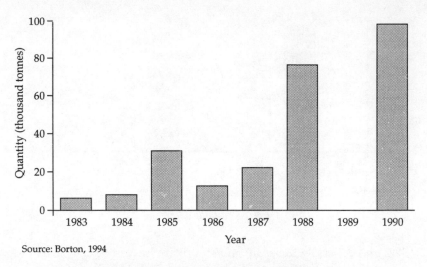

Source: Borton, 1994

Figure 2.3 *Food aid distributions by REST*

THE ROLE OF NGOS ON BOTH SIDES

On the GOE side, western bilateral donors deliberately channelled the bulk of their assistance through NGOs and avoided the government's Relief and Rehabilitation Commission (RRC). Such channelling decisions were due primarily to the anti-western stance and Marxist policies of the GOE and the fear that assistance channelled through the RRC might be used in support of the controversial Resettlement Programme or by the Ethiopian army. A key period was late 1984 and early 1985 when, at a time of a massive increase in the volume of assistance provided (belatedly) in response to the famine, the predominant position of the RRC as a channel for the transportation and distribution of relief assistance was replaced by that of NGOs.

Available data indicate that approximately 70 per cent of food aid and 50 per cent of non-food emergency assistance was provided by or channelled through NGOs during the period 1985–91, with the Red Cross Movement accounting for about 10 per cent of both and the UN and GOE accounting for the remainder of both *(Borton, 1994)*. NGO operations in the GOE areas were conventional in the sense that agencies took responsibility for specific activities in geographically defined areas. However, they were on a larger scale than previous NGO relief operations and involved many NGOs in trucking and dry ration distribution as well as the more traditional intensive feeding and health care activities.

In the areas controlled by the Fronts, the role of NGOs was quite different in that all distributions were undertaken by the Eritrean Relief Agency (ERA) or the Relief Society of Tigray (REST) – agencies which were closely linked to the EPLF and TPLF respectively. The role of international NGOs was that of conduits for western assistance, the bulk of which from 1984 onwards was provided by bilateral donor organisations. Such assistance was provided in the form of funding and in-kind assistance (principally food aid) for the relief operations managed by ERA and REST. While some food and seeds were purchased in Tigray and to a much lesser extent in Eritrea, the bulk of assistance was provided by Cross-Border Operations (CBO) from Sudan.

Initially, the CBOs were small scale operations undertaken by the ICRC and a few international, mainly church-affiliated, NGOs using their own resources. Though such agencies undertook periodic monitoring of the assistance they provided, they played no effective role in the planning and implementation of the relief activities within Eritrea and Tigray. Prior to 1984, bilateral donors did not support such operations for fear of being seen to be aiding and providing tacit recognition to the EPLF/TPLF. However, the 1984–85 famine and the evident need for humanitarian assistance in areas outside GOE control forced bilateral donors, led by the USA, to modify their previous position.

In order to maintain a 'diplomatic distance' bilateral donors channelled their humanitarian assistance through international NGOs acting as low-profile, almost covert, intermediaries. As a result of the monopoly of the relief operations held by ERA and REST inside Eritrea and Tigray, the role of international NGOs was effectively as conduits between donors and ERA and REST, which the international NGOS referred to as 'implementing agencies' or 'implementing partners'. Food aid shipped to Port Sudan was generally consigned to the intermediating NGO which would either hand it over immediately to ERA or REST, or transport it to the Sudanese border where it would then be transferred to ERA or REST trucks. When food was available for bulk purchase in Sudan, international NGOs would procure the food from Sudanese merchants and arrange for delivery to the border. REST also undertook substantial 'Internal Purchase' programmes in western Tigray. Initially, international NGO personnel took suitcases of Ethiopian Birr into Tigray where they would supervise the purchases from Tigrayan merchants. Subsequently, the funds were simply transferred into REST bank accounts and the Internal Purchase programme monitored through periodic visits into Tigray.

With bilateral donors distancing themselves from such activities and the UN resolutely refusing to play any role in relation to areas under the control of the Fronts, the coordination mechanisms that developed were the NGOs' own creations and did not operate within the UN/donor coordination framework usually present in relief operations. With ERA and REST undertaking the coordination of relief delivery within their respective areas, cooperative mechanisms that developed among the international NGOs were consortia formed to coordinate the procurement and delivery of assistance to ERA and REST and the monitoring of ERA and REST's use of such assistance within Eritrea and Tigray. Not only did such consortia 'coordinate' the various activities, they also avoided the duplication costs that would have been incurred if agencies had operated independently, setting up their own offices in Sudan and undertaking monitoring visits only in relation to their own particular shipments or funded activities.

For relief assistance, the principal consortia were:

- the ERD, through which ERA and REST received the bulk of their food aid;
- the Tigray Transport and Agriculture Consortium (TTAC);
- and the Eritrean Inter-Agency Agriculture Consortium (EIAC).

The latter two provided resources for transport and agricultural recovery programmes within Tigray and Eritrea respectively. During its 11-year existence, ERD provided some 685,000 tonnes of food to ERA, REST and a small amount to the Oromo Relief Agency (ORA). 54 per cent of this amount was supplied by United States Agency for International Development (USAID) which channelled its assistance through Lutheran World Relief (*Duffield & Prendergast, 1993*). From 1983–92, the TTAC provided REST with a total of 302 trucks and 65 trailers together with spares, garage equipment, road construction equipment and funding for labourers, etc.

Not all of the assistance provided to ERA and REST was from members of these consortia. For instance Oxfam did not join ERD even though at certain points it was responsible for channelling substantial volumes of food aid to Tigray. The reasons for this are not entirely apparent but in part it stemmed from Oxfam-UK's secular status, whilst ERD was a consortium of agencies affiliated to Protestant churches. It was also in part because REST wanted to avoid a situation where it was faced with a single 'monopoly' supplier. Interestingly, much of the food aid provided by Oxfam-UK was donated by the EC which also provided food aid to the ERD, channelling the assistance through Dutch Interchurch Aid (DIA), one of ERD's member agencies.

Though the experience of the CBO is interesting from a number of perspectives, its lessons for NGO coordination in future relief operations appear to be limited, as the instances where international NGO serve as conduits to monopoly 'implementing agencies' are likely to be infrequent.

COORDINATION ARRANGEMENTS IN GOE-CONTROLLED AREAS

In the GOE controlled areas, NGOs operated within a broad coordination framework provided by the GOE and the UN. By any account, the GOE's RRC played a central role in the relief efforts during the period. Though the ability of the RRC to control and coordinate the relief operations was substantially weakened by the use of NGOs as channels for bilateral relief assistance, it was at least able to exercise considerable control over the activities of NGOs through its registration procedures, controls over expatriate staff and internal travel, and the requirement that the RRC Head Office and RRC provincial representatives approve new projects.

Because of the poor relations between many of the international bilateral donors and the GOE, the RRC's role in terms of donor coordination was limited and it was here that the UN played a key role. In late 1984, at the peak of the famine, the United Nations Office for Emergency Operations in Ethiopia (UNOEOE) was formed, headed by the Special Representative of the UN Secretary General – Kurt Jansson. The location of the UNOEOE in Addis Ababa rather than in Geneva or New York increased the involvement of the UN in operational coordination. The Head of UNOEOE had access to the President and Ministers which was generally denied to representatives of international donors and NGOs. The UN was thus able to represent their interests and concerns at this level *(Jansson, 1987)* In 1987 the UNOEOE was closed but many of its functions and some of its staff transferred to the United Nations Emergency Preparedness and Prevention Group (UNEPPG) within United Nations Development Programme (UNDP) Ethiopia.

Such 'macro' coordination was complemented among the NGO community by the CRDA, regarded by many as the best example of an NGO operational coordination mechanism.[3] An additional arrangement was made by several members of CRDA who joined together to form a consortium – the JRP – which proved remarkably successful in mobilising resources and utilising church structures to distribute relief assistance. The development and operation of the CRDA is discussed below, and for the purposes of comparison a brief description of the JRP is also provided.

THE CRDA[4]

The CRDA originated in a forum known as the 'Christian Relief Committee' which was formed in mid-1973 following the Imperial government's belated acknowledgement of the famine then underway in Wollo and Tigray and its request to local churches and missions to help in the response. Following the request, 20 representatives of churches and missions, including the Ethiopian Catholic Secretariat (ECS) and the Evangelical Church Makene Yesus (EECMYH), held

---

3. For example, a 1987 study of NGO coordination mechanisms in seven African countries, *Duell and Dutcher (1987)*, found the CRDA to be 'the most sophisticated voluntary cooperative body encountered in this study.'

4. The information contained in this section was obtained from CRDA bi-annual reports, annual reports on relief and rehabilitation activities and from interviews with Brother O'Keeffe (Executive Director), Hagos Araya (Assistant Executive Director) and Liz Stone (Information Officer) in November 1992.

their own meeting and agreed to hold regular meetings to pool information and coordinate their relief activities. Other agencies, including a number of secular agencies such as Concern, SCF-UK and Oxfam-UK subsequently joined the Committee. To fill gaps in the resources of member organisations, contact was made with overseas funding agencies and the funds received were allocated on the basis of decisions by the Committee. With the growth of membership, particularly after the showing of Jonathan Dimbleby's documentary film *Unknown Famine* in September 1973, and the need to expedite the allocation process, an Executive Committee and full-time Coordinator were appointed in December 1973.

During 1974, the Committee began to support members' rehabilitation activities and the geographical area of the Committee's coordination and support activities was widened to include the relief and rehabilitation activities of member agencies in other areas of Ethiopia, such as Eritrea, Hararghe, Sidamo and Illubabor. In September 1974, the Committee was officially registered under the new name – Christian Relief and Development Association – and a Memorandum of Association drawn up which declared CRDA's purpose to be 'to promote and encourage relief and development activities in Ethiopia'. In March 1975, a special agreement was signed with the RRC, which had been established the previous August, that defined the relationship of CRDA to the government's relief and rehabilitation activities.

Many of the significant features of CRDA's subsequent development were laid during the life of the Christian Relief Committee, particularly during its first three months. Key features of this framework were the regular sharing of information, the creation of a Secretariat, the ability to receive funds and material assistance from non-members and the creation of a mechanism to allocate such funds between members.

CRDA described its primary role as being:

- to coordinate the activities of its members for the purposes of joint decision-making and action;
- to supplement members' resources with financial and material assistance from donor partners; and
- to provide common services to its members *(CRDA, 1992)*.

The coordination function was undertaken by providing mechanisms for the exchange of information and by exercising control over significant material and financial resources which could be allocated to members' programmes. The principal forum for information exchange during the large scale relief and rehabilitation operations of the 1980s and beginning of the 1990s, not only for the NGO com-

---

5. During 1987, the government restricted attendance at the meetings to members and certain UN officials as it believed that certain media reports which were critical of the government had originated at General Meetings *(Duell & Dutcher, 1987)*.

munity but also between the NGOs and the UN agencies and donor organisations, were CRDA's monthly General Meetings. These were open to anyone and it was normal for representatives of the RRC, UN agencies, and interested foreign embassies and the media to attend.[5]

During the General Meetings, information was exchanged on the situation in different areas and developments relevant to the relief, rehabilitation and development activities of members. After the General Meeting, member agency representatives remained for a closed Members' Meeting to conduct CRDA business. This involved, for instance, discussion of issues arising from the open session and planning CRDA's response to them possibly by coordinating actions by member agencies operating in particular areas of need and identifying ways in which CRDA might support them.

Ad hoc committees were also set up by CRDA to coordinate action in response to particular emergencies. In recent years, these have included the Meningitis Task Group in 1989 and the Committee on Transport Requirements in the Northern Regions and the Emergency Task Group, both of which met throughout the 1987–8 relief operations. In addition to the committee structure, CRDA organised workshops on particular subjects to encourage the sharing of experience and ideas. Workshop reports were prepared and disseminated to members. For the Health, Development and Children's Programmes the Workshops were held on a quarterly basis.[6]

The practice of receiving material and financial assistance from donor partners and using them to supplement the resources directly available to members was an important function since CRDA's creation and substantially empowered its coordinating role. The assistance may either have been actively requested by CRDA in the knowledge of a particular resource need among its member agencies or it may have been offered to CRDA by donors wishing to support NGO activities and trust CRDA to serve as a 'clearing house' for their assistance. While some assistance came from privately raised funds of non-operational partner agencies, a substantial proportion represented resources requested from bilateral donors by partner organisations on CRDA's behalf. Some foreign governments consigned material aid directly to CRDA without channelling it through Northern NGO partners, but it was rare for CRDA to receive financial assistance directly from bilateral donor organisations.[7]

---

6. A selection of workshop reports over the last few years include: 'Fighting Aids Together'; 'Small Scale Income Generation – Does it Really Pay'; 'Environmental Impact Assessment'; 'Monitoring and Evaluation of Rural Water Projects'; 'Special Needs of Children in Disasters'; 'Integrated Basic Health Services: Collaboration in the Health Services by the MoD, RRC, UNICEF and CRDA Members'; and 'Lessons Learned' (from the 1984-5 relief operation).

7. One of the exceptions is that of the US Office of Foreign Disaster Assistance (OFDA) grant to CRDA which is held by the US Embassy in Addis and can be released on approval of funding proposals submitted by CRDA.

Non-operational funding partners which have provided substantial support to CRDA's activities over the years include Christian Aid, Catholic Fund for Overseas Development (CAFOD) and Band Aid in the UK, Church World Service and USA for Africa in the USA, Interchurch Coordination Committee for Development Projects (ICCO) and Catholic Organisation for Joint Financing of Development Programmes (CEBEMO) in the Netherlands, Brot für die Weld and Zentralstelle fur Entwicklungshilfe (Protestant Association for Cooperation in Development), (EZE) in Germany, DanChurchAid in Denmark and Cardinal Leger and Peace and Development in Canada. This pattern of support reflected the traditional association of CRDA with church-affiliated organisations in the North.

The value of financial and material relief and rehabilitation assistance channelled through CRDA to member agencies was substantial (see Table 2.1). In 1986, for instance, the material assistance provided (food aid, tents, shelter material, medicines etc) was valued at US$9.4 million and US$520,000 was provided in financial assistance for CRDA's relief activities. Much of the amount shown for relief during 1988 was accounted for by a donation of 25,000 tonnes of wheat from the EC allocated to programmes of 27 member agencies working in ten regions of the country. In 1985, member agencies agreed that the CRDA Secretariat should provide a central procurement service purchasing seeds, tools and oxen for the recovery efforts and this resulted in a programme which provided 6000 tonnes of seed. It was agreed that this should be considerably expanded during 1986. Seed requirements of member agencies were collated in October 1985 and distributions began in February 1986. In total, 16,700 tonnes of seeds and 437,000 tools were distributed that year in all 12 provinces of Ethiopia.

Table 2.1 *Value of relief and rehabilitation assistance from CRDA,*
(1986–88)

Year	Relief	Rehabilitation
	(cash and in-kind allocations measured in US$m)	
1986	10.3	10.3
1987	6.2	4.1
1988	24.0	7.7

Source: CRDA 'Relief and Rehabilitation Reports 1986–8', Addis Ababa.

CRDA is also an important provider of transport services to its member agencies, particularly the smaller agencies that are unable or unwilling to set up and operate their own truck fleets. In 1982–3, CRDA transported 8700 tonnes of RRC grain from Addis Ababa to programmes run by member agencies in Eritrea, Wollo and Tigray as a way of assisting the RRC with the severe transport shortage it was facing at that time *(CRDA, 1983)*. The truck fleet grew rapidly during 1985 and stood at 54 trucks in 1986 *(USAID, 1987)* and 66 by 1992. In 1989, CRDA contributed 22 trucks from its fleet to the JRP Southern Line Operation north of Dessie. The vehicle workshop set up to maintain this fleet also serviced vehicles belonging to member and other agencies on a cost recovery basis and in 1992 this service was a net earner of funds for CRDA.

Membership of CRDA was open to any church or voluntary agency in Ethiopia engaged in promoting relief and development activities. Applicant agencies had to have a signed agreement with the government and had to have been working in the country for six months. When it was registered in 1975, CRDA had 22 member agencies. By 1988, the number had increased to 53. In 1989, associate membership was introduced for all new members. Associate members were able to receive assistance from CRDA and use the range of services available but they could not vote or hold office for the first three years of membership. The category of associate membership was introduced partly as a response to the number of small new agencies being set up whose activities were often limited to the provision of assistance and care to orphans and children. After the fall of the Mengistu regime in 1991, REST and ORA became associate members of CRDA. In 1992, CRDA had 61 member agencies and 23 associate members. (See Box 2.1)

Analysis of the 1988 Directory of member agencies indicates that just over half (28 out of 53) of the member agencies were secular whilst the remainder were church-affiliated. The Directory also contains information on the year in which member agencies were established in Ethiopia and this has been plotted in Figure 2.4. This reveals the

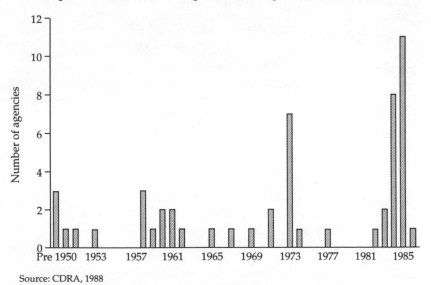

Source: CDRA, 1988

Figure 2.4 *New NGOs established in Ethiopia*

Box 2.1

CRDA's STRUCTURE

The principal elements of CRDA's structure were the Secretariat, the General and Members' Meetings, the Executive Committee and Sub-Committees. The Secretariat had a total staff of 240 in 1992 of which 40 were based in the Head Office. As noted above, the General and Members' Meetings were held monthly with the General Meetings serving an important information sharing role and being followed by closed Members' Meetings. The Members' Meetings represented the supreme governing body of CRDA and all decisions reached by the Executive Committee and the sub-committees were subject to approval by the Members' Meetings. The Executive Committee comprised 12 members elected from the official delegates to the Membership Meetings. The Executive Committee met every two weeks to formulate policy and approve projects costing more than 100,000 Birr (approximately US$50,000) which were screened by the Secretariat.[8]

The role of the Sub-Committees was to review requests for financial and material support submitted by member agencies in relation to particular areas of activity. Prior to 1989, there were three sub-committees for Material Aid, Relief, Rehabilitation and Development and in that year a fourth was added, the sub-committee on Children's Programmes. The Material Aid sub-committee allocated the substantial quantities of food, medicines and shelter materials which were donated to CRDA by partner agencies and occasionally by bilateral donor organisations. The Material Aid sub-committee was made up solely of Secretariat Personnel. Requests involving comparatively modest resource allocations could be approved by the sub-committees. For requests of greater value members of the Executive Committee were co-opted to evaluate the proposals. All decisions taken by the sub-committees were ratified by the full monthly Members' Meeting.

---

long history of NGOs in Ethiopia – particularly the indigenous church based agencies and foreign missions and church affiliated agencies. Thus 21 of the 53 member agencies in 1988 were established prior to the 1973–4 famine and three (the Society of International Missions, St Matthew's Church and the Kale Heywet Church Development Programme) were established during the 1920s. The impact of the famine relief programmes of 1973–4 and 1984–5 on the number of NGOs commencing work in the country is clearly visible.

Members were required to make an annual contribution towards CRDA's overhead costs. Contribution levels in 1992 were 5000 Birr for members and 2500 Birr for associate members. Some members contributed

---

8. The financial authority of the Executive Committee and the various Sub-Committees has varied over time. During 1986, for instance, the secretariat staff could authorise allocations up to a level of 30,000 Birr. Allocations between 30,000 and 70,000 Birr could be approved by three members of the Executive Committee. Allocations above 70,000 Birr required the approval of the full Executive Committee.

above this requirement. This source of funding only covered a proportion of the overhead costs. The remainder of the overhead costs together with the funding of CRDA's various services and projects was met by contributions from international non-operational funding partners.

CRDA did not have a foreign exchange account as a matter of policy. As a result it developed mechanisms in conjunction with its main funding partners whereby CRDA requested them to use their contribution to CRDA funds to procure and transport materials and equipment needed by CRDA and its member agencies which could not be obtained locally. For instance, ICCO might have requested to use its contribution by tendering for suppliers in the Netherlands to send plastic sheeting and medical supplies to CRDA. For some of the partner agencies the mechanism became more sophisticated. For instance, if CAFOD was requested to procure £15,000 of stationery supplies, the Birr equivalent of the CRDA foreign exchange saving was credited to CAFOD as its contribution to the CRDA micro-project fund.

In 1982, CRDA fielded a team of four nurses to run an intensive feeding programme at Ibnat. As the situation worsened during 1983 and 1984, so CRDA increased the number of such teams and at the peak of the relief operations in early 1985 was directly involved in 17 feeding centres and shelters. This move into a directly operational role was questioned by member agencies who felt CRDA was putting too much of its energies into its own projects at the expense of its support to member agencies. In addition, larger member agencies felt that it was inappropriate for CRDA to undertake such directly operational activities which overlapped with their own and effectively competed with them for scarce donor resources. By 1986, CRDA had withdrawn from such operations and thereafter confined itself to the range of activities detailed above. Duell and Dutcher, *(1987)* see this episode and differences over the growth of CRDA's vehicle fleet as being a dispute between the interests of large agencies and small agencies over the proper role of a consortium.

THE JRP

The JRP was formed in late 1984, initially under the name of Churches Drought Action Africa/Ethiopia (CDAA/E), by Catholic Relief Services (CRS), Lutheran World Federation (LWF), the ECS and the EECMY. Later, these four agencies were joined by the Ethiopian Orthodox Church (EOC).

From 1985–86 the JRP was responsible for distributing 428,000 tonnes of relief food, representing approximately 22 per cent of total relief food distributions in GOE areas. Its development and operation during the period 1984–86 is described in detail by *Solberg, (1991)*. During 1990–91, the JRP ran a 'cross-line' operation into areas of northern Wollo and Tigray under the control of the TPLF/EPDM using food supplied through the Southern Line Operation from Assab which distributed 153,000 tonnes over a 15 month period *(JRP, 1992)*.

The principal features of JRP's structure were:

- **'International' members used their existing donor relationships on behalf of all members** – ie CRS and LWF submitted requests for assistance on behalf of the whole JRP programme to USAID and the EC respectively.
- **Member agencies took responsibility for supervising JRP operations in particular provinces** – for example, ECS supervised operations in Eritrea, Tigray, Gamo Gofa and Kefa.
- **Within their areas of responsibility member agencies were free to pass on food to other agencies** for use in their emergency programmes once they had become affiliated to JRP and agreed to the terms and conditions prescribed by USAID for the use of Title II food commodities. By mid-1985, 29 agencies had become affiliated.
- **Member agencies adopted a standard distribution method** modelled on the Nutrition Intervention Programme (NIP) take-home supplementary ration system previously developed by CRS.
- **There was provision for member agencies to continue their ongoing rehabilitation and development activities separate from their JRP relief activities**.

For the first few months, CRS tended to dominate the partnership but the partnership's ecumenical nature was asserted, in part by changing some of the individuals initially involved. Donors and other NGOs also at first feared that CDAA/E was becoming a 'super-agency'. However, as a result of legal difficulties over its status – ie whether it represented a new autonomous agency and would therefore be required to register as such under Ethiopian law – the JRP was not allowed to develop substantial autonomy from its member agencies and the size of its secretariat was deliberately limited.

CONCLUSION

There are some lessons from the Ethiopian experience for NGO relief coordination. The JRP showed how a consortium of Northern NGOs capable of accessing the substantial food aid resources of the USA and the EC, coupled with the infrastructure of local churches, can mobilise and distribute substantial quantities of relief and rehabilitation resources. However, as a coordinating body of over 50 agencies rather than an exclusive consortium of five agencies, it was CRDA's experience that held the greatest lessons for NGO coordination in emergency operations.

CRDA's provision of common services to its members, such as

vehicle maintenance, seed purchasing and transport services, reduced the costs of duplication among NGOs in these areas of their activity. The value of such common services was probably proportionately greater for the smaller member agencies than the larger ones, many of which ran their own trucking fleets and procured their own seeds.

CRDA's ability to receive resources and allocate them between its member agencies appears to be a highly positive attribute which other coordination bodies might consider emulating. It appears to have increased the access of the smaller, locally-based NGOs to donor resources and to have facilitated a degree of decentralisation of resource allocation decisions from the head offices of donor organisations located in Europe and North America to the Addis Ababa level. Control over a proportion of the relief resources being deployed in the GOE controlled areas of the country would appear to have enhanced CRDA's coordination function within the country by enabling it to support member agencies in meeting additional needs and filling 'gaps' in assistance. CRDA was often able to provide such support to its members more rapidly by bypassing the usual process of agencies having to seek support from donor organisation head offices.

For donor organisations, CRDA offered a valuable 'clearing house' facility enabling them to deal directly with only one agency rather than several, thereby reducing their administrative requirements and possibly leading to the provision of higher levels of resources than would otherwise have been the case.

The case for coordinating bodies to have control over the allocation of at least a proportion of the relief resources being provided is supported by the experience during the hectic, emergency period of late 1984 to mid-1985 when Wollo, one of the provinces most severely affected by famine, was severely under-supplied. From the evidence available, it would appear that the reduction in the proportion of food aid channelled through the RRC (resulting from the switch of resources to NGOs) reduced the ability of the RRC to play the vital role of 'sweeper', ie covering needs in those areas not covered by the expanding NGO programmes. Because such a large proportion of the bilateral food aid entering the country was earmarked for particular NGO programmes in particular areas, but not necessarily Wollo, the province was undersupplied by both NGOs and the RRC for several months. This experience points to the need in rapidly expanding, dynamic relief contexts for coordination mechanisms capable of receiving and storing a pool of unearmarked relief resources and allocating them to areas not covered by earmarked bilateral assistance. The point is valid in relation to all coordination mechanisms whether they are operated by the government, NGOs or the UN. In those situations where the proportion of resources being handled by government agencies is limited, it is logical that such a pool should be managed by either the UN or by an NGO coordinating body where the latter has the necessary capability. Such 'pools' are often discussed in relief contexts but rarely implemented, largely as a result of the unwilling-ness of bilateral donors to relax their accounting requirements and preference for their assistance to be distributed by agencies of the same nationality. How large such pools need to be in order to be effective will naturally vary depending on the particular circumstances of an operation, but, at a guess, somewhere between 10–30 per cent of the total flows would probably be adequate for most operations. Further investigation is needed on the appropriate size of such pools and how donors can be encouraged to provide resources to them rather than providing assistance directly to individual NGOs.

Developments since 1991

The fall of the Mengistu regime in 1991 ended the conflict in the north of the country, though instability continued in southern and eastern areas. The research upon which this chapter is based (*Borton, 1994*) did not examine the period since the change of government, but it is apparent that the change has brought with it some important implica-tions for NGOs in Ethiopia. The new government has allowed the formation of alternative political parties and introduced a new admin-istrative system based on five ethnically defined regions. Previously exiled groups have returned to the country and established new NGOs to assist in the rehabilitation and development efforts.

A result of these changes has been an increase in the number of indigenous NGOs, many associated with particular political parties or ethnic groups. This has led to the development of other umbrella organisations amongst NGOs besides CRDA and JRP, notably the Committee for Ethiopian Voluntary Organisations (CEVO). For their part, donor organisations are now keen to work with and support the rehabilitation and development activities of the new government and this has resulted in increased levels of government-to-government assistance. With the scaling back of relief efforts the amount of resources channelled through NGOs has decreased, though informa-tion on the extent of this reduction was not available for the preparation of this chapter.

ACRONYMS AND ABBREVIATIONS

CAFOD	Catholic Fund for Overseas Development
CBO	Cross-border Operations
CDAA/E	Churches Drought Action Africa/Ethiopia
CEBEMO	Catholic Organization for Joint Financing of Development Programmes
CEVO	Committee for Ethiopian Voluntary Organisations
CRDA	Christian Relief and Development Association
CRS	Catholic Relief Services
DIA	Dutch Interchurch Aid
ECS	Ethiopian Catholic Secretariat
EECMY	Ethiopian Evangelical Church Mekane Yesus
EIAC	Eritrean Inter-Agency Agriculture Consortium
EOC	Ethopian Orthodox Church
EPDM	Ethiopian People's Democratic Movement
EPLF	Eritrean People's Liberation Front
EPRDF	Ethiopian People's Revolutionary Democratic Front
ERA	Eritrean Relief Association
ERD	Emergency Relief Desk
EZE	Zentralstelle fur Entwicklungshilfe (Protestant Association for Co-operation in Development)
GOE	Government of Ethiopia
ICCO	Inter-church Coordination Committee for Development Projects
JRP	Joint Relief Partnership
ODA	Overseas Development Administration
ODI	Overseas Development Institute
ORA	Oromo Relief Association
NIP	Nutrition Intervention Programme
REST	Relief Society of Tigray
RRC	Relief and Rehabilitation Commission
SCF	Save the Children Fund (UK)
TPLF	Tigray People's Liberation Front
TTAC	Tigray Transport and Agricultural Consortium
UNDP	United Nations Development Programme
UNEPPG	United Nations Emergency Preparedness and Prevention Group
UNOEOE	United Nations Office for Emergency Operations in Ethiopia
USAID	United States Agency for International Development
LWF	Lutheran World Federation

REFERENCES

AfricaWatch (1991) *Evil Days: 30 Years of War and Famine in Ethiopia* AfricaWatch, London

Borton, J (1989) 'Food Aid to Tigray: a Review of Oxfam's Involvement in the Provision of European Community Food Aid to the Relief Society of Tigray', Relief and Development Institute, London

Borton, J (1994) 'The Changing Role of NGOs in the Provision of Relief and Rehabilitation Assistance: Case Study 3 – Northern Ethiopia and Eritrea' *Working Paper 76*, Overseas Development Institute, London

Centre of Development Studies (1988) 'Eritrea Food and Agricultural Production Assessment Study', Final Report, University of Leeds, UK

Centre of Development Studies (1992) 'Peace in Eritrea: Prospects for Food Security and Problems for Policy', University of Leeds, UK

CRDA (1983) 'Brief Report on CRDA Activities in the Drought Affected Regions of Wollo, Tigray, Eritrea, Gondar and Sidamo', CRDA, Addis Ababa

CRDA (1988) 'Directory of Members', CRDA, Addis Ababa

CRDA (1989) 'CRDA Review 1986–88', CRDA, Addis Ababa

CRDA (1992) 'CRDA Review 1989–91, CRDA, Addis Ababa

Duell, C B and Dutcher, L A (1987) *Working Together* InterAction, New York and Washington DC

Duffield, M and Prendergast, J (1993) 'Neutrality and Humanitarian Assistance: The Emergency Relief Desk and the Cross-Border Operation into Eritrea and Tigray' University of Birmingham, UK and Center of Concern, Washington DC

Jansson, Kurt et al. (1987) *The Ethiopian Famine* Zed Books, London

JRP (1992) 'Bi-Annual Report 1990 and 1991' JRP, Addis Ababa

Solberg, Richard (1991) *Miracle in Ethiopia: a partnership response to famine* Friendship Press, New York

USAID (1987) 'Ethiopia Drought/Famine: Final Disaster Report FY 1985–86' USAID, Addis Ababa

3

ERITREA AND TIGRAY: CHANGING ORGANISATIONAL ISSUES IN CROSS-BORDER RELIEF ASSISTANCE 1983–92

Mark Duffield

The People: Population: 3.5 million approx. Eight major ethnic groups, the Amhara, Tigre and Oromo being in the highland areas and the Afar, Somali, Niloti, Beni Amar and Gurage being mostly in the lowlands. The majority are shepherds or nomads; 20 per cent are urban workers. Half a million Eritreans live as refugees in Sudan.

Religion: Mostly Muslim or Coptic Christian.

The Government: Isaias Afewarki led the Eritrean People's Liberation Front (EPLF) to victory over the previous communist government of Ethiopia. Following a referendum, Eritrea became an independent country in 1993.

Development Aid: Figures not available.

The Emergency Relief Desk (ERD), an ecumenical NGO consortium formed in Sudan in 1981, was part of a unique, initially controversial, effort to deliver cross-border relief assistance into the war-ravaged, non-governmental areas of Eritrea and northern Ethiopia. Throughout the 1980s, ERD was dogged by internal division over the levels of individual NGO representation in the consortium and debates over whether it should remain purely a relief operation. However, the common denominator of war and the necessity of working through exclusive and well-organised indigenous agencies kept the alliance together. By the mid-1980s the Cold War was all but over in Africa and funding shifted away from governments towards NGOs. In Ethiopia, a de facto legitimacy was conferred upon the cross-border operation and the ERD became much more effective. At the end of the war, ERD transferred its offices to Eritrea but closed shortly thereafter. NGO members reverted to their more traditional bilateral relations with the government and thus perhaps missed an opportunity to build upon their unique historical relationship with the rebel Fronts who now assumed power.

BACKGROUND

During the 1980s, the background to the war in the Horn was complex. It was defined by the opposition of popular liberation struggles in Eritrea and Tigray to an authoritarian military regime (the Dergue) claiming sovereignty in Ethiopia. Before the mid-1980s, the Dergue enjoyed the support of western donors, notably what is now the European Union (EU) and its members. Soviet military assistance to Ethiopia also encouraged the West to compete with developmental aid and, increasingly, humanitarian relief. In contrast, since the Dergue was the recognised government, the peoples of Eritrea and Tigray were isolated. Most international agencies did not provide assistance to these areas outside of government control.

In the mid-1980s, an historic shift in donor policy occurred. Increasingly, relief aid was channelled away from the Dergue and through NGOs. Importantly, this included the few agencies then engaged in the cross-border humanitarian operation from Sudan into Eritrea and Tigray. The most important of these were formed into an ecumenical consortium called the ERD. Not only did the change in donor policy increase the amount of aid crossing the border, but also it conferred a *de facto* legitimacy on an operation that had previously been seen as diplomatically suspect. Furthermore, it established in Ethiopia and Eritrea a situation that has since become increasingly common – that is, the attempt by international agencies to supply both sides in an internal conflict with humanitarian aid.

When the war ended in 1991, ERD and other agencies were presented with a new challenge – the issue of programme adjustment and post-war reconciliation that was particularly acute in Ethiopia. This chapter examines the changing organisational issues facing ERD during the above stages. Among other things, it suggests that NGO coordination is not a fixed or optimum reality. It is contingent upon a host of factors, ranging from conditions on the ground to the current shape of international relations.

THE ERD

ERD was formed in Sudan in 1981. It was an ecumenical NGO consortium delivering cross-border humanitarian assistance into the war-ravaged, non-government areas of Eritrea and northern Ethiopia. With an administrative base in Khartoum, its nine core members were:

- Brot für die Welt/Diachonisches Werk (BFW), Germany
- Christian Aid (CA), UK
- DanChurch Aid (DCA), Denmark
- Dutch Interchurch Aid (DIA), The Netherlands
- Inter-Church Coordination Committee for Development Projects (ICCO), The Netherlands
- Lutheran World Relief (LWR), USA
- Norwegian Church Aid (NCA), Norway
- Sudan Council of Churches (SCC), Sudan
- Swedish Church Relief (SCR), Sweden

Apart from SCC and LWR, the agencies were European Protestant organisations.[1] As for providing continuity and an administrative focus, NCA played a lead role throughout the life of ERD. ERD wound down its relief operations with the end of the war in 1991. It did not formally close, however, until June 1993.

ERD was the main NGO consortium providing cross-border assistance from Sudan. From its own resources, and especially after the mid-1980s from donor governments, ERD mobilised around 3/4 million tonnes of food aid for Eritrea and Tigray. The total value of ERD's cash and in-kind assistance was in the region of US$350 million. Although small when compared to the total aid channelled through the government side, ERD accounted for more than half of the total cross-border assistance from Sudan.

Apart from spanning several historic stages, an important feature of ERD lies in the fact that it worked with indigenous relief agencies, most notably, the Eritrean Relief Association (ERA) and the Relief Society of Tigray (REST). ERD was a conduit for outside assistance to these implementing agencies (IAs). In turn, the IAs played an important role in developing locally-managed participatory relief systems. Unusually in today's emergency operations, no expatriate staff from the outside operational agencies were involved in managing programme implementation in non-government areas; their input was entirely under the direction of the IAs.

---

1. After its formation, the only new members were Canadian Lutheran World Relief (CLWR) which joined in 1989, and the Mennonite Central Committee (MCC) and Finchurchaid (FCA), which both joined in 1990.

ERD DURING THE COLD WAR PERIOD

ERD's limited humanitarian mandate

At the end of the 1970s, the cross-border operation was confined to Eritrea. Two parallel relief conduits had emerged. One involved SCR that worked through SCC and supported the humanitarian efforts of the Eritrean Liberation Front (ELF). The other involved NCA that worked with ERA, the humanitarian wing of the other rebel force in Eritrea, the EPLF. The negotiations to create a coordinating group for the cross-border operation (CBO) began in 1980. Despite several difficulties, the agencies eventually signed an agreement in Khartoum in February 1981.

ERD was established as a limited independent body within the SCC *(NCA & SCC, 1981)*.[2] Although this structure was an improvement on the previous situation, it was fraught with contradictions. Due to the sensitivity of having to operate from Khartoum, the agreement established SCC as the 'legal' cover for ERD's operation. In practice, however, it was NCA (which supplied the ERD Executive Secretary) which effectively ran the operation.

From the outset, ERD perceived itself as non-political and having a strictly humanitarian brief. It avoided publicity for its cross-border relief activities and maintained a low profile in Khartoum. In relief terms, ERD was seen as a 'temporary instrument, subject to annual review and only providing aid in kind and at a reasonable level'. Transport, for example, was not provided by ERD. The cost of transporting relief goods, moreover, was only met either to Port Sudan or the border. It was not covered to the point of distribution. ERD also excluded cash payments.

Within this limited brief, the indigenous humanitarian organisations were to be treated on an equal basis. Due to the prevalence of earmarked funds for ERA, however, a rough equality was not achieved between ERA and REST until 1986. The agreement also established no formal mechanism for the consultation or involvement of what became known as the implementing agencies (IAs).

Essentially, ERD was established as a logistical and monitoring organisation to receive requests from the IAs for assistance, to verify need through field visits, pass on requests to member agencies and, when necessary, arrange procurement in Sudan. It also cleared shipments, kept regular accounts, received distribution reports, provided members with information on developments in Eritrea and Tigray, and so on. It is important to note that the original agreement to form ERD was made between SCC and NCA. It was on the basis of this agree-

---

2. In this chapter, organisation and mandate issues are the main focus. For the wider position see *Duffield, M and Prendergast, J (1994)*.

ment that other agencies were approached. Apart from SCR, however, the other supporting agencies were not formally involved in the organisational structure until 1985. In the first half of the 1980s, ERD was a low-key, informal consortium.

Emergence of other cross-border consortia

By 1983, the growing need in Eritrea and Tigray had led to an increasing demand for relief inputs. It had also produced broader demands for rehabilitation and especially transport assistance (*Jacobsen, 1984*). Because of its limited relief mandate, ERD was unable to fully address these needs and came under increasing pressure from the IAs (*Willemse, 1984a.*)

Lobbying by ERA and REST drew other agencies into these fields. In 1983, the Eritrean Inter-agency Agricultural Consortium (EIAC) and the Tigray Transport and Agricultural Consortium (TTAC) were formed. Unlike ERD, both consortia were non-denominational. They drew their initial organisational impetus from some of the agencies associated with what was then Euro-Action Accord (EAA).

Having rehabilitation and transport mandates, EIAC and TTAC could be seen as complementing the relief work of ERD. Until around 1987, however, when mutual observer status was established, there was little formal contact between the cross-border consortia.

Growing contradictions within ERD

By 1983, not only had relief needs clearly outstripped ERD's ability to respond but also the local political conditions that initially shaped its formation had changed.

In 1981, following the demise of the ELF in Eritrean politics, ERA, the humanitarian wing of the now-dominant EPLF, became the only relief association operating in Eritrea. The defeat of the ELF coincided with a major reduction in Swedish funding.[3] This fell from over 60 per cent of the total ERD budget in 1981 to 10 per cent in 1983. There was thus a significant decline in ERD's total contribution. In relation to ERA, ERD was meeting 15 per cent of its total estimated need at the beginning of the 1980s. By 1983 this had fallen to 5 per cent. For REST, the comparable proportion was 1 per cent (*ERD, 1984*).

Despite this fall in performance, 1983 was also the year that the contributions of ERD members other than NCA and SCR first began to clearly manifest themselves (see Figure 3.1). LWR, for example, at around US$1 million was now providing 20 per cent of ERD donations. Impressed with the IAs' efficiency and concerned over US

---

3. The Swedish government and Swedish NGOs and contractors had a long history of involvement in Ethiopia, particularly in educational and infrastructural programmes. They had been working in areas under ELF control from the outset of the war but, in 1981, were forced to reassess this assistance, hence an initial drop in overall spending.

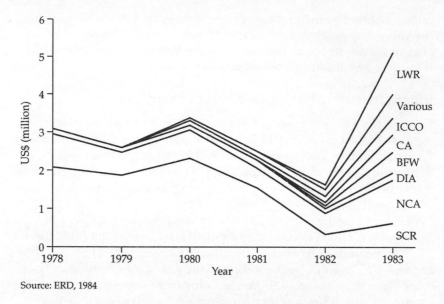

Source: ERD, 1984

Figure 3.1 *Member donations, 1978–83*

neglect of Eritrea, it had begun to take over from the Swedes. The importance of LWR's material contributions would continue to grow. The structure of ERD, however, based upon an agreement between NCA and SCC, did not reflect adequately the demand that emerged for greater member representation.

SCC's position had also begun to change. SCC had previously worked in association with the ELF. This did not make for good relations with ERA *(Willemse, 1984)*. SCC's organisational capacity had also been shown to be lacking. This tended to accentuate the role of NCA, making ERD a one-sided organisation. Finally, with re-emergence of civil war in South Sudan in 1983, SCC, with its roots in the south, fell from favour with the Khartoum government.

The 1984 evaluation

Due to building tensions, by mid-1983 it was already felt that ERD needed to adapt. A short evaluation completed in February 1984 *(ERD, 1984)*, initiated a lengthy and sometimes difficult process of negotiation. It was not resolved until October 1985 when members signed a new agreement. This extended interregnum is notable for the fact that it corresponded with a substantial increase in the workload of ERD's Khartoum office which struggled to survive. The discussions, including conflicting members' views, highlighted the many difficulties that such NGO consortia face.

The main consequence of the evaluation was to highlight the poor performance of ERD. The consultants called for a significant increase in budget and the recruitment of extra staff for the Khartoum office. It was also realised that member representation would have to be enlarged, given the increased contribution planned. Regarding ERD's mandate, the evaluation advocated both change and reinforcement. It was further recommended that ERD's relief mandate should be broadened to include rehabilitation. This covered agricultural inputs, continued support for internal purchase and funding for transport costs.

As for neutrality and public profile, discretion remained the key word. The quiet, neutral stance of ERD was reaffirmed. While this was accepted by members, pressure from the IAs for greater advocacy and mounting public concern had an effect. Some ERD members became increasingly vocal in an individual capacity. A distinction was drawn between the neutrality of ERD as a consortium and the views of individual member NGOs.

THE MID-1980S TRANSITION

Internal debate

The ERD evaluation was discussed by member agencies in May 1984 (*ERD, 1984*). This was the first occasion that members had all formally sat together on ERD business. The meeting did not resolve what became the main issue, that is, the need to improve member representation and strengthen organisational capacity. It did, however, set the scene for the lengthy process of meetings and discussions that were not resolved until October 1985.

That such an important agreement took so long to reach shows not only the difficulty of the issues, but also that once representation is increased, the different philosophies of member NGOs come into play. One difficulty concerned the role of SCC and its reluctance to accept a reduced position. Other issues related to the continuing internal debate on the scope of ERD's mandate. For those agencies favouring development work, the period was one of forming bilateral links with the IAs.

For their part, the IAs supported both the moves to broaden ERD membership and for members and other agencies to establish bilateral relations with them. While appreciating the support of ERD, the IAs were always concerned lest ERD became a monopoly supplier. By 1983, ERA, for example, had established links of various forms with 120 international agencies. Internationalisation and bilateralism increased IA access and representation.

Even when humanitarian relief provides the common denominator, the history of ERD would suggest that collaboration through consortia is not a natural state for NGOs. For most of its history, ERD was kept afloat by the personalities involved. The fact that member representatives knew each other and had shared disappointment and success served as a bond and sense of solidarity. This often overlays policy differences. Apart from the ecumenical nature of the agencies, this fractious solidarity was also maintained by the exigencies of the war.

Internationalisation of ERD

By mid-1984, it had become evident that ERD needed to redefine its position in relation to SCC. An alternate view had emerged in which ERD was to be recast as an international relief consortium working in Eritrea and Tigray alongside other consortia, that is, EIAC and TTAC. A cross-border division of labour would be established (*Willemse, 1984c*). Partly because of SCC's limited participation in the discussions that followed, however, the issue of ERD's relation to SCC proved difficult to resolve. Feeling threatened by the changing nature of ERD, SCC often prevaricated on issues raised and, on several occasions, simply failed to turn up to meetings.

Crisis point was reached in early 1985. Delay on agreeing a new structure was negatively affecting the relief performance of ERD. Out of desperation, the Executive Secretary proposed a new structure designed to overcome the difficulties with SCC. Within this structure, member agencies would elect a lead agency that would appoint an additional member to the SCC-dominated Executive Committee. The resulting administrative arrangement was an interim measure that members would vote on at the next Board Meeting. Meanwhile, NCA would provide the point of coordination outside Sudan. In many respects, this proposal was a holding measure that confirmed the existing arrangements.

Growth of bilateral development links with the IAs

The inability of ERD to reach a decision on its reestablishment contributed, in some members' eyes, to its marginalisation during the momentous year of 1984. Besides EIAC and TTAC, other agencies began an involvement in the CBO. While remaining the monopoly food aid supplier until around 1987, ERD's total share of CBO activity began to decline. From this period, agencies began increasingly to establish bilateral relations with the IAs. Even some ERD members moved in this direction. This trend contributed to the diversification of internationally supported programmes in Eritrea and Tigray.

By mid-1985, a clear division had emerged between the ERD agencies. Roughly speaking, this contrasted agencies wishing to maintain a strictly relief-based operation with those wishing to widen ERD's mandate to include either development work, or work with refugees in Sudan. The first group, which included NCA, SCR and LWR, for various reasons worked almost exclusively through ERD on a relief basis (*ERD, 1985a*). While not having a monopoly of the argument, this group clearly articulated the need for a relief brief to maintain the neutrality of ERD. The second group included DIA, CA, ICCO and DCA.

Several of these agencies were keen to develop bilateral relations with the IAs due to what they perceived as restrictions in the ERD mandate. Discussions between the two groups, rather than the issue of SCC, dominated the agenda (*ERD, 1985b*).

The eventual outcome was significantly influenced by the attitude of the IAs. Their interests lay in transforming ERD into an international consortium but, simultaneously, limiting any extension of its mandate lest ERD should become a monopoly supplier. The IAs therefore supported the restriction of ERD to a relief brief, preferring to handle development work bilaterally (*ERA, 1985*). This position stemmed from longstanding criticism of ERD's failure to speak out about the real causes of the famine and Ethiopia's violation of human rights. Some ERD members were also individually accused of the same shortcoming. An enlarged or monopoly ERD, apart from restricting the IAs' external contacts, threatened to stifle the IAs' aim of mobilising Western public opinion.

The re-establishment of ERD

Between the evaluation and the signing of a new agreement, ERD members had come a long way. Due to the fast changing social and political climate, member agencies themselves were engaged in a media and political learning process. The increasing involvement of strategic donors increased the diplomatic links of ERD members. Simultaneously, although ERD itself maintained a low profile, some members had established the precedent of more active individual campaigning. The events of 1984 and 1985 saw a loosening of some caution surrounding cross-border work. Over this period, it became an international consortium defining itself as working in Eritrea and Tigray and not, as before, in areas that were unable to be reached from the government side.

When the agreement was finally signed, it was to reestablish ERD's relief and rehabilitation brief (*CA, 1985*). NCA was elected the lead agency. NCA's role was confirmed as giving general administrative support to ERD and, as appropriate, to member agencies. This included providing office space in Khartoum and furnishing the Executive Secretary.

To internationalise the organisation, the agreement established a Board that consisted of all signatory agencies, including SCC. Under a rotating Chairperson, the Board was charged with meeting once a year to decide issues of general policy. It also elected an Executive Committee that consisted of the Chairperson and a representative from SCC, NCA and two other member agencies. The Executive Secretary was a non-voting ex officio member.

The responsibilities of the Executive Committee included the approval of reports, consulting regularly with IAs and arranging Board

Meetings. The ERD Office, which in turn convened the Executive Committee meetings, was headed by the Executive Secretary, who ran the day-to-day business of ERD:

- financial procedures;
- purchasing and transport;
- the clearance of goods;
- reporting and field visits;
- maintaining regular consultation with the IAs, and so on.

As for improved involvement, the agreement made some concessions to IA demands. They were given the right to approach the Executive Committee for consultation through the Executive Secretary. They could also request administrative assistance from the ERD Office and their opinions would be heard in the recruitment process of ERD staff when the outcome was of direct concern. Although the IAs were free to form bilateral links with member agencies, it was reiterated that ERD could not speak out on behalf of any IA.

Fault lines in the new ERD

The new agreement weakened the link with SCC – it became little more than an ordinary member. Simultaneously, it reconfirmed a limited relief and rehabilitation mandate as a necessary base for holding such a disparate group together. The main weakness lay in the fact that the 'legal' basis for ERD's existence in Sudan became NCA's country agreement. Due to political sensitivity, however, this did not mention ERD. The existence of the consortium remained an informal understanding with the Sudanese government.

Through the process of widening member representation, however, ERD increasingly appeared as an independent body (*Erichsen, 1993*). With the growing prominence of NGOs generally during the latter part of the 1980s, this spurious independence would increase and have important implications for member agencies, the IAs and the Government of Sudan.

POST-COLD WAR TRENDS AND TENSIONS

The increasing effectiveness of the IAs and ERD

By the mid-1980s, the Cold War in Africa was all but over (*Clough, 1992*). Events of this period represented a major change in international relations. An historic shift took place in donor funding away from governments and towards NGOs. In Ethiopia, it had the effect of simultaneously weakening nation-state sovereignty and conferring a *de facto* legitimacy on the CBO. This shift initiated a significant organisational growth of the IAs and ERD. In operational terms, from this period ERD and the CBO became much more effective.

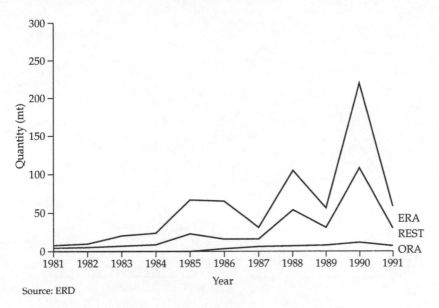

Source: ERD

Figure 3.2 *ERD food donations to IAs*

ERD's ability to increase the flow of food aid and funds was beginning to have a beneficial impact on the relief situation within Eritrea
and Tigray, as early as 1986 (Figure 3.2). Monitoring reports suggested
improved health, reduced internal migration and some indication of
increased herd sizes *(ERD, 1987)*. Increased relief assistance alone,
however, was not the only factor. The IAs had undergone a period of
organisational growth and development that helped them stabilise the
situation in Eritrea and Tigray.

Detailing these changes is beyond the scope of this chapter (see
Duffield & Prendergast, 1994). In Tigray, however, a sophisticated and
integrated approach to disaster management had emerged by the mid-
1980s. Transport capacity had been increased and an effective system
for targeting food aid developed. Simultaneously, REST blended relief
aid with food-for-work programmes and wage labour. These measures, and internal purchase, supported important sectors of the
agrarian economy. The outcome was that Tigray could weather famine
conditions equal to those of the early 1980s without seeing mass
migration into Sudan. In Eritrea, while privation continued, similar
evidence of stabilisation was forthcoming *(Bondestam, 1988)*.

ERD emerged from the mid-1980s as a powerful fund raising tool,
able to secure large grants compared to other NGO operations (see
Figure 3.3). Its dynamism in resource mobilisation was much greater
than the sum of its parts *(Overby, 1993)*. It also had access to unique
sources of information and possessed great flexibility in the contributions that different members could make *(Hendrie, 1993)*.

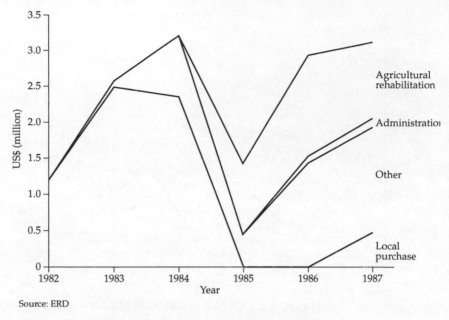

Source: ERD

Figure 3.3 *Cash programmes in Eritrea, 1982–87*

An important factor that emerged from the 1986–87 period was the pressing need to co-ordinate the CBO with relief assistance in government areas (*Hendrie, 1988*). Until this time, there had been few contacts and no serious attempt to coordinate activities, or even share information, between agencies working on the two sides. Towards the end of 1987, propelled by the growing military success of the Fronts, piecemeal contacts began to develop. This is an indication of the growing impact of ERD and the CBO.

Move toward ERD independence

The demands of 1984 saw a significant increase in ERD's Khartoum staff. In mid-1984, the first USAID shipment prompted the opening of ERD's Port Sudan office. In response to these demands, the re-establishment of ERD in October 1985 allowed for the appointment of an expatriate Assistant Executive Secretary. By mid-1987, ERD employed six senior staff, mostly expatriates, with 11 local staff in Khartoum and 30 local staff in Port Sudan.

The expansion of CBO activity also served to attract other ecumenical partners to join ERD. In practice, however, ERD only attracted three new members and these relatively late: CLWR joining in 1989, and the MCC and FCA in 1990.

Following the publicity of the mid-1980s and the emergence of famine conditions in Sudan, the NGO community in Khartoum grew rapidly. Although officially ERD kept a low profile, by 1985 its existence was widely known in Khartoum. Its activities were increasingly discussed in NGO and donor circles (*Abadi Zemo, 1993*). The growth of ERD,and its links with what were seen as effective indigenous agencies, produced internal pressures to change its image.

ERD's administration in Khartoum wished to 'professionalise' the consortia's activities. This endeavour was tantamount to the administration seeking a more independent role by weakening ERD's links with NCA. In 1987, the boundary between the administration – that is, the Executive Secretary and his staff – and the Executive Committee was more clearly drawn so that the latter only dealt with major policy issues (*ERD, 1988a*).

This allowed the administration to establish direct relations with member agencies. At this stage, NCA's Resident Representative in Sudan and ERD's Executive Secretary was the same person. In April 1988, ERD's Board decided to separate the NCA Resident Representative position from that of ERD Executive Secretary. Following the appointment of an NCA Resident Representative based in Khartoum with responsibility for NCA's programme in the south, the split between the ERD and NCA administrations was completed in September 1988 (*ERD, 1988c*).

The main problem, however, was that ERD continued to have no legal existence within Sudan. Its only cover was NCA's country agreement. Even then, this existence was the subject of an informal agreement with the government.

Antagonism with the Sudanese State

During the mid-1980s, scores of NGOs entered Sudan. Until this period, Sudanese policy had been to restrict the involvement of international agencies. The crisis of 1984–85, however, with the political flux that followed the fall of the Nimeiry regime, was the basis upon which this virtual 'humanitarian invasion' took place. With 80 or so NGOs appearing in Sudan within the space of a couple of years, by 1986 the NGO question had reached a critical mass in domestic politics.

Within months of the election of a new government in April 1986, it was made clear that the Sudanese intended to control NGOs. This attitude hardened further due to NGO humanitarian involvement in the war zone of South Sudan. The developing antagonism between the Sudanese state and international and national Christian NGOs had important implications for ERD. NCA, for example, felt that by association its programme in South Sudan could endanger the ERD activities (*ERD, 1986*). However, the geo-political reasons for Sudan maintaining an open border with Ethiopia remained and, indeed, strengthened since Ethiopia was aiding the Sudan People's Liberation Army (SPLA) in South Sudan. The main difficulty for the Sudanese government was that the CBO was run by international NGOs.

Although the government made its intention clear in 1986, due to political in-fighting it took several years for measures to take formal shape. From the start, however, there was a steady increase in the difficulties faced by NGOs. ERD, for example, faced growing problems in importing vital equipment and supplies. Earlier and more generous arrangements became increasingly restricted. Beginning in October 1986, the first inconclusive attempt to register NGOs took place (*ERD, 1987a*). While pressure mounted on NGOs in Sudan, the IAs were not affected. Having separate agreements with the government, they carried on much as before.

Re-merging of ERD with NCA

At the beginning of 1988, the internal struggle around the right to register NGOs was settled in favour of the Ministry of Social Welfare. In mid-1988, the Ministry set a deadline for all NGOs to be registered. This represented a great problem for ERD since, technically, it did not exist. Earlier agreements with the Sudanese government to operate had been verbal: none of the parties had wished anything to be recorded on paper. Moreover, successive changes of government and purges within State Security had dimmed institutional memory.

Arguing that NCA was now unable to cover for ERD, the ERD administration pushed for the consortium to seek registration separate from NCA (*ERD, 1988b*). Over the next couple of months several meetings took place with government officials. They revealed that the government was not interested in a separate registration. This was also resisted by ERD's Executive Committee. To resolve the matter, NCA was invited by the Committee to re-establish links with the government and take direct responsibility for ERD.

At the beginning of 1989, NCA secured the agreement of the Sudanese (*Abuoaf, 1989*). NCA's direct control of ERD was also supported by the IAs. Given the anti-NGO climate that existed in Sudan, the IAs appreciated that NCA was taking a risk. The IAs at this time had regular high-level political contact with the Sudanese government and doubtless exerted a degree of influence on the government to allow ERD to continue its operations.

In mid-1989, ERD became part of NCA's Sudan programme. ERD's Executive Secretary now reported to the NCA Resident Representative. The status of the Board was changed to that of an Advisory Group. Significantly, the following year saw the IAs admitted as full members. This merger represented a difficult period for all involved and several ERD staff quit. The crisis was compounded by the great increase in CBO activity that was then taking place.

In many respects, the merger represented the end of ERD as a clandestine CBO made necessary by the limitations of sovereignty. From the mid-1980s, it had progressively become more assertive. By 1989, its activities were public knowledge. Earlier *de facto* donor legitimisation of the CBO meant that a single agency could now acknowledge having management responsibility.

THE TRANSFER OF RESPONSIBILITY

Southern Line Operation

Between March 1990 and the months immediately following the end of the war in May 1991, the CBO relief operation in Eritrea and Tigray was at first complemented and then progressively supplanted by aid from the government side. Initially this was provided by Ethiopian church agencies and then the UN. Before the end of the war, the negotiations that were necessary to achieve this replacement conferred further *de facto* donor and eventually UN recognition on the Fronts.

Regarding Tigray, the main Ethiopian NGO consortium was the Joint Relief Partnership (JRP). It was formed in late 1984 (see Chapter 2). JRP's members were the Ethiopian, Catholic, Lutheran and Orthodox churches with the American-based Catholic Relief Services (CRS).

The return of Tigray famine conditions in 1989 prompted JRP to propose a free passage plan that would require the agreement of the Tigray People's Liberation Front (TPLF) and the Ethiopian government. To the surprise of the JRP agencies, the Dergue eventually agreed. With ERD support, discreet negotiations were begun in February 1990. This was the first time that REST and JRP representatives had met together. Safe passage terms were eventually agreed in March 1990, allowing the so-called Southern Line Operation to begin (*JRP, 1992*). During 1990, when the CBO reached its peak, the JRP Southern Line Operation was also delivering an average of 9,000 mt per month to Tigray and 3,000 mt to Northern Wollo.

The Northern Line Operation

For Eritrea, the Northern Line Operation involved the delivery of World Food Programme (WFP) food aid from Massawa. The Port of Massawa fell to the EPLF in February 1990, just when the JRP Southern Line negotiations were taking place. Initially, the Dergue tried to hide the fact that it had lost control of Massawa. Largely because of Ethiopian government intransigence, it was not until January 1991 that a ship successfully docked at Massawa.

Within the Northern Line Operation, ERA regarded its relations with the UN as generally poor. Reflecting common procedure, the UN managed the operation by telling other parties as little as possible and revealing few of its own intentions.

With the opening of the port in January 1991, donors in Addis Ababa began to press for the closing of the CBO. Many were for directing all assistance through Massawa and Assab. A fierce debate took place within USAID. This resulted in the channelling of all resources through Massawa. It marked the end of US support for the CBO. The IAs unsuccessfully opposed this development.

With the withdrawal of USAID support, the level of CBO activity dropped markedly in 1991. Largely because of institutional inertia, however, the EU maintained its commitment. Following the end of the war in May, ERA also began to route its supplies through Massawa. ERD closed its Port Sudan office in June and moved its entire office to Asmara in October. By the end of 1991, the CBO had almost finished. The task of coordinating relief assistance was taken over by WFP. Relief operations in Eritrea and Ethiopia had normalised, so to speak.

THE CHALLENGE OF THE POST-CONFLICT SITUATION

Proposal for Ethiopia

The transfer of ERD's office from Khartoum to Asmara in October 1991 took place in record time (*ERD, 1992a*). Moving to Asmara decided the fact that ERD should divide its remaining programme responsibilities between Eritrea and Ethiopia. Reflecting this division, the AGM of November 1991 took place in Addis Ababa and Asmara. They were historic occasions, being the first time an ERD meeting had been held in Ethiopia and Eritrea respectively. This chapter is only concerned with the phase-out of ERD in Ethiopia.

The fall of the Dergue left most of the aid community in Addis Ababa waiting for something to happen. Besides mandating REST to oversee JRP operations in Tigray and Wollo, the new government established a short-lived Relief Coordination Committee that included REST. Following the disbanding of this committee, REST began to assume the role of a regional NGO among other indigenous and international agencies within Tigray and Ethiopia. In these circumstances, ERD felt that an agency forum for bridge-building between those groups from different sides of the line was required.

With this in mind, ERD adopted a Statement of Principle setting out its future in Ethiopia (*ERD, 1991*). This limited the life of ERD to the political transition period, with formal closure by June 1993. A similar agreement was reached in Eritrea's case. In both situations, it came as something of a surprise to the IAs and was accepted with reluctance. Part of the phase-out would involve members gradually moving into bilateral relations with the traditional IAs and other local agencies as required. During this transition period, ERD would continue to provide several functions including institution building with the IAs. It would also maintain a forum for coordination and debate.

Importantly, however, the transitional role also included the promotion of ERD experience within the wider NGO community. This involved the initiation of a dialogue between ERD members, traditional IAs and the Ethiopian church agencies to develop cooperation and greater understanding. A key feature of these proposals was the appointment for a six-month period of a Liaison Officer attached to NCA's Addis Ababa office.

Argument for a liaison function

Compared to Eritrea, the political difficulties faced by ERD in passing on its experience in Addis Ababa were great. Few NGOs had an easy time in Ethiopia under the Dergue. Among the Church agencies, the Lutheran Ethiopian Evangelical Church Mekane Yesus (EECMY) had a particularly difficult experience. It had, however, survived and had played an important role in the relief programmes on the government side.

There was little real knowledge in Addis Ababa of operating conditions or methods in the former non-government areas. EECMY, for example, having a large Oromo and southern following, had never been sympathetic to the Eritrean struggle and opposed the demand for independence (*Erichsen, 1993*). Moreover, it saw the IAs and the Fronts as the same. EECMY therefore felt that the ERD members, some of whom were its partners, had forged links with suspect and secular agencies. More generally, there was a widespread suspicion among Addis Abba NGOs that the new government established by the Ethiopian People's Revolutionary Democratic Front (EPRDF) – a coalition with the TPLF as the dominant member – would exact some form of retribution. This was not helped by REST becoming part of the short-lived Relief Coordination Committee. There were frequent silences and other forms of non-communication at inter-agency meetings when ERD or REST representatives attended. Furthermore, widespread misconceptions prevailed concerning the role of ERD. Many thought, and still think, that ERD was politically linked to the 'rebels' and led by a few powerful personalities (*Abdul Mohammed, 1993*).

Sometimes, ERD was cast as a tool of anti-Dergue donors. Consequently, it was alleged that it operated with few reporting requirements (*Assab Tekle, 1993*). For a time, there were also widespread rumours that the EPRDF would systematically transfer all resources from the rest of Ethiopia to Tigray. Some donors were themselves not immune to this syndrome. The EU, for example, whose Addis Ababa office had consistently argued against the CBO over the years, was keen to highlight any perceived shortcomings of the new government.

This general antipathy concerning ERD and the EPRDF government lay at the heart of the decision to appoint a Liaison Officer in November 1991. The post had a bridge-building mandate. Within weeks of this appointment, however, the sensitivity of the position had become apparent. REST, also undergoing a process of reorganisation, stayed in the background during negotiations. Even the NCA Addis

Ababa representative had expressed reservations about the liaison role. NCA in Ethiopia has programme links with EECMY. This is thought to have influenced this critical position. By January 1992, not only did ERD feel that Ethiopia lacked a general coordinating body but, due to lack of interest among local Church agencies, the question was raised ...do they have a wish for ecumenical cooperation? (*NCA, 1992*).

The underlying rationale for a liaison role lay in the singular character of the CBO. Through the IAs, ERD had enjoyed a unique relationship with the political Fronts in Eritrea and Tigray. The locally-managed disaster mitigation systems that emerged in Eritrea and Tigray have few parallels in Africa. For some ERD agencies, the collapse of the Dergue established the possibility for NGOs to enter a collaborative relationship with the new Ethiopian government. Seizing this opportunity, which ran counter to the usual NGO practice of working independently of the state, was fraught with difficulty. ERD felt that its many years' experience could be utilized in this respect.

One can understand that the ending of a vicious civil war would leave a legacy of mutual misunderstanding and suspicion. In grasping the subsequent failure to develop the Liaison Officer role, it is important to realise that the proposal faced both external and internal difficulties. Concerning the former, it is necessary to examine the major organisational differences between the relief operations in the former government and non-government areas. In many respects, these differences reflect the wider political challenge that the EPRDF government currently faces.

Differences between relief operations in former government and non-government areas

Compared to the integrated and participatory relief programmes that developed in non-government areas, different forms of aid organisation had emerged in the rest of Ethiopia. A detailed discussion of these differences is beyond the scope of this chapter (see *Duffield & Prendergast, 1994*). A summary outline is given below.

Government operations
Until the mid-1980s, donors channelled the bulk of relief assistance through the government and its Relief and Rehabilitation Commission (RRC). The RRC was established by the Dergue in the mid-1970s to coordinate and carry out national relief activities. By the mid-1980s, it had a staff of over 12,000 and trucking fleet of around 1000 lorries. In contrast to the situation in Eritrea and Tigray, this huge operation functioned on a highly centralised basis. Even decisions concerning local-level food distributions were taken in Addis Ababa (*Villumstad & Hendrie, 1993*). Rather than empowering populations, the RRC concentrated power within itself. After the mid-1980s, its share of relief commodities declined as donors began to switch to NGOs.

NGO operations
From the mid-1980s, when NGO relief operations began to significantly develop, one can again detect contrary forms of organisation compared to non-government areas. Within Ethiopia, the Nutrition Intervention Programmes (NIP) developed by the CRS had a great influence on the practice of NGO consortia (*Solberg, 1991*).

Unlike the integrated community-based relief systems developed in non-government areas, NIP is based upon the family. That is, a 'family' defined as a mother and children under five years old. As far as it targets this group, NIP defines itself as a family-oriented food distribution system operating through a network of distribution centres. Unlike the peer-group targeting in non-government areas, NIP depends upon NGOs defining the at-risk population. It can, therefore, be argued to disempower the community and its individual members. It is NGO representatives who make all the key decisions concerning entitlement.

In NIP relief systems, moreover, there are no relations of political accountability between the NGO representatives and the beneficiaries. Within Eritrea and Tigray, however, relations of accountability existed between the elected village committees, the IAs and the political administration. In NIP systems, accountability usually flows from NGOs to donors. Typically, this assumes the form of a relief subcontracting relation.

As a power relation, subcontracting enhances the strength of the NGO at the expense of beneficiaries and often the host government. Relatively little attention has been devoted to the study of relations of accountability and power in relief operations.

Relations between NGO consortia and the Dergue
The Christian Relief and Development Association (CRDA), which was established in the mid-1970s, was a forum composed of national and international NGOs in Addis Abba. Rather than being in dialogue with the Dergue, it was often seen as opposing it. It was never active in formulating national relief policy. The other Ethiopia-based consortia were also not in policy dialogue with the government. They were operational bodies whose main links were with donors. Relations with government, if they existed at all, tended to be bilateral. In fact, NGOs within Ethiopia liked to keep their distance from the Dergue. They hid, rather than discussed, their activities. This is a marked contrast to the relations that pertained between the IAs and the Fronts.

ERD members and the post-conflict challenge

Besides differences in relief systems, there were also internal ERD difficulties facing the liaison proposal. With the end of the war, ERD as a consortium began to fragment and lose coherence, ceasing to have a function for many members in peace time (*Borden, 1993*). For these members, the resumption of traditional bilateral relations as quickly as possible was the desired outcome. Other agencies – for example,

DIA and NCA – were drawn by the political complexities of the situation. They felt that ERD should attempt to develop a new supportive mandate and help the transition to peace and development (*Villumstad & Strand, 1993*).

That ERD members should have been divided on the question of a wider liaison role in Ethiopia is not surprising. Throughout the 1980s they had differed on the question of relief versus development. Now, in an entirely new context, agency positions could, to varying degrees, be related to their links with Ethiopian partners.

Only a few ERD members, such as DIA, had little or no contact with Ethiopian Church agencies (*ERD, 1992b*). The majority had various relations. With the exception of NCA, most members with Ethiopian Church links (the majority) tended to be wary of adopting a liaison role in 1992. They preferred establishing bilateral relations with all agencies. One can discern in this posture the assertion of conventional NGO neutrality in the face of political complexity. The demand for a wider liaison and advocacy role, on the other hand, had grown out of the recognition that peace had not created a level playing field.

FAILURE OF THE LIAISON ROLE

At the beginning of 1992, the NCA-appointed Liaison Officer believed that REST, CRDA and other Church agencies were obvious partners in seeking a wider supportive role. Unlike Eritrea, in Addis Ababa it was argued that NGO institutions already existed. ERD did not have to pioneer new organisations. There was also the awareness, however, that peace had brought together contrasting forms of NGO organisation (*Villumstad, 1992a*). In these circumstances, the need for bridge-building was felt to be a real one.

This feeling was reinforced by emerging trends in post-war Ethiopia. These included the ambitious reform of the RRC that began in 1991. Also, in 1992, the World Bank started negotiating more flexible terms and conditions with the new government. This created an opportunity for NGOs to share their global experience with the EPRDF. Finally, in June 1992, reflecting earlier differences, the Oromo Liberation Front (OLF) withdrew from the transitional government. This created a fear of continuing political instability.

In relation to these developments, the Liaison Officer argued that Addis Ababa lacked an NGO forum that could reflect ERD experience. What was required was an Ethiopian NGO working group that included national and international NGOs. This would not be in competition with existing consortia and, moreover, only required the support of a reasonable number of ERD members. Despite these arguments, by April 1992, clearly there was little enthusiasm among most ERD members for such a venture (*Villumstad, 1992*).

As a final attempt to increase dialogue, the Ethiopian Church agencies were invited to attend the May 1992 ERD Advisory Group meeting in Addis Ababa. Here, the need for a new forum was put forward by the Liaison Officer. This was opposed by some ERD members and the Ethiopian Church agencies. Their grounds were that such structures, for example, CRDA, already existed. In attempting to inject some cross-border experience into the NGO debate in Addis Ababa, the meeting was a failure. By July, it was evident that there was insufficient interest to justify the extension of the Liaison Officer role (*Villumstad, 1992c*). With the end of this post, although not formally disbanded until June 1993, ERD in Ethiopia had come to a close.

CONCLUSION

In terms of NGO coordination, an important feature of ERD is that it spanned major changes in the nature of international relations. Notably, from Cold War superpower rivalry to the uncertain direction of the present post-Cold War era. The organisational form of the consortium changed over time. ERD's experience would suggest that NGO coordination in relief situations is not simply a technical matter. It is contingent upon a number of factors, many of them political. Apart from internal relations, the international attitude to sovereignty was instrumental in shaping ERD and defining its effectiveness.

In a practical sense ERD did not survive the end of the war. Internal differences among members soon surfaced without this common denominator. These differences propelled ERD towards dissolution and the establishment of bilateral relations with, and beyond, the former IAs. For many former members, the rationale for phasing out ERD was to re-establish more traditional links and forms of NGO activity. The irony, however, is that the continuing crisis in Eritrea and Ethiopia is far from traditional.

The move to create a liaison function in Addis Ababa by a few ERD members was an important attempt to break new ground. It represented a willingness to find a novel way positively to engage the changing post-war situation. The liaison function has as its rationale the seeking of a collaborative relationship with the new government. The attempt failed, largely due to the reassertion of conventional ideas of NGO neutrality.

Failure aside, the wish to establish a liaison role appears to be part of a growing mood among NGOs. In facing the complex political emergencies of today, ideas of neutrality no longer seem enough. NGOs are facing situations where traditional mandates fall short of reality on the ground. New ways have to be found of engaging and working in countries undergoing long-term crisis. Establishing new forms of solidarity rather than maintaining a spurious notion of neutrality is urgently required. Perhaps not always consciously, ERD has provided some important pointers in this emerging debate.

ACRONYMS AND ABBREVIATIONS

BFW	Brot für die Welt
CA	Christian Aid
CBO	Cross-Border Operation
CLWR	Canadian Lutheran World Relief
CRDA	Christian Relief and Development Association
CRS	Catholic Relief Services
DCA	DanChurch Aid
DIA	Dutch Interchurch Aid
EAA	Euro-Action Accord (now ACORD)
EECMY	Ethiopian Evangelical Church Mekane Yesus
EIAC	Eritrean Inter-Agency Agricultural Consortium
ELF	Eritrean Liberation Front
EPLF	Eritrean People's Liberation Front
EPRDF	Ethiopian People's Revolutionary Democratic Front
ERA	Eritrean Relief Association
ERD	Emergency Relief Desk
EU	European Union
FCA	Finchurchaid
IAs	Implementing Agencies
ICCO	Inter-Church Coordination Committee for Development Projects
JRP	Joint Relief Partnership
LWR	Lutheran World Relief
MCC	Mennonite Central Committee
NCA	Norwegian Church Aid
NIP	Nutrition Intervention Programmes
OLF	Oromo Liberation Front
REST	Relief Society of Tigray
RRC	Relief and Rehabilitation Commission
SCC	Sudan Council of Churches
SCR	Swedish Church Relief
SPLA	Sudan People's Liberation Army
TPLF	Tigray People's Liberation Front
TTAC	Tigray Transport and Agriculture Consortium
WFP	World Food Programme

REFERENCES

Abadi Zemo (1993) Interview on January 28
Abdul Mohammed (1993) Interview on January 25
Abuoaf, I (1989) Letter to General Secretary, NCA, January 29
Assab Tekle (1992) Interview on January 26
Bondestam, L, Cliffe L, and White P, (1988) 'An Independent Evaluation of the Food Situation in Eritrea Submitted to the Emergency Relief Desk' *Eritrea Food and Agricultural Assessment Study, Final Report*, Centre of Development Studies, University of Leeds
Borden, J (1985) Memorandum 'ERD Meeting in Geneva on 14/15 October', October 3, London
CA (1985) 'Notes on ERD Board Meeting: 14th/15th October 1985', CA, London

Clough, R E (1992) *Free at Last? US Policy Toward Africa and the End of the Cold War* Council on Foreign Relations, New York

Duffield M and Prendergast J (1994) *Without Troops or Tanks: Humanitarian Intervention in Eritrea and Ethiopia* Red Sea Press Inc/Africa World Press Inc, Trenton NJ

ERA (1985) Encl. 3 *To: ERD Ex. Comm.* Khartoum

ERD (1984a) 'Evaluation Report: 30 January–8 February 1984' March 5, Oslo

ERD (1984b) 'Minutes of a Meeting of Representatives of Agencies Associated With the Sudan Council of Churches Emergency Relief Desk' ERD, May 28, Geneva

ERD (1985a) 'Agencies Perspective on ERD' May 8, Khartoum

ERD (1985b) 'Minutes of Emergency Relief Desk Meeting' May 8–9, London

ERD (1986) 'Minutes of Board Meeting' October 24, Stuttgart

ERD (1987a) 'Minutes of Executive Comittee Meeting' February 4, ERD, Khartoum

ERD (1987b) *Annual Report, 1986* ERD, Khartoum

ERD (1988a) *Annual Report, 1987* ERD, Khartoum

ERD (1988b) 'Minutes of Executive Committee Meeting' October 21, Khartoum

ERD (1988) *Annual Report 1988* ERD, Khartoum

ERA (1991) 'Minutes From Emergency Relief Desk/Advisory Group Meeting' Novenber 7, ERA, Asmara

ERA (1992a) *Programme Up-Date no 012*

ERA (1992b) 'Minutes From Emergency Relief Desk/Advisory Group Meeting' May 4, ERA, Addis Ababa

Erichsen, J (1993) Interview on March 16

Hendrie, B (1988) 'Disaster Management in Tigray: Report on a Visit to the Non-government Held Areas of Tigray Province From January-February 1988' Khartoum

Hendrie, B (1993) Interview on February 5

Jacobsen, A, (1984) *Executive Secretary Annual Report No 1: 1983* Khartoum

JRP (1992) *Annual Report 1990 and 1991* JRP, Addis Ababa

NCA (1992) 'Minutes of Meeting at NCA Oslo with Jacques Willemse' (DIA) January 17, Oslo

NCA and SCC, Signatories (1981) 'Agreement Concerning Formation of an Emergency Relief Desk'. February 21, Khartoum

Overby, T (1993) Interview on February 4

Solberg, R W (1991) *Miracle in Ethiopia: A Partnership Response to Famine* Friendship Press, New York

Villumstad, S, (1992a) Liason Officer 'Preliminary Reflections on Possible Future Relationships Between AG Members and Local Partners in Ethiopia' Addis Ababa

Villumstad, S (1992b) Liason Officer 'Update From NCA/ERD Liason Officer in Ethiopia For March 1992' Addis Ababa

Villumstad, S (1992c) Memorandum to Strand, R and Ofstad, A, NCA, July 6

Villumstad, S and Hendrie, B (1993) 'New Policy Directions in Disaster Preparedness and Response in Ethiopia' *Disasters*, vol 17, no 3, pp 122–132

Villumstad, S and Strand, R (1993) Interview on March 17

Willemse, J (1984a) *Travel Report Visit, Rome: 3-7 March 1984* Utrecht

Willemse, J (1984b) Letter to Renshaw, P, CA

Willemse, J (1984c) Letter to Telex to Renshaw, P, CA

4

MOZAMBIQUE: POST-WAR RECONSTRUCTION AND THE LINK NGO FORUM, 1987–94

Jon Bennett

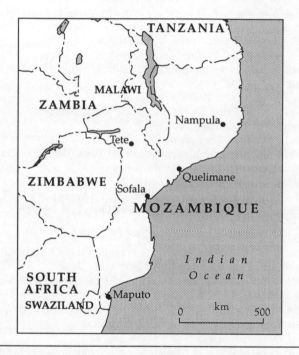

The People: Population 15.6 million approximately. Comprises a variety of ethnic groups, mainly of Bantu origin.

Religion: Most of the urban population is Christian with Islam prevailing in the north. The rural population profess traditional religions.

The Government: Joaquim Chissano became president in 1986 heading the Front for the Liberation of Mozambique (FRELIMO) government which has held power since independence in 1975. Since independence, an armed struggle has been maintained with South African backing, by the Résistência Nationàl Moçambicana (RENAMO). The fighting ceased in 1992, though tensions between RENAMO and the FRELIMO government still exist.

Development Aid: US$946 million (1990); US$60 per capita; 65.7 per cent of GNP.

Mozambique in the early 1990s was slowly recovering from one of the most destructive wars Africa has seen this century. The country had all the hallmarks of a complex and chronic emergency: bitter internecine warfare, internal and external displacement and wholesale destruction of life and property. Initially, the international community responded generously. Perhaps too generously, some have argued, for Mozambique was to become a magnet for a large number of foreign aid agencies who rapidly assumed responsibility for nearly all aspects of the relief operation. Ill-equipped and under-staffed, the government gradually lost the support of major donors, who preferred to channel money and goods through NGOs and the UN. In response to the pressing need for coordination of a complex repatriation programme, the NGOs set up the LINK Coordination Unit in 1993, the first attempt to create an umbrella body specifically to represent NGOs at a national level. The initiative was applauded by donors and the UN alike. LINK was soon to assume a key role in promoting NGO interests in a peace process that depended as much upon local goodwill as it did upon political reconciliation.

BACKGROUND

The signing of the General Peace Agreement on 4 October 1992 marked the end of 17 years' brutal civil war in Mozambique. To a large extent the laying down of arms was the last viable option for exhausted combatants faced with devastating drought and starvation. The war left an estimated one million persons dead, 250,000 children orphaned, thousands of homes and farms destroyed and mines strewn across the country. Half the war's fatalities were children. One-third of the fighters were also children.

In accordance with agreements reached by the Government of the Republic of Mozambique and the RENAMO, the Peace Accords envisaged a cease-fire followed by large scale demobilisation of troops and an electoral process timetabled initially for one year after the signing of the Accords.[1]

Under the same agreement, the United Nations Operation in Mozambique (UNUMOZ) was set up to monitor and coordinate the political, military, electoral and humanitarian aspects of the General Peace Agreement.

The Accords were to alter fundamentally the setting in which humanitarian assistance had been conducted over the previous decade. For the first time, provision was made for international aid to be delivered to government as well as RENAMO areas; indeed, this assistance was regarded as part of the dynamics of peace-making under which contacts could be recreated between communities separated by years of warfare. UNOMOZ was to chair the Humanitarian Assistance Committee (HAC) and oversee operations relating to refugees, internally displaced persons, demobilised soldiers and a rehabilitation programme encompassing almost the entire fabric of the country (*AWEPAA, 1993a*).

---

1. The elections were subsequently delayed until October 1994.

About 1.5 million Mozambicans had taken refuge in neighbouring countries during the war, with a further four to five million being internally displaced. Their return implied not only the logistics of moving, feeding and rehousing a massive population but also the attendant problem of an estimated two million mines spread over the country. Under-employment, compounded by the demobilisation of some 370, 000 combatants from both sides of the conflict, was to present long-term challenges to the government and aid community.[2]

By mid-1993, there was general recognition of the need to move away from food aid and the provision of relief items towards a more consolidated rehabilitation programme and a restoration of essential services for the returning population. For their part, the NGOs had already initiated many 'cross-line' contacts in RENAMO areas and travel throughout the country became easier. In spite of delays in implementing the peace agreement, there was a positive climate of reconciliation which would lend itself to medium-term planning of integrated aid programmes. The time was ripe for coordination initiatives from both the NGOs and the UN that were to become an essential part of the peace process itself.

COLONIAL LEGACY

Many factors that led to economic and social decline in Mozambique can be traced back to the Portuguese colonial experience that left the country with a distorted and weakened economy with few indigenous skills and industries. Independent in 1975, the victorious FRELIMO government undertook a radical programme of nationalisation, promoting communal villages and organising collective production methods. As elsewhere in Africa, these proved both unpopular and untenable, especially given the increasing amount of resources being absorbed by the insurgency fuelled by neighbouring South Africa.

1985 marked the beginning of a critical period for Mozambique. RENAMO had stepped up its offensive at precisely the time when a severe drought threatened the entire country. A 25 per cent reduction in grain production and a 70 per cent drop in livestock produce was reported to the UN by President Somora Machel. It was at this time that some of the major foreign NGOs began to open offices in Mozambique (*ITEM, 1992*).

The FRELIMO government had inherited a largely centralised government machinery from the Portuguese that was inflexible and demanded bureaucratic skills not easily found, especially at regional levels. Their social policy was, nevertheless, perceived as broadly progressive. Thus several foreign NGOs began working closely within

---

2. The demobilisation process was delayed for some months, due mainly to reticence on the RENAMO side. The first RENAMO soldiers to surrender their arms to the UN did not present themselves until October 1993.

government structures to avoid setting up parallel programmes or structures (see for example *Thomas, 1992*, an examination of Save the Children Fund (UK)'s (SCF) institution-building work in Mozambique). The government had already established a close relationship with political solidarity organisations and their workers (*cooperantes*) by placing them within the institutional framework of national and regional government. Indeed, for foreign NGOs there were initially no alternate community structures or indigenous NGOs through which to work.

The situation changed quite dramatically towards the end of the decade. Rendered bankrupt by debt and an expensive war, FRELIMO was forced to accept reforms prescribed by the Bretton Woods institutions. The government's previously hard-line Marxist stance considerably softened and new political parties emerged. Economic liberalisation was promoted through the government's acceptance of the Economic Rehabilitation Programme (PRE) drawn up by the World Bank and the International Monetary Fund (IMF) in 1987 (*World Bank, 1993*). In line with new political pluralism, national NGOs emerged no longer linked to FRELIMO, although they were not formally legalised until 1989.

AID 'EXPLOSION'

Mozambique has often been described as the most aid-dependent country in the world. From 1989 to 1993, international aid to the country approached US$1 billion per year with reliance on external assistance representing three-quarters of the gross domestic product (GDP). Indeed, the state had little capacity to carry out any investment except with recourse to foreign aid. The need for massive food imports was mainly due to the war that wrecked normal commerce and distribution. Domestic food sales amounted to only 10 per cent of the country's requirements, while defence and security still absorbed 38 per cent of the national budget in 1993 (*De Coninck, 1993*).

In 1992, Mozambique received US$700 million in grants and concessionary loans, including US$190 million in emergency assistance, or US$47 per capita, one-third above the average levels for sub-Saharan Africa (*UNOHAC, 1993*). Ironically, although money pledged for 'the emergency' bolstered the state and its institutions, it also contributed to their further disintegration. Individual agencies, multilateral and non-governmental, often forged privileged links with specific government departments at the expense of overall coherence and capacity development.

Several studies have accorded aid a central role in weakening the capacity of the state to pursue progressive development policies. The contention is that aid served to secure the virtual collapse of FRELIMO's socialist programme (*Brochman & Ofstad 1989* and, for a critique of NGO policies, *Kanji, 1990*). The demands of the myriad donors, their different agenda, procedures and policies lent credence to the charge that Mozambique was simply a hostage to foreign intervention (*Hanlon, 1991*).

In line with similar developments abroad, donors were intent upon developing a two-tier support system: institutional government support through the UN and more flexible and 'conditional' support through the NGOs. Throughout the 1980s, western donor commitment to funding NGOs was premised on the assumption that too much government power had been a major constraint to humanitarian intervention in Africa. NGOs were a safety net enabling relief assistance in particular to be carried out directly, thus avoiding channelling money through national governments. This two-tiered welfare system and its implications in Africa in general have been explored elsewhere (*Duffield, 1992*).

Like Ethiopia and Sudan, Mozambique was to become a 'testing ground' for massive operational NGO relief programmes backed by significant Northern government and multilateral aid. True, there could be no lasting peace without a thorough review of the chronic level of underdevelopment facing Mozambique and in this respect the skills offered by NGOs were at a premium. Their profile, however, was soon far to exceed that of small-scale development activities.

Impact of foreign NGOs

From 1987–90, the number of foreign NGOs opening offices in Mozambique rose to over 100. The momentum was maintained by a series of fundraising campaigns abroad. Mozambique was at the epicentre of a regional displacement and drought crisis and the general slackening of regulations by the government allowed increasing freedom to foreign relief operations.

The new open-door policy had two main consequences in Mozambique: first, the government found it almost impossible to retain control over policy while securing vital donor assistance; second, long-term, low-profile development activities were increasingly out of favour as the government sought to attract more visible (and larger) material inputs. The notion that NGOs were 'invited' to participate in the country's development is rather spurious in this context: their presence was more or less a *fait accompli*. Their role as the government's 'working partners in development' is questionable. As we have seen, they were an increasingly independent 'Trojan Horse' for donor interests in the country as a whole.

Yet, the growing power of Northern NGOs was not necessarily a signal for greater cost effectiveness and appropriate aid. There were many reported cases of lack of coordination, growing inter-agency competition and arbitrary changes in donor fashions (*Zetter, 1992*). These were to influence NGO priorities and collective endeavours regionally as well as in Mozambique itself.

Mozambique Government capacity

From the early 1980s, the Mozambique government became increasingly astute in explaining to donors the structural nature of the emergency in the country and the necessity for linking the goals of emergency relief and rehabilitation. In the four appeals carried out under the auspices of the UN between 1987 and 1990 the executional strategy was to emphasise the use of existing institutional structures and to reinforce them with training and appropriate resources (*Government of the People's Republic of Mozambique and the United Nations, 1989*).

Despite overwhelming need, there was a significant fall-off in donor response to the appeals of 1989 and 1990, not least because evidently government effectiveness was declining. The cumulative effect of cuts in World Bank assistance, a marked increase in FRELIMO corruption and the first signs of donor 'fatigue' were to plunge the country into ever-deepening crisis. When the devastating Southern Africa drought hit in 1991–92 the capacity of the government to deal effectively with the complexity of the relief operation was further questioned by the aid establishment.

The issue was compounded by the increasing time spent on 'humanitarian diplomacy', notably the complex negotiations to secure free passage of relief items to RENAMO areas. For years, Mozambique had been subject to a cynical, often ruthless, use of food as a weapon of war by both government and RENAMO.[3]

Aid to the countryside

While most commentators have lamented the negative impact of aid on the state at a national level, its effects at provincial and district levels are more complex. Here, we encounter the interplay between local government and the aid community, particularly the NGOs. By 1993, there were over 180 registered NGOs in the country, overwhelmingly foreign agencies.[4] Although many opened administrative offices in Maputo, it was at provincial and district levels that their impact was most felt. Here, NGO resources invariably exceeded what the government could muster. Provincial authorities were normally allocated less than 5 per cent of all public sector investment resources. Virtually their only source of funds for local projects (mainly relief work) was the NGOs.

What was the impact of this on local structures? Some have argued that, over time, NGOs undermined the coordinating role of the provincial emergency commission by increasingly executing programmes for

---

3. For a more thorough analysis of the use of food as a weapon of war, see *Duffield, 1990*. For a review of literature and evidence, see *Macrae and Zwi, 1992*.
4. Author's discussion with Rogerio Marrime, Deputy NGO Coordinator in the Ministry of Cooperation, 20 August 1993. The figure of 180 NGOs included donor NGOs without offices in the country. Marrime was able to point to 18 local NGOs who had registered with the government but it was unclear how many of these were active.

themselves rather than channelling aid through government institutions (*Egan, 1991*). However, it is not sufficient to categorise NGOs as all-powerful players who sweep aside government authority and structures to impose an homogenous (even 'conspiratorial') aid strategy. NGOs are very different in terms of internal dynamics and there can sometimes be a significant disparity between what they claim to have achieved and what local beneficiaries on the ground perceive as happening.[5]

It has been argued that only when NGOs like Oxfam-UK and SCF-UK became involved in Mozambique was it possible for the government to set up workable mechanisms for relief distribution (*Borton et al, 1988*). The enormous increase in aid in the mid-1980s often empowered government at district level by providing inputs for reconstruction and daily operations far beyond what was available to a state whose revenue base had been destroyed (*Wilson & Numes, 1992*).

Paradoxically, the massive explosion of aid to Mozambique may have played an important role in the expansion of government military control in the north during the 1987–90 period. Government representatives overseeing the distribution of aid in rural centres acquired an important level of power and legitimacy in their relations with the peasants and displaced people. Moreover, the IMF's structural adjustment programme and new aid contracts had encouraged the re-emergence of a commercial elite, who became a key ally of the state against RENAMO at district level. It has been argued that it was the fruits of commerce, not aid directly, that sustained the army and administration. The re-invigorated local economy was perhaps the major means of sustaining and integrating the displaced and returnees (*Wilson & Numes, 1992*).

Coordination efforts by the government

Throughout the 1980s, the government built up a framework of coordinating bodies in a bid to retain responsibility for planning, execution and monitoring of emergency work. Dealing with donors at national level was the National Executive Emergency Commission (CENE), which came under the Ministry of Cooperation. At provincial level was the Provincial Emergency Commission (CPE) and at district level was the Emergencies Operations Committee (COE). Relief distribution was to be handled at all levels by the Department for the Combat and Prevention of Natural Disasters (DPCCN), set up in 1983.

---

5. Some interesting studies have been done on NGOs' *de facto* weakness in the face of rapidly changing situations where beneficiaries have ideologies and skills quite capable of subverting unwelcome activities by external agents. For instance, in Zambezia province the 'grand design' strategy of NGOs working with artisan associations during the war – to strengthen government, help the artisans and local community and boost the local economy – was either over-ambitious or had mutually contradictory objectives (*Thomas & Hallam, 1992*)

As we have seen, about US$1 billion a year poured into Mozambique from 1987 onwards to provide relief to some 1.5 million people. Not surprisingly, the task of effective coordination was beyond the capacity and resources of the various government structures. They were general highly centralised, with poorly paid and low-skilled staff who could only look with envy at the resources and money available to the international aid establishment. Moreover, the World Bank's PRE structural adjustment programme of 1987 resulted in the forced shedding of many government jobs and the weakening of all emergency bodies.[6]

From 1989–91 a huge amount of relief materials was sent to the provinces, particularly Zambezia and Tete. The government's stock controls and information systems were weak and transport was poor. This prompted several NGOs to set up their own warehouses and assume greater responsibility for the delivery of goods. Able to pay higher salaries, the NGOs attracted better educated and more motivated Mozambicans to work with them. Invariably, these people reported to an expatriate manager. The DPCCN warehouses began to be used only for food, whereas previously all relief items were channelled through them.

Meanwhile, several important gestures were made to enhance the DPCCN's performance. For example, CARE International set up a logistics unit within DPCCN and SCF-UK placed expatriate counterparts in the provincial Directorates of Health and Social Action in Zambezia as well as helping to build up the capacity of DPCCN in the province.[7] Nevertheless, the trend was towards increasingly interventionist approaches by the NGOs with the tacit approval of a weakened government administration.

In arguing for a more coherent nationwide strategy, several NGOs reported a degree of confusion between the authority of the government coordinating bodies and that of the line ministries, which already existed to cater for more traditional activities of government.[8] In most provinces it was the Planning Department of the provincial government that retained the coordinating role in emergencies. The exception was Zambezia Province where the CPE assumed a dominant role. It 'borrowed' civil servants from existing ministries, pronounced on the

---

6. The World Bank has often avoided accommodating the impact of conflict in their planning. Its removal of food rationing and subsidies in Mozambique (supposedly to boost production and stimulate the market) is a case in point. The reasons for low production levels lay not simply in poor marketing policies but in the interruption of production by the war, especially by direct targeting by RENAMO. This is not acknowledged in the Bank's structural adjustment programme (see, for example, *Green, 1987*)
7. SCF was, in fact, one of the few NGOs whose stated objective was to work within government departments so as to avoid setting up parallel structures. From 1990 they placed technical advisors within the Ministry of Health and the State Secretariat for Social Action (SCAS) at national level as well as a number of advisors in government departments in Zambezia (see, for example, *SCF, 1992*).
8. For example, the author's interview with Nathan Simonson, Lutheran World Federation, 19 August 1993.

priorities of construction programmes, and monitored the distribution of drugs by the provincial health structures and the selection of school materials by the provincial Education Directorate. In doing so, it created obstacles between NGOs and their usual government partners. More important, by rendering the various line ministries relatively moribund and inserting an additional stratum of government, a potentially short-sighted strategy was put in place (*Thomas, 1992*).

In spite of these constraints, or perhaps because of them, international NGOs enjoyed a quasi-autonomous role in several provinces. In Tete and Zambesia, for instance, districts were 'carved up' among a handful of prominent NGOs, resulting in a degree of surrogacy and substitution of the government's role. In creating zones of primary influence, these NGOs cut across their traditional sectoral specialisations to become 'jacks of all trades'. By building donor support for such activities it is difficult to see how NGOs will revert to their more specialised roles in the post-emergency period.

By local NGOs

Mozambique does not have a history of indigenous NGOs operating at a national level. With a few notable exceptions (Mozambique Red Cross, for example) the NGO sector before the mid-1980s comprised cooperatives, trade unions and social welfare institutions that were, for the most part, linked to government political institutions. The exceptions were those linked to professional, confessional or commercial interest groups.

In 1990, the Ministry of Cooperation invited 12 local NGOs to form a cooperative umbrella that could represent the rather loose body of national NGOs. Three organisations were elected to lead this – Organizaçaõ para o Desenvovimento socio-económico Integrado (KULIMA), Conselho Cristáo de Moçambique (CCM) and Liga Internacional das Concepçöes Globais do Consenso (LICGC). A survey was conducted of all known national NGOs and published by the Ministry of Cooperation, (*Ministry of Cooperation 1992*).[9] Meanwhile, the Institute of Rural Development (INDER), a government body linked to the Ministry of Agriculture, set up an NGO database and coordination unit that, by 1993, had performed only marginal activities.

Attempts at coordinating national NGOs were confounded by mutual suspicion and unease about the political connections of several

9. The Ministry of Cooperation lists 87 national NGOs, though non-governmental here means non-commercial or simply 'representational bodies'. Only 36 were listed as development organisations, though many were only at provincial level. Ten were listed as humanitarian (presumably emergency relief, etc). An unknown number were closed by 1993 (*see also KULIMA, 1993*)

prominent NGOs.[10] Those close to FRELIMO pushed for the government to take the lead in information sharing. In a climate of potentially profitable relations being developed between individual NGOs and foreign donors, it was inevitable that 'contacts' were jealously guarded. Yet the general neglect of institutional support of local NGOs by international donors pre-empted their ability to keep pace with rapid developments in the relief operation. Few, if any, studies were undertaken to assess the capacity of Mozambique NGOs as viable partners of either the UN or international NGOs, although the UN's various offices had irregular meetings with local NGO representatives.[11]

THE LINK NGO FORUM

Origin

An original proposal for an NGO coordination unit comprising national and international NGOs came from the Norwegian Refugee Council (NRC) following a mission to the region in June 1992. Contacts with various international NGO colleagues had established the need for regional cooperation among aid agencies on issues related to Mozambican refugees in neighbouring countries and the displaced within Mozambique. It was also recognised that NGOs should become involved in the various commissions being set up through the General Peace Agreement. With the likelihood of large-scale repatriation and reintegration taking place in 1992–1993, closer cooperation was of paramount importance.

In October 1992 the proposal was endorsed by the Executive Committee of the International Council of Voluntary Agencies (ICVA) in Geneva. The Chair of ICVA's Working Group on Humanitarian Affairs was also the Secretary-General of NRC. Although the original notion was to establish a refugee-centred coordination body, its mandate was soon extended to include other issues of general concern to NGOs in Maputo. NRC was asked to lead an ICVA Task Force whose brief included three elements: general development related issues; implementation of the General Peace Agreement; and refugee related work (*Ngabonziza, 1993*).

---

10. Dominico Luizzi, Executive Director of KULIMA, reported to the author (22 August 1993) that four local NGOs were particularly resistant to the notion of coordination: Progresso, Associação Desenvolvimento da Comunidade (ADC), Associação Mozambicana para o Desenvolvimento Urbano (AMDU) and Associação Mulher Lei e Desenvolvimento (MULEIDE). Each was very pro-FRELIMO; in fact, ADC was headed by ex-President Samoro Machel's widow.
11. There were a few more successful coordination attempts at sectoral levels. The Mozambique Organisation of AIDS Associations (MONASA), for example, brought together 15 NGOs, mostly from the refugee sector, to coordinate efforts in aspects of AIDS and family planning education (author's interview with Eleuterio Fenita, Director, Amodeff Association, Maputo, 20 August 1993).

The first informal meetings of NGO field directors in Maputo signalled a widely felt need to improve contacts between them. Several *ad hoc* arrangements had already proved successful, particularly at provincial levels, but there had rarely been an opportunity for NGOs to come together to discuss policy and programmes other than infrequent UN meetings, where detailed exchange of information was impractical. For example, there was no existing database of NGO activities either regionally or nationally, although Médecins Sans Frontières (MSF) had, since August 1992, issued a fairly comprehensive monthly update of health and security issues drawn from information provided by NGOs countrywide.[12]

LINK was formally established in February 1993 after the formation of an Interim Steering Committee (ISC) in January.[13] The ISC was 'self-appointed' in that it comprised a handful of interested NGOs: ActionAid, KULIMA, Lutheran World Federation (LWF), Oxfam-UK and NRC. The Mozambique Red Cross and CARE International were soon to join, bringing the ISC membership to seven. In April, NRC provided initial funding, office space and the secondment of a staff member as the first LINK coordinator. The 1993 secretariat budget was US$156,000 for a staff of three persons. Except for US$30,000 provided by three other ISC members, NRC (through its own funds and those of the Norwegian Ministry of Foreign Affairs) provided the bulk of LINK expenses for 1993.

Upon its formal establishment in February 1993, LINK saw itself as both an ICVA Task Force for regional consultation on refugees and a coordination unit for NGOs in Mozambique. It soon became clear, however, that an ICVA Task Force could not comprise non-ICVA members. LINK therefore soon dropped the idea of setting up a task force, though it did retain a brief for developing regional contacts in Southern Africa (*ICVA, 1993*).

Mandate and membership

In March 1993, the ISC issued a brief Agreement of Understanding that was to form the first commonly agreed mandate for the coordination unit (*LINK, 1993a*). At this stage membership of LINK was open to all NGOs engaged in humanitarian assistance in Mozambique. It was stressed, however, that members should provide a basic outline of their activities to LINK and that they should be recognised by the government as a 'bona fide' NGO. In early March the first LINK open meeting

---

12. The *Boletim Mensal CIS* was initially a project set up for MSF of Belgium, France, Holland, Spain and Switzerland. By 1993 at least 40 per cent of its information came from surveys regularly submitted by other NGOs and collected by staff paid by MSF. MSF also maintained a well-stocked resource centre in Maputo.
13. LINK initially carried both the Anglo name and the Portuguese name, LIGAÇAO, but this was later dropped.

took place with 35 international NGOs and seven local NGOs (invited through the Mozambican NGO, KULIMA). The meeting was addressed by the UN Secretary-General's Special Representative and head of UNUMOZ, Aldo Ajello, thereby signifying the importance the UN attached to NGO coordination in the region.

Having established the secretariat in April, the new coordinator set about developing a register of known NGOs in the country. Since the original mandate was remarkably inclusive, LINK was not seen to be a threat to individual NGO interests and many larger foreign NGOs were firmly behind the initiative. The issue of coordination versus control was not yet brought to the fore. However, these were very early days; LINK had yet to set up any regional or sectoral coordination groups, preferring to concentrate on co-opting potential members and establishing a profile in the aid community in Maputo. (See Box 4.1)

Box 4.1
GENERAL ASSEMBLY

The first General Assembly, the 'coming of age' for LINK, took place on 29 September 1993. Formal statutes and membership criteria were, with a few revisions, accepted by majority vote of the 56 NGOs present. An NGO would be considered a member once it had fulfilled basic criteria, submitted information on its activities and paid membership dues. A new Steering Committee comprising three Mozambican and six international NGOs was elected. The new budget for 1994 would be approximately US$180,000, US$15,000 of which would be met by membership dues, the remainder by major NGOs, donors and the UN.

LINK was soon to establish a number of working groups chaired by interested agencies. These included mine clearance, repatriation, reintegration of demobilised soldiers, food aid, education, health, and regional groups for Tete Province and the southern provinces (*LINK, 1994a*)

Countries of asylum

One of the first LINK initiatives was a two-day NGO seminar held in May 1993 entitled 'A Regional Approach to NGO Coordination in the Repatriation and Resettlement of Mozambican Refugees'. The main objective was to encourage regional cooperation between NGOs working with Mozambican refugees in countries of asylum and NGOs working in Mozambique. Major items for discussion included NGO cross-border activities and NGO participation in the implementation of the United Nations High Commissioner for Refugees (UNHCR) Plan of Operation for the repatriation of Mozambican refugees.

The seminar was attended by 60 NGOs (including 25 national NGOs) and representatives from international NGOs working with refugees in Malawi, Zimbabwe, Swaziland and South Africa. Various UN, government and RENAMO representatives were also present. This was perhaps the first opportunity for LINK to present itself as a viable channel of information and advocacy on NGOs' concerns.

It has been estimated that up to seven million Mozambicans were displaced during the war at one point or another, including nearly two million who took refuge abroad. Mozambicans officially designated as refugees were those who fled their homes near an international border and crossed it to safety, though on average they were no further from their area of origin than were the internally displaced. By the time the Peace Accords were signed in 1992, approximately 1.2 million refugees remained outside the country (ie Malawi 1,058,500; Zimbabwe 137,900; Zambia 25,400; Swaziland 24,000 and Tanzania 20,000, according to official UNHCR figures, *UNHCR, 1993a*).

With few exceptions, camps and settlements were not welcomed by refugees and local people. Although refugees enjoyed relatively greater security than internally displaced persons, the majority were confined to crowded camps, highly dependent on free food and other services. They enjoyed relatively superior health, water and education but camp life caused a host of complex social problems that often accompany high population density and confinement.

Several studies have shown that Mozambican 'assistance dependence' can be attributed to the overriding institutional concern for security and the willingness of UNHCR and other donors to provide significant aid only to those refugees who were separated from their local hosts. Indeed, repeated suggestions for assistance to self-settled refugees and their local hosts have been ignored by donors, NGOs and local governments alike (see, for example, *Pruitt & Marama, 1988*, and *Mupedziswa & Makanya, 1988*). It has been argued elsewhere that refugee policies framed by security considerations have been a major constraint on useful development interventions, since they limit engagement in the wider economy and society (*Harrell-Bond, 1992*).

The majority of refugees were to be found in camps in Malawi and Zimbabwe. Some 80 per cent came from only 12 districts or about 10 per cent of the districts in Mozambique (*DHA, 1993*). The mid-1980s saw a rapid penetration of the Malawi and Zimbabwe programmes by northern NGOs and an attendant drop in vetting by the host governments of these agencies' activities.

As in Mozambique itself, NGOs began to develop their own initiatives, linked principally with donors and local administrative authorities rather than with central government. Local NGOs who were the main implementing partners in the early years of the operation were increasingly undermined by the opening of programmes under direct Northern NGO engagement. The extent to which this may have undermined indigenous coordination structures has yet to be examined.[14]

Repatriation

From the beginning of 1993, the NGOs had asked LINK to help clarify the roles of the various UN bodies responsible for repatriation and rehabilitation of the hundreds of thousands of people likely to return to their homes in the near future. Attention was drawn to a degree of frustration with UNHCR, in particular, whose plans did not take account of the increasing level of spontaneous repatriation taking place from Malawi and Zimbabwe. NGOs pointed to a policy vacuum in which the reasons for UNHCR's delayed plans were unclear. Was it because of economic constraints in preparing travel grants, transport, etc, or had UNHCR assessed that security constraints meant that protection could not be guaranteed? There was a lack of transparency in the criteria used for a UNHCR promotion of repatriation. Indeed, an exaggerated 'legalistic' approach towards a perceived threshold of safety for returnees deprives refugees of international protection if and when they do decide to spontaneously repatriate (*NRC, 1994*).

It was not until May 1993 that the UNHCR launched its appeal for returning refugees. By then some 300, 000 people had already returned with little assistance. The UNHCR's three-year appeal totalled US$203 million for an expected 'registered' return of 1.3 million people by 1995. At the time of the launch, only US$6 million was in the coffers (*UNHCR, 1993b*).

Many of these population movements were taking place in RENAMO areas at a time when there was still no protocol between the Government of Mozambique and RENAMO concerning the restoration of basic services such as health provision and education. LINK was asked to promote such a protocol via the UN in an effort to avoid NGOs setting up parallel structures in RENAMO areas (*LINK, 1993b*).

A series of Tripartite Agreements between UNHCR, the Mozambique government and the various countries of asylum took place between December 1988 and October 1993 which dealt with the practical arrangements for voluntary repatriation. The last of these agreements – that with South Africa – allowed for the formal repatriation of some 250,000 Mozambicans to begin in 1994 (*UNOHAC, 1993*).

---

14. An interesting model for 'scaling up' the activities of a local NGO coordination body was provided by the Council for NGOs in Malawi (CONGOMA). Early in 1992 it recognised the need to enhance its capacity to deal with the drought crisis that had hit the country. Thus the Drought Relief Coordination Unit (DRCU) was created, headed by an expatriate, and funded by United States Agency for International Development (USAID), United Nations Children's Fund (UNICEF), United Nations Development Programme (UNDP) and several NGOs. Apart from taking on a representational and informational role for NGOs, DRCU also began a series of management training programmes for local NGOs. By mid-1993, its role within CONGOMA was phased out but not before a plan for further NGO (and CONGOMA) upgrading had been instigated. It has been argued that without DRCU, donors and the large number of newly arrived international NGOs would almost certainly have bypassed CONGOMA and set up a parallel structure. However, the impact of DRCU and its success in restructuring CONGOMA have yet to be assessed (*Barbee, 1993*).

The May 1993 LINK seminar highlighted several themes that were to recur in the coming months and were to give direction and emphasis to the organisation's role in Mozambique. These included a general advocacy and lobbying role, particularly regarding NGO inclusion in the commissions related to the peace agreement. Forthcoming LINK meetings were also to emphasise NGO potential in conflict resolution at local levels. Critical in this respect was the increasing contact with RENAMO and NGO involvement in issues such as land tenure and human rights.[15]

Cooperation with the UN

From the outset, LINK aimed at improving cooperation between NGOs and various government departments, RENAMO and the UN in efforts to establish its credentials as an impartial facilitator of inter-agency contacts. Most important, it immediately made a strong bid to be a representative NGO voice in humanitarian aspects of the General Peace Agreement.

In December 1992, the UN Secretary-General recommended that UNOMOZ should have a humanitarian component based in Maputo with sub-offices at regional and provincial levels. Thus the United Nations Office for the Coordination of Humanitarian Assistance (UNOHAC) was opened. With six UN agencies under its umbrella, UNOHAC was to be a temporary replacement for the more usual Special Coordinator's office under UNDP. It was expected that after the elections UNDP would again assume a lead role.

UNOHAC's prime responsibility was to buttress the role of humanitarian aid in promoting the process of national reconciliation. A declaration on 'Guiding Principles for Humanitarian Assistance' had been signed by the warring parties on 16 July 1992, three months prior to the peace agreement. It allowed for the free passage of relief items to all areas. RENAMO, however, insisted on airlifting the food; the UN and government refused on the grounds of cost and security. Finally, after three months' delay, land routes were agreed. Not only had the situation worsened but also people were forced to travel long distances to food distribution points and were thus unable to plant seeds for the next year's crop.

The Guiding Principles included a commitment towards a neutral commission to oversee the fair distribution of the massive material aid now pouring into the country. UNOHAC was to become the principal body ensuring an equitable 'cross-line' distribution. It coordinated the distribution of over 18,000 tons of food and seeds to RENAMO areas in the first six months of 1993.

---

15. NGOs were usually required to report any violations of the General Peace Agreement to the UN. In early 1993, Amnesty International submitted a proposal on a Human Rights Commission to be held under the auspices of the agreement, a matter strongly supported by NGOs in Mozambique.

One of UNOHAC's early tasks was the management of the Trust Fund for Humanitarian Assistance in Mozambique, a fund set up by the Department of Humanitarian Affairs (DHA) in Geneva. The Trust Fund was to meet requirements not covered in the much larger 1992 appeal, the Consolidated Humanitarian Assistance Programme (initial pledges – nearly US$500 million).[16] In particular, it enabled donors to give voluntary contributions to sectors such as demining, reintegration of demobilised soldiers and an institution-building programme for NGOs in RENAMO areas. Donors who were not operational themselves (or did not have operational partners) preferred to pledge money through the Trust Fund.

By November 1993, the fund had reached nearly US$34 million.[17] A significant achievement of LINK was its successful lobby to get an NGO representative on the Trust Fund Approval Committee responsible for allocating unearmarked funds. In others areas of the world (for example, Afghanistan) this had proved remarkably difficult.

From UNOHAC's point of view, LINK was a useful organisation with whom to deal since it simplified the process of dealing with NGOs while demonstrating a 'democratic' representation of the wider NGO community. Backed by the larger funding NGOs, LINK also bolstered the confidence of the UN system in dealing with international donors predisposed to NGOs. The DHA and UNOHAC fundraising documents were at pains to stress the important role NGOs played in the country. Pressed for funds themselves, they were all too aware of the symbiotic relationship they had with NGOs. The UNHCR, for example, was still struggling with protocol arrangements with neighbouring countries.[18]

Severely short of money and personnel, it was initially unable to do more than simply monitor the spontaneous return of thousands to Mozambique. Only the NGOs at this stage could begin rudimentary assistance to the thousands of people recrossing borders.

Humanitarian Assistance Committee (HAC)

Among the many commissions set up in Maputo in the aftermath of the peace agreement there was none on humanitarian affairs. In October 1992, an HAC was formed which brought together the International Committee of the Red Cross (ICRC), World Food

---

16. The Consolidated Humanitarian Assistance Programme was updated in November 1993, with priority needs estimated at US$609.7 million from May 1993 to April 1994. Donor response up until that time had been quite good (*UNOHAC, 1993*).

17. Author's interview with Mr Bernt Bernander, Director of UNOHAC office in Maputo, 25 August 1993.

18. The tripartite agreement to regulate organised repatriation from South Africa was not signed until 15 October 1993. Some interesting 'spontaneous' repatriation had taken place across the Kruger Park border before then under the direction and assistance of the local South African Defense Force. Although UNHCR was wary, NGOs welcomed the initiative.

Programme (WFP) and UNICEF, but since it had not included a REN-AMO representative it was abandoned by the end of the year. One of LINK's early tasks on behalf of the NGO community was to press for the re-establishment of HAC as a policy unit to include NGOs, government, RENAMO and the UN.

Despite the good will of UNOHAC (including an invitation to LINK to nominate NGO representation to the HAC) there were long procedural delays. The HAC's integral link with the peace agreement meant that it was one of several negotiating ploys by RENAMO, who retained a deep-seated mistrust of FRELIMO. Of the eight commissions established under the peace agreement, only four functioned by the end of March 1993.[19]

In a further dramatic setback, RENAMO withdrew even from these. The head of UNOMOZ, Aldo Ajello, suggested the indefinite postponement of elections. RENAMO was widely accused of 'playing for time and money'. RENAMO president, Alfonso Dhlakama, cited 'logistical problems' as the reason for his stalling of the peace process. Meanwhile, the Italian and British governments rushed to provide food, rent and office equipment for the several hundred RENAMO officials entering Maputo in advance of their leader. Dhlakama remained at his base in Maringue while castigating the international community for their 'preferential' treatment of government areas (*AWEPAA, 1993b*). He was not to come to Maputo until 21 August 1993.

Meanwhile, LINK was caught in the impasse. The HAC was finally reactivated in December 1993 with an increased membership including RENAMO as well as all UN agencies, 18 bilateral donors, the World Bank, European Union, ICRC, International Organisation for Migration (IOM) and three NGO representatives (including LINK). It was to be a sub-committee of the Control and Supervisory Committee (CSC) under the chairmanship of the UN.[20]

NGOs and RENAMO

Throughout the 1980s, the UN channelled aid exclusively through government structures. This was never really questioned. UN objectives were defined in terms of accountability to the government rather than the people of Mozambique (however difficult that is to define). One consequence was that no UN aid was distributed in RENAMO areas, which accounted for as much as 50 per cent of the country. There

---

19. UNOMOZ was also plagued by delays within the UN system. It was not until March 1993 that the initial US$140 million budget was approved. The first UN troops (Italian) were not in place until April. Priorities elsewhere in the world were cited as the main reasons for the delay.

20. There had been some opposition to the NGO presence in HAC, particularly from the Italian and Spanish donors who argued that since NGOs were not party to the peace agreement their inclusion on the commissions would not be valid. However, the views of UNOMOZ head, Aldo Ajello, a strong advocate of a high NGO profile, held sway.

was, however, a small amount of NGO activity in these areas by several right-wing South African Christian groups. The ICRC was also active in some RENAMO areas. Interestingly, this meant that RENAMO became nowhere near as dependent on aid as the government.

The promotion of the HAC represented a fundamental departure in UN policy, in line with the principles of the peace agreement. Its thrust was a cross-line, cross-party attempt to ensure an equitable distribution of assistance throughout the country. Land routes were opened in 1992 but the political squabbling caused constant delays in the delivery of aid to RENAMO areas. Although the cease-fire held, the obligations of all parties towards safe delivery of aid were contained in the mandates of the various paralysed commissions. Only a handful of NGOs and the ICRC were able regularly to access the disputed areas. Without any higher-profile assistance, international donors hesitated in contributing to the Consolidated Humanitarian Assistance Programme before a resolution of these difficulties was found. For its part, UNOHAC was increasingly anxious to break the impasse.

Long delays in the implementation of the peace process undoubtedly benefited RENAMO. Caught between the cutting of supply lines from neighbouring countries and an ill-prepared and still hostile capital, it is not surprising that RENAMO held out for a longer planning period. The extent to which government troops were to be replaced with UN troops was a main sticking point that delayed RENAMO's handing-in of weapons for many months. Dhlakama's negotiators continued to demand large monetary payments as a condition of its transference from a guerilla movement to a political party.[21] To some extent, donors acceded to such demands since they feared a repetition of the Angola débacle.

LINK had already met with RENAMO officials in Maputo in March 1993 when issues of coordination, access and security were discussed with RENAMO's Coordinator of Humanitarian Affairs (*LINK, 1993c*). However, NGOs continued to experience difficulties when travelling to RENAMO areas. The basic problem was one of false expectations and perceptions of minor RENAMO officials who, over the years, had very little contact with the international community. NGO insistence on assessment missions, monitoring and reportage, for instance, was not fully understood. The 'numbers game' was also being played, with both RENAMO and government claiming to administer greater numbers of people than the NGOs and UN were prepared to acknowledge as recipients of food aid. Although the WFP began to develop its own census, UNILOG, the UN logistics body, was often accused of 'dumping' food in RENAMO districts without proper distribution and monitoring.

---

21. Donors became increasingly alarmed at reports of corruption and excess on the part of RENAMO (*AWEPAA, 1993a*).

Some interesting NGO initiatives took place in spite of bureaucratic obstacles. District-level RENAMO and government commanders and administrators were far more amenable to NGO missions than their bosses in Maputo. Information was shared on mine hazards, bridges were built and roads were repaired. By bypassing formal procedures, it was possible for NGOs to tap the good will of people in the countryside anxious to find their own ways of making peace with long-time adversaries.[22]

LINK, supported by UNOHAC, decided to push for a meeting with Dhlakama himself. Armed with anecdotal evidence of good will on the ground, they were to stress the importance of regional coordination, a 'basic services' protocol between government and RENAMO and the urgency of setting up the HAC. A delegation comprising the Christian Council of Mozambique, MSF, SCF-UK and World Vision was chosen to represent the NGO community in the negotiations. It met with Dhlakama in November 1993. The meeting highlighted some fundamental differences in approach between the NGOs and REN-AMO, with the former emphasising access to the beleagured population in RENAMO areas and the difficulty of identifying a single authority with whom to negotiate. For its part, RENAMO was more concerned to emphasise the imbalance of inputs between government and RENAMO areas, wishing to address this balance to its favour before any real progress could be made in its relations with international aid organisations. Several follow-up meetings were suggested with LINK acting as the facilitator (*LINK, 1993e*).

CONCLUSION

The degree of success of any coordinated approach to humanitarian assistance in Mozambique in 1992–93 was inevitably tempered by two immutable facts. First, the geography of Mozambique and the relative autonomy of aid operations in the provinces made effective sectoral coordination from Maputo neither possible nor desirable.[23] At best, LINK could bolster its advocacy and information roles through closer contacts with NGO administrative offices in Maputo and play a lead role in policy discussions with the various inter-governmental bodies. It could also bring to the attention of the government and the new political parties (notably RENAMO) the important role of NGOs in post-war Mozambique.

---

22. See, for example, reports from the British NGO, ACTIONAID, on their relief programme, 1989–93.
23. In November 1993, LINK established, with a LINK-paid secretary and a 3-member steering committee, a provincial coordination group in Tete. As well as working with NGOs in Tete province, its brief included liaising with NGOs working with refugees in Malawi.

Second, the fluidity of political events and the yet undetermined outcome of the peace process meant that donors and their client NGOs were reluctant to begin longer-term programmes requiring three to five years' funding. Apart from the DHA's Consolidated Programme, there was neither the facility nor the expectation for sectoral planning of rehabilitation and development programmes at a national level. As we have seen, access to RENAMO areas was limited and the demining programme had hardly begun.

With its small staff (one expatriate and two Mozambicans in 1993), LINK could not at this early stage envisage more than a supportive role very much confined to institutional and structural aspects of the aid operation. From the outset, it was well supported and encouraged by international NGOs and the UN system. Interestingly, the level of such support pointed to a frustration with the lack of coordination in previous years. Anecdotal evidence of this was abundant. The only remaining worry for LINK was whether expectations would outstrip performance.

Representatives of Mozambican NGOs pointed to the technical bias of LINK and its dominance by foreign NGOs. The process of dialogue among local NGOs was, they claimed, different. Cooperation may in some cases have political overtones, in others it may involve associations of a more pastoral nature. LINK had not given priority to establishing a training programme for local NGOs.[24] Its potential support role in this respect, some claimed, has been overshadowed by the priority given to dealings with UNOHAC and the 'international agenda'. Here, as in other major aid operations, local NGOs were unable to keep pace with initiatives launched and maintained by a temporary but powerful relief hierarchy.

For its part, the government's weak NGO division in the Ministry of Cooperation was no match for the potential informational role LINK hoped to build up in 1994. From its inception, LINK's regular contact with various government departments was mostly confined to issues of customs regulations, import of NGO relief supplies, vehicles and equipment, and rent increases in office areas.[25]

The handful of international NGOs who had, over previous years, paid close attention to bolstering the performance of the government's DPCCN relief arm – usually through expatriate secondments – were, by the end of 1993, beginning to question the relative advantages of such an approach.

By 1994, Mozambique was already moving from emergency to development priorities, from a centrally planned to a market economy and from a one-party state to a multiparty political system. Hopes

---

24. In January 1994, LINK began discussions with donors about funding a professional trainer for Mozambique NGOs.
25. The Deputy Director of DPCCN, Mr Silva Langa, addressed the first LINK General Assembly in September 1993 and stressed that the government had no problem working with the parallel structure that LINK represented (*LINK, 1993d*).

were raised that economic self-reliance would soon replace aid dependency and thus the role of NGOs would change significantly. It was hoped that such changes would encourage greater discussion of policy, methodology and strategic planning on the part of NGOs, yet LINK saw little evidence of this by mid-1994 (*LINK, 1994b*).

In part, this may have been due to a chronic lack of government initiative. Donors and their client NGOs had, to a large extent, dictated the scope and pace of the Mozambique aid operation. Given that continued funding would undoubtedly depend upon maintaining this momentum, it was unlikely that an ill-equipped government could recapture the initiative in the foreseeable future. The dilemma – in so far as it was recognised at all – was, as in so many complex emergencies in the last decade, easier to define than to surmount.

ACRONYMS AND ABBREVIATIONS

ADC	Associação para o Desenvolvimento da Comunidade
AMDU	Associação Moçambicaca para o Desenvolvimento Urbano
CARE	Co-operative of American Relief Everywhere
CCM	Conselho Cristao de Moçambiquo
CENE	National Executive Emergency Commission
COE	Emergencies Operations Committee
CONGOMA	Council for NGOs in Malawi
CPE	Provincial Emergency Commission
CSC	Control and Supervisory Committee
DPCCN	Department for the Combat and Prevention of Natural Disasters
DRCU	Drought Relief Co-ordination Unit
FRELIMO	Front for the Liberation of Mozambique
GDP	Gross Domestic Product
HAC	Humanitarian Assistance Committee
ICRC	International Committee of the Red Cross/Crescent
ICVA	International Council of Voluntary Agencies
IMF	International Monetary Fund
INDER	Institute of Rural Development
IOM	International Organization for Migration
ISC	Interim Steering Committee
KULIMA	Organização para o Desenvovimento Sócio-económico Integrado
LICGC	Liga International das Concepções Globais do Consenso
LWF	Lutheran World Federation
MSF	Médecins Sans Frontières
MONASA	Mozambique Organisation of AIDS Associations
MULEIDE	Associação Mulher Lei e Desenvolvimento
NRC	Norwegian Refugee Council
PRE	Economic Rehabilitation Programme
RENAMO	Résistência Nationàl Moçambicana
SCAS	State Secretariat for Social Action
SCF-UK	Save the Children Fund (UK)
UNDP	United Nations Development Programme
UN-DHA	United Nations Department for Humanitarian Affairs

UNHCR	United Nations High Commissioner for Refugees
UNICEF	United Nations Children's Fund
UNILOG	United Nations Logistics Body
UNOHAC	United Nations Office for the Coordination of Humanitarian Assistance
UNOMOZ	United Nations Operation in Mozambique
USAID	United States Agency for International Development
WFP	World Food Programme

REFERENCES

AWEPAA (1993a), *Mozambique Peace Process Bulletin* AWEPAA (European Parliamentarians for Southern Africa), Issues 2,3, 4, 5, and 6, March 1993 onwards

AWEPAA (1993b), *General Peace Agreement of Mozambique 1992* African-European Institute, The Netherlands

Barbee, J (1993), 'Report on the Drought and NGO Coordination in Malawi: the role of the DRCU/CONGOMA', paper presented to the *Southern Africa Disaster Management Workshop*, Harare, Zimbabwe, April

Borton, J et al (1988), *Evaluation of ODA's Provision of Emergency Aid to Africa, 1983-86* Relief and Development Institution, London

Brochman, G & Ofstad, A (1989), *Mozambique: Norwegian Assistance in the Context of Crisis* Chr. Michelen Institute, Norway

De Coninck (1993) 'Towards a CSP: programme review, contextual description and interim strategy statement', unpublished, ActionAid, Maputo

DHA (1993) *Post-War Population Movements in Mozambique* DHA, Maputo, June 1993

Duffield, M. (1990) 'War and Famine in Africa: An exploratory report for Oxfam', mimeo, Oxfam-UK

Duffield, M (1992) 'Famine, Conflict and the Internationalisation of Public Welfare', in M. Doornbos et al (eds), *Beyond Conflict in the Horn*, ISS, The Hague

Egan, E (1991) 'Relief and Rehabilitation work in Mozambique: institutional capacity and NGO executional strategies' *Development in Practice*, vol 1, no 3

Government of the People's Republic of Mozambique & the United Nations (1989), *The Emergency Situation in Mozambique: Priority Requirements for the Period 1989–90*, UN Office for Emergencies in Africa, New York

Green, R H (1987) *Killing the Dream: the political economy of war* Discussion paper 238, Institute of Development Studies, University of Sussex.

Hanlon, J (1991) *Mozambique: who calls the shots?*, James Curry, London

Harrell-Bond, B E (1992) 'Refugees and the Re-formulation of International Aid Policies: what can Britain and Japan do?', *Background Paper for the UK-Japan 2000 Group*, Refugee Studies Programme, Oxford

ICVA (1993) 'ICVA Task Force, Mozambique', memorandum to ICVA from Nanna Thue, NRC Regional Coordinator, Maputo, 28 June 1993

ITEM (1992) *Third World Guide 93/94* Instituto del Tercer Mundo, Uruguay

Kanji, N (1990) 'War and Children in Mozambique: is international aid strengthening or eroding community-based policies?' *Community Development Journal*, vol 25 no 2

KULIMA (1993) 'NGOs in Mozambique: A challenge for the new

Mozambique society', paper presented by Kulima at the *Southern African NGO Development Organisation (SANDON) Conference*, Kulima, unpublished

LINK (1993a) 'Draft Agreement of Understanding', 8 March 1993, Maputo

LINK (1993b) *Conclusions and Final Recommendations* report of the Seminar: 'A Regional Approach to NGO Coordination in the Repatriation and Resettlement of Mozambican Refugees', 12-13 May 1993, Maputo

LINK (1993c) Minutes of the meeting with Renamo, International NGOs and UNOHAC, 23 March, Hotel Rovuma, Maputo, LINK, unpublished

LINK (1993d) 'General Assembly Minutes', LINK, 29 September 1993

LINK (1993e) 'LINK/RENAMO meeting minutes', 18 November

LINK (1994a) 'Summary of Activities', 20 February

LINK (1994b) 'Summary for the ICVA Seminar', Oxford 7-9 April

Macrae, J and Zwi, A (1992) 'Food as an instrument of war in contemporary African famines: a review of the evidence', *Disasters*, vol 16, no 4

Mupedziswa, R & Makanya, S J (1988) 'Refugee protection in Zimbabwe: local integration - a permanent solution to a temporary problem?', paper presented at the *Silver Jubilee Conference of the African Studies Association (UK)*, 14–16 September, Refugee Studies Programme, Oxford

Ngabonziza, D (1993) ICVA Task Force, Mozambique, General note to the ICVA Sub-group on Africa, 28 June, ICVA, Geneva

NRC (1994) 'Partnership and Protection', paper presented to the PARinAC conference, Norwegian Refugee Council, Addis Ababa, unpublished

Pruitt, J & Marama, D (1988) *Mtwara Report: Mozambican Refugees in Tanzania* TAMOFA, Tanzania

SCF (1992) 'Mozambique Country Strategy Paper', (internal document), SCF, Maputo

Thomas, S (1992) 'Sustainability in NGO relief and development work: further thoughts from Mozambique', *Development in Practice*, vol 2, no 1

Thomas, S & Hallam, A (1992) 'Associations as a means of organising small enterprises in war-affected areas of Mozambique - reflections after four years of working with displaced people', *Small Enterprise Development*, ITDG, London

UNHCR (1993a) 'Repatriation and Reintegration of Mozambican Refugees' *Executive Summary*, UNHCR Geneva, May

UNHCR (1993b) 'Appeal for the Repatriation and Reintegration of Mozambican Refugees' *UNHCR Fund Raising Service*, Geneva, 3 May

UNOHAC (1993) *Mozambique Report, Humanitarian Activities in a Post-War Mozambique*, Monthly Bulletin, 1993 onwards, Maputo

Wilson, K & Numes, J (1992) 'Repatriation to Mozambique: refugee initiatives and agency planning' in Allen, T and Morsink, H (eds), *When Refugees Return*, James Curry, London

World Bank (1993) 'Macroeconomic Perspectives for Mozambique in the Post-War Period' discussion draft, 2 June

Zetter, R, Bonga, V, Harrell-Bond, B E, Machikaika, M R E, Makanya, S and Mupedziswa, R (1992) 'Governments, NGOs and Humanitarian Assistance for Refugees in Southern Africa', draft report to funders, ESRC and the Pew Charitable Trusts, Refugee Studies Programme, Oxford

5

KENYA:
NGO COORDINATION DURING THE
SOMALI REFUGEE CRISIS, 1990–93

Monika Kathina Juma

The People: Population 25.3 million. Kenyans are descended from the main African ethnic groups: Bantus, Nilo–Hamitics, Sudanese and Cushites. Numerically and culturally the most significant groups are the Kikuyus and the Luos.

Religion: 60 per cent profess Christianity, 30 per cent are Muslim and 10 per cent practice traditional religions.

The Government: Daniel Arap Moi has headed the predominently Kenya African National Union (KANU) government since 1978. First multi-party elections for 25 years were held in 1992.

Development Aid: US$1,000 million (1990); US$41 per capita; Aid 11.4 per cent of GNP.

1991 was the most turbulent year in Somalia's history. The year began and ended with the Somali capital, Mogadishu, engulfed in violence. Thousands of Somalis were killed as rebel groups from the north and south launched a succession of offensives against the beleagured government of dictator Mohammad Siyad Barre. Hundreds of thousands fled to Ethiopia, Djibouti and Kenya. Over a two year period more than 500,000 refugees flooded into Kenya, settling in camps and being absorbed into the local population. At the height of the crisis, more than 900 refugees were entering Kenya each day. A coordinated response took place in three main regions of the country with a 'lead agency' being appointed by United Nations High Commissioner for Refugees (UNHCR) in each.

A critical factor throughout was the role of the Kenyan government. The Presidential appeal for aid and the passing of the NGO Coordination Act were clear manifestations of the assertive position of the government. This was a fundamental factor in shaping not only the nature and scope of government–NGO coordination, but also NGO–NGO coordination, which was – undoubtedly as a direct result of government policy – strengthened over this period. In spite of antagonism at policy levels, NGOs utilised government infrastructure, services and personnel quite fully. This did not, however, preclude competition at field level, an impediment to extending coordination beyond simple information sharing. In a highly complex environment, dominated by foreign NGOs, the scope and potential of coordination was not fully realised. In the absence of consistent evaluation, it was also unlikely to be fully appreciated.

BACKGROUND

The Somali refugee emergency began in 1990. Prior to this, Kenya hosted a refugee population of about some 15,000. The number rose dramatically during the emergency to an estimated (and contested) 360,000–700,000 people at the height of the inflow (*UNHCR, 1992*) Although a proportion of these people were individual asylum seekers from a number of other African states, the largest number were Somalis. They were assigned refugee status on the basis of group determination criteria as provided for by Article 1 (2) of the Organisation of African Unity (OAU) Convention Governing the Specific Aspects of Refugee Problems in Africa (*OAU, 1969*).

The presence of a large refugee population severely strained Kenyan social services and created competitive tensions between refugees and local residents over food relief, housing, water and police protection from rising crime. Owing to the small refugee population in the past, Kenya lacked both the administrative and legal capacity to handle the emergency. The Refugee Draft Bill had yet to be debated and passed. Although a signatory to all the main international conventions on refugees, Kenya's response to this influx, like others in the past, had been criticised internationally with repeated accusations of violations of the refugees' human rights (*Daley, 1994; Human Rights Watch, (HRW) 1991*).

In addition to its limited capacity to manage the refugee inflow, the Government of Kenya faced intense domestic and international pressure on a number of issues. Internally, the government was being

pushed to permit multi–party politics. This pressure was compounded by the donor governments' accusations of corruption and
undemocratic practices within the Kenyan government, which resulted in a cut in international aid in 1989. To restore its credibility, Kenya
was pressed to institute 'good governance' and implement a structural
adjustment programme (as prescribed by the International Monetary
Fund (IMF) and World Bank) as a condition of the resumption of aid
(*Weekly Review, 1990 and 1991c*).

Although unstated, the government attitude was unsympathetic
towards the Somali refugees. This resulted from historically hostile
relations between the Kenya and Somali governments following the
unresolved territorial dispute over the North Eastern province of
Kenya, where the population is ethnically Somali. After independence,
Somalia propounded the 'Greater Somalia' ideology, the implication
of which was the expansion of the Somali state into those areas where
Somalis had been incorporated, by colonial boundaries, into Ethiopia,
Djibouti and Kenya (*HRW, 1991; Weekly Review, 1991a*).

To the dismay of the Kenya government, which could not distinguish
between the Somali Somalis and the Kenyan Somalis, the ideology of
'Greater Somalia' was popularly embraced by the Somali population in
the North Eastern province. This led to a general fear within the government that the Kenya Somalis were more loyal to the Somali state and,
therefore, posed a security risk to the nation state of Kenya.

The hostility between the two states manifested itself in the *shifta*
(bandit) war during the 1960s and a declaration of a state of emergency
in the North Eastern province since independence which was only lifted
in 1990 (*HRW, 1991*). Troubles in the region persisted, however, particularly in the form of bandit attacks. To combat these, the government
deployed security forces which have often been accused of routine
excesses against the population within the region (*HRW,1991*). In
September 1992, for instance, the United States Committee for Refugees
(USCR) charged that UNHCR and Kenyan officials deliberately with-
held assistance at two remote camps in northeast Kenya as part of a
policy to discourage 70,000 Somali refugees from remaining there. The
policy of 'light intervention' at the two camps, Mandera and El Wak,
allegedly resulted in at least 2000 avoidable deaths (*USCR, 1993*).

The view of the government has been reinforced by the general
perceptions of the non-Somali Kenyan population, which sees Somalis
as 'trouble makers'. This attitude translated into a lack of enthusiasm
within the non-Somali Kenyan population to offer asylum to the
Somalis. It also explains, in part, the lack of public pressure upon the
government to be sensitive to the Somali refugee issue.

The Somali influx into Kenya came at a time when many parts of
the country were experiencing drought. Significantly, all the districts
through which the Somali refugees entered and settled (Mandera,
Wajir, Garissa, Isiolo and Marsabit) were among the 26 districts mostly

affected by drought (*UN, 1993*).

The UNHCR had to increase its capacity from fewer than ten officers dealing with the entire East African region in 1989 to 40 by mid-1991, and 162 by mid-1992 (*UNHCR, 1992*). At the beginning of the emergency there was almost a total absence of either local or international NGOs. The few existing refugee-assisting organisations were largely concentrated in the main urban areas (Nairobi and Mombasa). Yet Somalia was to become very quickly the centre of massive international media attention and the consequent pressure and momentum to deal with this – the latest aid crisis.

It was against this background that the President uncharacteristically called a press conference to appeal for international assistance (*HRW, 1991, p341*). The appeal, coupled with another by UNHCR, attracted attention from foreign NGOs in particular who began arriving in Kenya. Most of the local NGOs responded by expanding their operations while some were created specifically for the emergency.

Early coordination efforts

Coordination efforts during the Somali crisis have to be seen in the context of what took place over the previous decades. As the number of NGOs increased during the 1970s and 1980s, the need to create a more effective method for coordinating their work became apparent. Prior to the emergency, the official body with the mandate to coordinate NGOs in Kenya was the Kenya National Council of Social Services (KNCSS), created within the Ministry of Culture and Social Services (MCSS) in 1964. A brief description of the KNCSS is given in Box 5.1.

A large number of NGOs and other voluntary and grassroots movements worked outside the KNCSS framework (see *Fowler, 1988; Kanyinga, 1990*). Most tended to concentrate on specific sectors; for example, Kenya Energy and Environmental Non-governmental Organisations (KENGO) in energy conservation, the Green Belt Movement in afforestation and the empowerment of the grassroots movement, the Kenya Rural Enterprise Programme (KREP) in small scale businesses, and the Voluntary Agencies Development Assistance (VADA) in consultancies for various NGOs. All these networks also acted as funding channels for member NGOs.

It could be argued that some networks compromised their autonomy and local credibility by allowing leverage by foreign donors (*Wellard & Copestake, 1993; Duell & Dutcher, 1987*). Moreover, they each lacked a mandate to cover the entire NGO spectrum and were, like the KNCSS, occasionally accused of being exclusive.

Efforts were also made to coordinate church-based organisations. For example, the Religious Superiors' Association of Kenya (RSAK) was a federation of Catholic parishes created in 1987 to focus on effective provision of assistance to urban refugees. This association weakened due to the increasing demand upon it and finally collapsed

---

BOX 5.1
THE KNCSS

The KNCSS was a membership organisation whose objective was regional emergency planning and coordination of meetings and working committees (*Duell & Dutcher, 1987*). It was required to operate under the supervision of the MCSS. This was regarded as a serious constraint to its independence, leading to the suspicion, among others, that its membership was vetted by the government. Moreover, the MCSS was itself not a government body with a priority portfolio; it was thus constrained by a lack of central funding. In turn, the KNCSS was expected to raise its own operational costs, leading to a mismanaged membership structure that demanded annual subscriptions without regard to the ability of NGOs to pay. Consequently, many could not qualify for membership and were left out of the coordination process.

In spite of these shortcomings, it was within KNCSS in the early 1980s that initial attempts at comprehensive coordination through a number of sectoral task forces took place. Most importantly, it was through the KNCSS that NGOs articulated their desire to have the government create a framework within which they could operate. In 1987, when the KNCSS reached a membership of 106 NGOs, it made the first recommendations to the government for a 'supportive policy and legislation for NGOs' (*KNCSS, 1990*). Significantly, the initial reaction to the NGO Coordination Bill came through the KNCSS and it was to continue to play an active role in facilitating NGO discussions with the government in the difficult months ahead.

---

in 1988 when one of its centres closed down (*Headly, 1988*).

Most of these early coordination attempts concentrated on local NGOs, focusing more on development than relief. Even then, their effectiveness was questionable. The particular interests of the dominant participants was often promoted above the cause of the collective.

THE GOVERNMENT NGO BILL AND NGO REACTION

The need for an umbrella body to coordinate NGO activity was one of the prime motives behind the government's introduction of the legislative process for an NGO bill. Between 1986–1990, the Office of the President, in collaboration with the Attorney General's office, began formulating legislation for NGO coordination. As the drafting advanced, KNCSS took advantage of the enthusiasm shown by the government and submitted its recommendations (*Kanyinga, 1991, p2*).

In spite of the KNCSS intervention, the government tabled The Non-Governmental Organisations Coordination Bill in Parliament in November 1990, without incorporating the KNCSS recommendations. The bill was debated, passed and became an Act of Parliament in December 1990. It received Presidential Assent in January 1991 and this set the scene for increasing NGO alarm and reaction.[1]

The NGO Coordination Act was interpreted by the NGO community as a 'controlling and punitive' piece of legislation rather than one that would facilitate NGO coordination. NGOs argued that it was inadequately drafted and therefore liable to a wide range of interpretations, in particular with regard to definitions and exemption criteria. The act allowed for the creation of an NGO Board but this also was controversial (see Box 5.2).

NGOs further feared that the Act could lead to an imbalance of power and responsibilities between the government and NGOs (*Muktaza, 1991*). Despite the provision for a KNCNGOs, supervised by the NGO Board, most NGOs interpreted the entire structure as unjust and saw the act as providing for no recourse to the courts of law.

The act, in its initial stages, required renewal of NGO registration after a period of 60 months of operation. While NGOs argued that this time span would be unconducive to NGO project continuity in relation to funding, the most contested aspect of this section was the condition that the misbehaviour of an NGO officer could lead to deregistration of the NGO for which they worked. Renewal was conditional upon a government review of the NGO operation. This was seen as punitive by the NGO community.

Following a General Meeting of the KNCSS in 1991, a large number of NGOs formed an Ad Hoc Standing Committee to represent their interests vis-à-vis the Government. In February 1991, the Standing Committee organised what was to become the largest documented meeting of NGO community in Kenya since independence, with an attendance of over 200 NGO representatives.[2] The meeting resolved that lawyers be employed to prepare a response, communicate the concerns of the group to other actors and dialogue with the relevant government departments (*Kanyinga, 1991, p16*).

This strategy succeeded, firstly, in slowing down the enactment of the Act until 1992 and, secondly, in securing amendments to two sections of the Act. The judicial powers of the Minister were reduced and hence NGOs could seek redress from the courts in arbitration of disputes. Further, NGO representation on the NGO Board was increased from five to eight members.

---

1. Whereas the NGO community was opposed to having this framework within the Office of the President, the government argued that this indicated the significance it attached to the sector (*Kanyinga,1991*).
2. This information is from interviews with members of the Ad Hoc Committee, 1994. See also the *KNCNGOs, Bulletin No 1, September 1993*.

BOX 5.2
THE NGO BOARD

One part of the 1990 NGO Coordination Act allowed for a consultative mechanism, the NGO Coordination Board. Its functions were:

- to facilitate and coordinate the work of all national and international NGOs operating in Kenya;
- to maintain the register of national and international NGOs operating in Kenya, with the precise sectors, affiliations and locations of their activities;
- to receive and discuss the annual reports of the NGOs;
- to advise the government on the activities of the NGOs and their role in development within Kenya;
- to conduct regular reviews of the register to determine consistency with the reports submitted by the NGOs and the NGO Council;
- to provide policy guidelines to the NGOs for harmonising their activities with the national development plan for Kenya;
- to receive, discuss and approve the regular reports of the NGO Council and to advise on strategies for efficient planning and coordination of the activities of the NGOs in Kenya; and
- to receive, discuss and approve the code of conduct prepared by the NGO Council for self-regulation of the NGOs and their activities in Kenya. (*Kenya Gazette, 1990*)

Concern was expressed over how the NGO Board was to be funded, for the suspicion was that NGOs would provide the bulk of the funding, which would then pass through the Treasury with little control being exercised by donors. The NGO Board, for instance, was to comprise 23 members including only five NGO representatives, the rest being government officials and appointees. The responsible Minister (to be decided) retained absolute judicial and executive powers. To offset some of the worries, the formation of the Kenya National Council of NGOs (KNCNGOs), run solely by the NGOs, was proposed; yet even this was to be supervised by the Board, headed by the Minister.

Still these amendments were regarded as inadequate by the NGO community. In a letter to the Attorney General, the Chairman of the Standing Committee noted that: 'the amended law did not go far enough in addressing the fundamental concerns [of the NGOs]'. The letter further expressed the intention of the NGOs to seek repeal of the law and recommended its replacement with a 'very basic legal framework' which catered sufficiently for the principal legal concerns and requirements (*Mbogori, 1992*).

The NGOs agreed among themselves to formulate an alternative and more concise piece of legislation. A Private Voluntary Organisations' Act (PVOs Act), described as a more enabling act, was thus drafted as an alternative to the governments' act.

Meanwhile, NGOs were utilising the acceptable structures provided for in the Act, such as the KNCNGO. Within six months of its establishment, the KNCNGO had developed rules and regulations and a code of conduct for NGOs. A secretariat was set up and charged with the task of producing a newsletter for announcing NGO events, creating a database of all NGOs in Kenya, and providing advice to new NGOs.[3]

By early 1994, nine quarterly meetings and a fund-raising workshop had been held under the auspices of the KNCNGO. This body further facilitated the creation of various sectoral networks. Three were already functioning by 1994: those for the internally displaced (a critical issue in Kenya today), refugee issues and human rights.

Ironically, the attempt at NGO coordination by the government had the effect of bringing them together in a more inclusive way. As noted by the KNCNGO, 'NGOs came together to deal with the turbulence created by the Act and constituted the *ad hoc* NGO committee. A network emerged.' (*KNCNGO, 1993*).

Trends in other African countries

Experience from elsewhere in Africa led the NGOs to suspect hidden motives behind the Kenya government's desire to legislate NGO activity. Many felt that the desire of the Kenya government to get involved in the voluntary sector was a rather heavy-handed attempt at control, following the example of several African governments who have in the past sought to direct the pace of the voluntary sector. For instance, in 1987 the Government of Uganda outlawed the use of radios by NGOs in communicating between their headquarters and up-country project sites. Again, in 1989, the same government, concerned about the security implications of NGOs working in the country, introduced a bill that required all NGOs to register or become illegal. The Ministry of Internal Affairs was charged with implementing the bill, placing NGOs alongside the departments of prison, immigration and the police.

African governments have also restricted specific NGO activities where these have been judged as being contrary to the 'national interest'. In 1983, the Zimbabwe government ordered the shutting down of operations of the Rural Associations for Progress (ORAP). In 1987 the

---

3. Information about 500 NGOs had, by 1994, been established. However, the process was held up by a tug of war over who should undertake the database project between the NGO council and the government bureau charged with registration. Doing the project jointly seems unacceptable to the government on the grounds that they would not wish to release 'security' information.

South African government passed the Disclosure of Foreign Funding Act to monitor the funding of NGOs by foreign donor organisations. And in Sudan, the Khartoum government prohibited NGOs operating in the civil war zones in the south from receiving foreign funds in 1986 (later rescinded).

In Kenya itself, the 1990 NGO Coordination Act was not the first attempt to regulate NGO activities. In 1987, politicians called for the deregistration of the National Christian Council of Kenya (NCCK) when it opposed the introduced queue-voting system of election. Similar calls were made in 1989 against the Green Belt Movement following the decision of its leader, Wangari Mathai, to seek an injunction to prevent the ruling party, KANU, from building a sixty-storey structure at the Uhuru Park Gardens in Nairobi.

Unlike other places, NGOs in Kenya undertook a massive campaign against the government, which involved other civil society sectors such as the lawyers' associations and the donor community. For their part, Northern donors provided the 'hidden' pressure for the Kenyan government to withdraw certain elements of the original legislation, an indication of the bargaining power foreign aid can sometimes have over domestic policy.

COORDINATION IN THE EMERGENCY

As the tension and conflict between NGOs and the government was unfolding, the refugee situation in Kenya was one of the fastest growing emergencies faced by UNHCR in 1992 (*UNHCR, 1993*). An average of 900 refugees entered Kenya each day throughout 1991–92 (*UNHCR, 1991*). When the influx began, Somali refugees entered the country along the entire Kenya–Somali border and also by sea. The situation was complicated by the inflow of about 80,000 Ethiopians following the fall of the Mengistu government and a further entry of about 24,000 Sudanese, of whom 12,400 were unaccompanied minors. These added to an existing urban refugee population of about 20,000 (*UNHCR, 1992; 1993*).

1992 saw an unprecedented immigration into Kenya (Figure 5.1). As we have seen, the majority of these immigrants were Somali refugees (Table 5.1). To cater for a refugee population of about 425,000, 11 camps and six border posts were hurriedly established at entry points along the border during 1992. The UN emergency-assistance response, organised to cope with programme support for the new arrivals, soared from US$12 million in 1991 to US$58 million in 1992 (*UNHCR, 1993*).

Table 5.1 *Breakdown of refugee populations in the camp areas in Kenya*[1]

Camp/border site	Estimated number	Main nationality
North Eastern area		
WALDA	47,334	Ethiopian
LIBOI	45,000	Somali
DAGAHALEY	45,218	Somali
IFO	46,000	Somali
HAGADERA	39,408	Somali
MANDERA[2]	50,000	Somali
BANISSA[2]	30,000	Somali
EL-WAK[2]	18,000	Somali
GURAR[2]	2,500	Ethiopian
RHAMU[2]	600	Ethiopian
Total	*324,060*	
Coastal area		
UTANGE	31,411	Somali
HATIMY	2,873	Somali
MARAFA	5,678	Somali
ST. ANNES	2,873	Somali
Total	*42,835*	
North Western area		
KAKUMA	24,000	Sudanese
Total	*24,000*	
Central Area		
THIKA	5,800	Mixed
NAIROBI	1,500	Mixed
Total	*7,300*	

Notes
1. The estimates above are for those refugees in designated camps and border sites. They do not include a further 20,000 or so urban refugees that were in Kenya before the onset of the 1990 emergency. They also do not include the Kenyan government's estimate of 100,000–150,000 refugees and asylum seekers outside organised camps and border sites.
2. Indicates border sites established as reception centres. Most of these were closed down by 1994 and populations transferred to the camps in the region.

Source: *Information Bulletin*, November 1992, UNHCR, Nairobi

As is often the case in emergency situations, the Kenyan crisis was characterised by lack of information, a government preoccupied largely with security concerns, limited resources in personnel and material terms and a general state of unpreparedness. This was further complicated by the influx of a large number of diverse agencies with different types of resources, all leading to a confusing mix of actors on the ground.

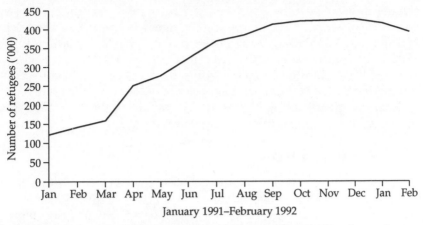

January 1991–February 1992

Note: The Government of Kenya estimated a further 100,000–150,000 asylum seekers and refugees outside the figures given by UNHCR

Source: *UNHCR Information Bulletin* February 1993

Figure 5.1 *Inflow of refugees into Kenya in 1992*

As illustrated by Harrell-Bond (1986) in the Sudan, Nicholds & Borton (1994) in Pakistan and Bennett (see chapter 4) in Mozambique, such variables determine not only the nature of response patterns but also the manner in which the response is managed. In the Kenyan case, the situation was one of 'muddling' through *ad hoc* arrangements. Certainly there was no predetermined comprehensive coordination strategy. Instead, the general response was to react to events as they arose without any form of coherent cooperation or collective action. At field level, coordination was left as a matter of initiative for the lead agencies.

The emergency was managed by UNHCR as the main actor, which contracted, funded (wholly or in part), coordinated and monitored activities of implementing agencies. Although a considerable number of local NGOs were involved, only three – the African Medical Research Foundation (AMREF), Appropriate Technology (Approtech), and the Kenya Red Cross Societies (KRCs) – were lead partners of UNHCR at various times during the emergency. The remaining lead agencies were international NGOs.[4]

The contracting of international NGOs as main implementing partners of UNHCR has been criticised both within and outside the humanitarian assistance structures in Kenya. The view held by the critics is that local competence and knowledge were sidelined in favour of the foreigners arriving during the emergency. Nevertheless, if UNHCR was drawing upon experience and ability of the NGOs, there was a marked deficiency of both within the local NGO community. Indeed, there were less than eight local NGOs operating in

---

4. Information from the author's interviews with the UNHCR, 1994.

refugee assistance in the entire country before the emergency. These NGOs dealt with small numbers of refugees in the urban areas of Nairobi and Mombasa. The majority of local NGOs operational by 1992 were created during the emergency. Thus, UNHCR was constrained by the limited capacity within the local sector. By contrast, international NGOs could offer experience of working with refugees (at least elsewhere) and resources, which was one of the UNHCR conditions for contracting implementing partners.

Coordination patterns

The patterns of coordination were largely determined by two factors: the pressure created by the influx and the number of the actors on the ground. At the outset of the crisis, the critical needs of the refugees and the inflow of many types of agencies created a 'free for all', a dilemma to UNHCR and others. The resulting confusion created the need for networking and information sharing between agencies, particularly at the field level. At the time, UNHCR chaired all the coordination meetings in the camps.

As time passed, the situation stabilised and clarity in terms of role differentiation was achieved. Field-level weekly meetings became bi-monthly and then monthly. By the end of 1993, meetings were being held when appropriate, except in Dadaab area where a monthly security meeting was chaired by UNHCR. This meeting, however, addressed issues specific to the security of the agency staff, and coordination took the form of information sharing rather than operational strategies and evaluation of the programme implementation.

By late 1993, one of the lead agencies complained of being increasingly frustrated by some of UNHCR's subcontracted agencies who made coordination impossible by failing to turn up for meetings. The general feeling among most agencies was that the emergency was over and, although there was a will to continue operating, the greatest challenge for the coordinators was how to sustain the momentum of the agencies in the face of obvious fatigue.

Is coordination desirable?

In a survey of international and local NGOs, donors, UN and government officials, conducted by the author in late 1993, 36 NGO respondents stated that they believed coordination was desirable, while 13 thought that it was not. There was support for the view that coordination avoided duplication and increased efficiency. Some operational NGOs saw coordination in terms of ensuring that refugees did not take advantage of the humanitarian assistance system. For instance, one reason given for the attempt at coordination in the 1970s, during the influx of Ugandan refugees following the military coup by Idi Amin, was to eliminate the possibility of a refugee making claims for multiple assistance to different NGOs.

Coordination was also seen as desirable for purposes of providing a mechanism for accountability and monitoring of activities. A member of the NGO Council Secretariat talked of the need to have a body to which NGOs are accountable. This perspective was most common with interviewees from the local NGOs. The question of the degree to which lack of coordination impacted negatively on the effectiveness of the relief operation was raised by several respondents, though in the absence of quantifiable data the suggestion remains hypothetical, though crucial.

Some respondents held the opposite view – that coordination could impede the operation of able NGOs. The argument here was that NGOs are independent organisations (especially international NGOs) and that they have resources, mandates, aims and objectives that are different and cannot be brought under one concerted approach.[5]

A respondent from one of the donor governments suggested that liaison and cooperation were important, but not to integrate activities. He further argued that the large NGOs, particularly the international NGOs, have the capacity to run their operations without any coordination as long as they did not interfere in each others' spheres of activities. Such views were also recorded by Anderson & Woodrow (1989), who argue that coordination can inhibit the effectiveness of a relief programme by destroying the chances of alternative approaches as well as advantages that accrue from different actors engaging differently in the same activity.

The argument that NGOs should not interfere with each others' spheres can be interpreted as a desire for limited coordination. Indeed, even those NGOs who, in our survey, disagreed with comprehensive coordination were represented in coordination meetings, perhaps to safeguard their interests!

There was little agreement on the ideal coordination model and which agency should take a lead in this respect. Interestingly, in spite of the 1991 Act, over 50 per cent of the respondents preferred the government as the ideal coordinator. The rest of the respondents recommended UNHCR for the role of coordinator during emergencies. Whether the desire for coordination reflected the relative effectiveness of NGOs on the ground is a matter for further study.

MODELS OF NGO COORDINATION IN THE REFUGEE SECTOR

Although coordination in the entire NGO field in Kenya was weak, coordination in the refugee sector was even weaker when compared to

---

5. The claim that international NGOs are independent organisations is also challenged by the fact that many of them depend to a large extend on funding from their home governments and are sometimes used as foreign policy instruments of their governments (*Nicholds, 1988*)

the development agency sector.[6] This was compounded by the lack of NGO and government experience in dealing with refugees. Most of the actors in the field were new arrivals with little knowledge of the refugee population, the political system in Kenya or humanitarian interventions generally. Field positions held were the first for more than half of the field staff interviewed in this study, who were, to a large extent, learning on the job.

Coordination at policy level

At the policy level, a four-way relationship was in effect. This was between the UN agencies themselves, the UN agencies and the government, UNHCR and the government and, between UNHCR and the main implementing partners (referred herein as lead agencies). At the inter-UN agency level, there was an interdependent relationship marked by reciprocity and exchange of views and opinions. For instance, the two most involved UN agencies, World Food Programme (WFP) and the United Nations Children's Fund (UNICEF), had been part of joint assessment teams to the refugee areas.

These and other UN specialised agencies also consulted with the government. However, the relationship here was one-sided, with the UN agencies tending to influence the government's position and not vice versa. This had the effect of weakening the legitimacy of the government in the eyes of the NGOs, since it was perceived also as a lack of confidence in the government from the UN. Consequently, NGOs sought coordination with the UN and donor agencies rather than the government.

The relationship between the government and UNHCR was ambivalent. Whereas there were consultations, particularly with the Ministry of Home Affairs and National Heritage, which deals with the refugee issues on behalf of the government, most of these were complaints and mutual recrimination.

The relationship between the UNHCR and the main implementing partners is based on two principles:

- a division of labour; and
- the appointment of a lead agency.

Whereas UNHCR concentrated on matters of legal protection, it delegated responsibilities related to social welfare provision to the lead agencies and only monitored the programme implementation process in the camp areas.

UNHCR had a contractual relationship with the lead agencies.

---

6. The development NGOs had created impressive networks of coordination in various regions of the country; for example, OXFAM with its Turkana Drought Unit and Action-Aid in the western part of the country following the displacement of the population as a result of ethnic clashes.

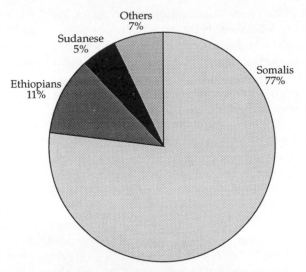

Note: This study concentrated on the Somali refugees who
comprised over two-thirds of the entire refugee population
during the last emergency (1989–1993)

Source: *UNHCR Information Bulletin* February 1993

Figure 5.2 *Proportion of refugees in Kenya by nationality in
mid-February 1993*

Terms and conditions of service were legally defined and the latter
operated with the guidance of project descriptions within specific time
frames, after which evaluations were done.

There were three lead agencies in the management of the refugee
camp areas in Kenya: the KRCs, working in collaboration with the
International Federation of the Red Cross and Crescent Societies
(IFRC) in the coast area; the Cooperative of American Relief
Everywhere (CARE-Kenya), in the north-eastern camp area; and the
Lutheran World Federation (LWF), in the north-western camp area. In
addition, AMREF was lead agency in the Marsabit area until the camp
was closed in 1993.

These lead agencies were selected on the basis of their ability to
respond to emergencies at short notice, local experience, ability to
maintain staff and hence ensure continuity, and, most importantly,
their ability to contribute resources to the programme. Lead agencies
were therefore expected to raise funds for part of their operations.[7] The
basic powers of the lead agencies included power to subcontract other
agencies for programme implementation on the ground. This arrangement was either legally binding or mutually agreed upon. The
subcontracted agencies were then accountable to the lead agencies.

---

7. According to the UNHCR Deputy Country Representative, interviewed by the
author in 1994, KRC/IFRC had raised up to 40 per cent of its total budget in 1992.

In spite of this clear organisation at the policy level, there were no established guidelines either by the UNHCR or collectively by the lead agencies to help coordinate or monitor operations of the subcontracted agencies. This vacuum gave enormous power to the lead agencies who employed different standards. As illustrated by Harrell-Bond & Voutira (1992), the concept of the lead agency allows innumerable variations in the context of power relations among actors.

Whereas the UN agencies had dialogue mechanisms, such as the Consultative Meetings, to confer with actors such as the government and encouraged informal consultations with each other, there was limited contact between the various lead NGO agencies. UNHCR was often used as the only point of contact and UNHCR was itself not always available for consultation.

Although UNHCR had a presence in all the refugee areas, its influence tended to decline until issues of protection arose. For instance, UNHCR was visibly present in the Dadaab region where protection, in terms of physical security of both refugees and agency staff, was a major issue.[8] This contrasts with its low presence in both the Coastal and the North-Western camp areas, where the influence of the lead agencies was far greater than that of UNHCR.

Coordination at field level

At the policy level one observes equal treatment of the lead agencies by the UNHCR. At the field level, however, operational coordination was a matter of the lead agency. The absence of an operational definition of coordination translated itself into different interpretations of what constituted coordination by the lead agencies. Coordination models were geographically specific.

In the Coastal area, KRC was in control of all the operations. It was KRC that called the first coordination meeting in the area. It also acted as a facilitator of contacts between refugees and UNHCR and between the other agencies and UNHCR. In its dealing with other NGOs, it drew up legal contracts with clearly spelt-out terms and conditions for both continuation and termination of services.

At the same time, KRC monitored operations of the subcontracted agencies very closely. One of its unique characteristics was the requirement that it monitor the project accounts of the subcontracted agencies. Thus coordination in this area took the form of accountability exercised in the form of financial control of project activities.

In the North-Western area, the LWF seemed to define coordination in terms of division of labour that allowed decentralised operations and a limited operational autonomy for the agencies under its 'con-

---

8. The project on Women as Victims of Violence had also increased the presence of UNHCR in the Dadaab area. At the time of the survey, there were over five officers attached to this programme, all of them in Dadaab area.

trol'. The argument advanced for this model was that it reduced bureaucratic delays and enhanced quick delivery of assistance. It was also argued that the model was responsive to the local refugee structures in the camp.

However, such a pattern carried the risk of creating parallel chains of command, where an agency would get instructions from various 'bosses'. According to both the LWF and UNHCR respondents, such tensions became apparent in the relationship between International Rescue Committee (IRC) and the LWF at the beginning of the operation. In this instance, UNHCR had to intervene to reinforce the position of LWF as the lead agency in the area.

In the North-Eastern area, where CARE was the lead agency, the model allowed for a measure of flexibility for the subcontracted agencies. Whereas some had signed contractual documents, others were operating on mutual agreement. Each operated their own accounts and dealt with their projects independently. The main requirement was the provision of progress reports to CARE. UNHCR had the largest presence in this area owing to problems of security and legal protection. For this reason, it chaired the monthly security meetings.

UNHCR preferred the single lead-agency approach because it created fewer procedural complications, particularly with budgeting and reporting. UNHCR could withdraw from close coordination in the camps, leaving it to deal primarily with protection issues and a low-key monitoring presence in the camps.

In answering the question why local NGOs were largely absent, UNHCR argued that emergencies do not allow for trying out relatively new NGOs with no track record. More worryingly, many of the international relief agencies were preparing to leave in the face of no local capacity and this was likely to lead to a breakdown of services. There was marked anxiety about the implications of the pull-out, which had already begun with some of the Médecins Sans Frontières (MSF) teams.

Looked at structurally, the set-up appears as shown in Figure 5.3. The structure as shown omits mention of the government. Before returning to this, it is important to introduce the relationships at the field level.

RELATIONS BETWEEN DIFFERENT GROUPS

Local and international NGOs

The relationship between the international and local NGOs was determined to a large extent by the way the former interpreted the presence of the latter. Relationships were cordial in so far as the local NGO was not deemed a threat, ie when there were clearly designated roles for each. This was the situation in Kakuma, where the agencies operated in a semi-autonomous way, only reporting to the lead agency at certain intervals.

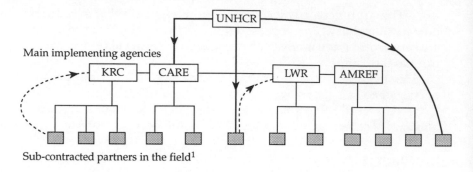

Note: 1 Local and international NGOs. There are also individuals and other smaller permanent or semi-permanent groups operating in the field.

➤ Feed-back loop
--➤-- Direct relationship

Figure 5.3 *Assistance implementation structure*

In the coastal region a different mode of operation was being practised. The demand that other agencies channel project funds through KRC, who for the most part controlled these funds, had two effects on its relationship with the agencies. Many agencies resented this level of control. They complained of problems with their donors, who were unable to see the NGO's 'profile' in the camps when they came for evaluations. The Red Cross, for their part, had no problem with this mode of operation, but NGOs dependent on a public profile in their home countries obviously were unhappy with it.

Secondly, the coordination strategy was interpreted as a means by which KRC/IFRC sought to have a dominant presence in the camps, and a way to ensure that all the credit for running the camps went to them. Subsequently, most of the subcontracted agencies were overly suspicious of the KRC/IFRC agenda. It is telling that the latter complained of some of its subcontracted agencies sabotaging its coordination effort by failing to attend meetings.

In all three areas, UNHCR saw issues of coordination as falling within the mandate of the lead agency. As long as the programme operation was satisfactory, UNHCR was not too concerned with the details of how coordination was achieved. This gave the lead agencies a wide remit, though it also carried the risk of impeding capacity building among the smaller agencies involved.

It also followed from the UNHCR perspective that the aggrieved agencies had either to accept the arrangement as it was or simply leave. Rather than take this option, some NGOs instead devised means of bypassing requirements of the lead agency. For instance, in the coastal region two agencies brought materials rather than monetary assistance.

Yet, even in these cases, KRC insisted on the agencies costing the materials for purposes of accounting and evaluation of the programme.

There were cases where the larger international NGOs were accused of harassing the smaller local NGOs, especially when they did not 'toe the line'. The author's survey revealed that one of the major agencies had not paid at least two of its subcontracted smaller NGOs.[9] The availability of resources is a critical factor in any emergency and even a short delay in payment can severely affect the operations of an NGO.

In these cases the smaller NGOs felt that their capacity was being undermined and this had a bearing on the level of their cooperation with the lead agencies in question. The smaller NGOs seemed to react to the perceived threat by being more critical about the structure under which they operated, claiming it to be unjust. In response, they consulted less with either the lead agencies or UNHCR.

There were also accusations from the smaller local NGOs of biased allocation of activities. This was attributed to the international NGOs' superior ability to canvass for the implementation of projects. In one instance, the Executive Director of one local NGO alleged that he been invited to a meeting to decide on cross-border projects allocations when, in fact, the allocations had already been done on paper. He argued that the claim that local NGOs lacked capacity could often be used as a means of impeding their operation whether they had capacity or not:

> 'If you up a 5 million shillings budget, you are told that, it reflects your lack of capacity. If you draw a 200,000 million budget, you are told, you do not have the capacity to handle such resources (sometimes you are 'advised' to look for a European partner for implementation). Whichever way you go, you lose!'

Although difficult to verify, these allegations highlight some of the concerns within local NGO circles that warrant attention if the relationship between NGOs is to be mutually supportive.

Local NGOs

The relationships among the local NGOs were mostly dictated by their funding bases and the activity in which they engaged. Those funded from the same source tended to be suspicious about one another and therefore less willing to share information. This in turn caused a level

---

9. One of the local NGOs interviewed by the author in 1994 was owed about 12 million Kenya Shillings – 1 US$ = 54 Kenyan shillings – and argued that this was a deliberate strategy to get it out of operation because it had been accused of transgressing the mandate of the lead agency on another occasion when it had indeed tried to operate in the camps without the permission of the latter. This claim, though not elaborated in this text, does support the argument that large field NGOs have tended to use their dominant position to undermine the smaller NGOs. Various studies have attested to this.

of frustration for the donors who were often unable to get their recipient NGOs to work together.

In response to the funding problem, the first NGO funding workshop, organised by the NGO Council in 1992, focused on ways and means of securing funds within the East African region. Although the workshop has not been evaluated in terms of resources mobilised, all the 18 respondents from local NGOs in this study agreed that they had, since the workshop, begun sharing funding information and felt that this was a positive development. Following this, it was decided that the funding workshop be an annual NGO event. Whether this activity will eliminate the suspicion between competitors remains to be seen.

There was close collaboration between NGOs which provided similar services. For instance, five NGOs concerned with education at university level established a network to avoid duplication in awarding scholarships to refugees. They did this by circulating lists of their beneficiaries. These agencies also lobbied the authorities when the fees for refugee (and foreign) students were raised from about US$650 to US$2000 per annum in 1992, as a direct result of fee restructuring necessitated by economic conditions imposed by the International Monetary Fund (IMF) and World Bank.

Although the dialogue with the university administration was going on at the time of the study, the group claimed that their success had been limited because they lacked adequate support from UNHCR. When interviewed, UNHCR agreed that at the time of the emergency university scholarships were not a priority.

This network was largely informal, and coordination seemed to be interpreted as a cost-saving measure by the agencies rather than an attempt to pool the resources, or to implement and evaluate programmes jointly. Each agency sought its funds, implemented its projects and undertook evaluations independently of each other.

In spite of these variations, there were common strategic challenges that faced the effort of coordination among the local NGOs. First, was the challenge posed by the government's attempt to weaken the local NGO sector by providing certain immunities to some of the stronger NGOs. For instance, all church-based NGOs were exempted from registration on the basis that they were charitable organisations.[10] By these and other actions, the government was accused of diluting, distorting or destroying potential solidarity among local NGOs. The need for a common strategy to deal with national and local government was apparent, perhaps in itself an argument for closer cooperation and coordination.

Local NGOs were further constrained by their dependence on for-

---

10. This was perceived as the government's strategy of dividing and weakening the NGO movement, by appeasing the church which had played a major role in the campaign for pluralism. See also the *Pastoral Letter to the Government*, by the Catholic bishops in 1992.

eign funding, usually through the larger international NGOs. Such funding usually had conditions attached to it. Local NGOs had to adjust to the criteria set by international NGOs and other funders.

NGOs and the government

The relationship between NGOs and the government from 1992 onwards was shaped by the introduction of the NGO Coordination Act and the subsequent reaction to it. Even before the introduction of the Act, relationships between NGOs and the government had been fairly tense. Several studies highlight this, arguing for the government and the NGOs to perceive each other as partners rather than competitors in development (for example, *Chepkwony,1988; Kanyinga, 1990*).

The introduction of the NGO Coordination Act was itself a climax of this tension and became a catalyst for perceptions of the government by NGOs. There was perhaps a need to create new social structures within which a redefinition of spheres of operation of both parties would be spelt out. One of these definitions would need to state what constitutes necessary and legitimate government intervention.

NGOs in Kenya have repeatedly viewed government intervention in the voluntary sector as arising purely from political security considerations that had nothing to do with capacity building, or indeed the issues at hand. Because NGOs often operate in remote and neglected areas of the country, such as the refugee centres, there was no comparative advantage to be claimed by the government in intervening directly in this area of work.

The fear of government involvement was based on the argument that the government lacked adequate knowledge of the voluntary sector and could only intervene in a reactive rather than supportive manner (*Weekly Review, 1991b*). This fear was further expressed by the reference to the previous government attempts at the control and cooptation of grassroots movements in Kenya.[11]

NGOs clearly favoured self-regulation, though the extent to which the voluntary sector was capable of such was highly questionable. This said, any government has a level of duty and responsibility towards national and international actors within its territorial borders. The extent to which it could legitimately set operational limits for NGOs would be premised upon its understanding of priorities on the ground and its actual ability to direct developments. This would, in turn, imply a greater knowledge of the complementary capacity of NGOs as partners in the process.

Another argument advanced to justify government involvement

---

11. This was in relation to the cooptation of the various NGO networks in the country such as the trade unions and the Maendeleo ya Wanawake, an umbrella organisation for women. It should also be noted that the government exercises undue influence on various other union organisations such as the Kenya National Union of Teachers.

was the necessity of coordinating an otherwise diverse and growing group. In 1988 (before the emergency), there were less than 15 NGOs concerned with refugee assistance. The number rose to over 60 by 1992, an increase of over 400 per cent (see *UNHCR Bulletins* from 1990–1992). This increase is partly explained by the retreat into Kenya of NGOs previously operating in 'insecure' countries, such as the Sudan and Somalia. Indeed, some of the existing friction between the state and the relatively new international NGOs was due to the latter's habit of operating in a 'classical' emergency fashion, where governments were either non-existent or part of the problem.

Allan Fowler (1991) summarises this debate in favour of monitoring NGOs in Kenya and identifies the main problems within the NGO sector as administrative and legal accountability, corruption and rivalries between executives of NGOs and potential suspicions between NGOs and donors. NGOs holding this view interpreted the uproar against the government as a fault on the part of the government for having waited too long before exercising its legitimate authority.

The government reacted to these accusations by largely keeping quiet and accepting dialogue with the voluntary sector. The voluntary sector on the other hand took advantage of this stance and launched a massive lobbying campaign of the government officials in both their official and personal capacities. As the government was bent on salvaging its image, particularly in the west, it became more cautious, and subsequently divorced itself from the some of the sectors where international presence was large, including the refugee sector. This reaction was interpreted by the NGO community as a manifestation of the government's lack of interest in protection and promotion of human rights, emanating from its history of harsh treatment of foreigners (*HRW, 1991; Daley, 1994*).

In spite of an often tense relationship, some NGOs made increasing use of government institutions. For instance, the International Relief and Rehabilitation Services (IRRES) launched two teacher training workshops with the use of government school inspectors in both Kakuma and Somalia, with the cross-border operation. In Walda, AMREF made use of government doctors and nurses throughout their refugee camp operation. KRC at the coast acknowledged the benefits accruing from the appointment of a Division Officer, responsible for refugee affairs within the provincial administration. Such arrangements may have been weak, provisional and temporary, yet they were generally applauded, suggesting that NGOs did, in fact, realise the need for government involvement at field level.

UNHCR and the government

In 1992, the Government created the Refugee Secretariat Unit in the Ministry of Home Affairs and National Heritage, as a unit to liaise with the

UNHCR. It was responsible for the running of the Thika transit camp, while UNHCR undertook all the procedures for determining asylum status and dealt with legal protection issues for the entire refugee population.

Conventionally, the government presence was felt when issues of physical security came to the fore. However, there was fairly close cooperation between it and UNHCR on issues of security. For instance, security in the Dadaab camps in the north-east was largely undertaken under the auspices of a government police post which UNHCR helped boost considerably by providing radio equipment. This police post provided escorts from one camp to the next every day.

Aware of the importance of greater government involvement, UNHCR encouraged the process of appointing government officers to all the camps throughout the country. It also urged the government to resume the process of status determination which had stopped in 1989. In order to clear the backlog, UNHCR was advising the Government to give full status to all persons who had entered the country before 1992.

Nevertheless, there was a marked absence of government presence in two critical areas – assistance provision and legal protection. The government insisted that contracted humanitarian agencies were responsible for all assistance rendered. On legal matters, UNHCR was deemed the responsible agency. The only other actor was a section of the Jesuit Refugee Services (JRS), a local NGO operating in Nairobi that screened non-Somali refugees before referring them to UNHCR. However, JRS lacked in legal expertise and its role was soon restricted.

In so far as the government's role was perceived as purely supportive, it was not involved in – and often not informed of – aspects of UNHCR and NGO cooperation. This was occasionally a source of irritation to the government (*DANIDA, 1991*).

Donor agencies and the NGOs

NGO lobbying activities clearly influenced the donor community over time, though several donor agencies were reticent about supporting NGO lobbying against the NGO Bill in 1990 and were cautious in their dealings with NGO activities for some time afterwards. However, this did not deter the NGOs, who continued to campaign strongly. Dependence on official aid was not of paramount importance, though the role of donors behind the scenes may have been important (*Fowler, 1991*). In time, the donor community felt the issue to be sufficiently important to elect a liaison officer for regular contact with NGOs, thus marking their increasing support for the issues at hand.

Donor agencies and the government

The attitude of the donor agencies towards the government varied according not only to the humanitarian issues at hand, but also the wider political climate in Kenya. Those governments regarded as 'hostile' by the

Kenyan authorities were generally opposed to government involvement in NGO coordination. Yet most international donors argued that the government lacked the capacity adequately to coordinate the operations of the NGOs and strongly advocated the use of UNHCR, which had both the mandate and ability to carry out the task of coordination.

On the other hand, some donors felt that the government had tried its best given the emergency situation. Reports on government activity from NGOs and others failed to appraise the situation. In particular, they were concerned that concentration of resources in the refugee sector, often at the expense of an even greater need in the local Kenyan population, was a problem compounded by the humanitarian regime. Others, however, have pointed to years of government neglect in marginalised areas now selected for refugee settlements.

Undoubtedly the selection of marginalised areas for refugee intake must be seen in the context of a deliberate government policy that has led to the neglect of these fragile ecological areas over many years. (*HRW, 1991*). The government decision to have 11 refugee camps in fragile areas in all three refugee regions further reduced the ability of a vulnerable local population to cope with an otherwise delicate environment.

Donor agencies' assessment of the government efforts
The World Bank led in the assessment of the Act at the request of the NGO Standing Committee. While equating it to the bills in India during Indira Gandhi's premiership and Bangladesh before democratic reforms, the World Bank found the Kenyan bill 'most disturbing'. The Bank's submission to the NGO Standing Committee read:

> 'The Kenya bill attempts to control NGOs, tax them in the guise of registration renewal, and repress any lobbying or advocacy which government deems not in the national interest. The bill would send wrong signals to the Bank and bilateral agencies which are placing more emphasis on pluralism, governance, privatisation and free association in the interest of development'. This standpoint gave a cue to most of the donor agencies who had by then begun holding donor agency meetings to monitor the events (*Williams, 1990*).

This perspective seems to have influenced most other donor agencies, who began regularly monitoring the relationship between the government and NGOs. When the donor community finally met to consider the bill in 1992, they concluded that it had failed to translate into an enabling atmosphere for NGOs.

The government was thus left will little alternative but to back down and, subsequently, make amendments to the Act. Some government officials expressed frustration at the fact that donors were clearly 'colluding' with NGOs and, in effect, weakening the government. NGOs had, from time to time, begun projects which, for various reasons, they had abandoned at a later stage, leaving the government to carry the project to its conclusion; this was cited as one of the main reasons for the government's promotion of a framework for NGO operation.

To facilitate an understanding with donor agencies, the government appointed a liaison person who was based in the National Refugee Committee, in the Office of the President. This person liaised with the UN National Disaster Management Team (DMT) in providing needs assessment, monitoring and information exchange as well as identifying and tackling problems encountered in relief operations. Together with the DMT, they organised donor consultative meetings and provided regular situational analysis. The extent to which this facilitated closer coordination with humanitarian officials is, however, debatable, since the input was primarily technical rather than political.

CONCLUSION

The refugee crisis in Kenya and the subsequent response by governments and NGOs is marked, above all, by a system of trial and error highlighted by the fact that this was an emergency that few were prepared for. The lack of a clear policy or administrative framework further hampered efforts to address the situation promptly and in an orderly manner in the early stages.

The crisis, when measured in terms of human needs and the large number of humanitarian agencies arriving in the country after 1991, seems to have made the desirability of coordination all the more urgent. A belated attempt by the government to provide a framework for coordination through the 1992 NGO Coordination Act was highly contested by the NGOs, creating unprecedented tension and hostility between both parties. Ironically, this move by the Government prompted greater cooperation among the NGOs as they put up a common front against what they perceived as a restrictive piece of legislation.

Coordination structures were set up by government and UN alike in an effort to deal with inevitable demand. At the policy level, the government's National Relief Coordination Programme (NRCP) and the UN's DMT acted as focal points for coordination within and outside the respective sectors. With these, coordination tended to take the form of consultations and information sharing.

At project implementation level, there was limited coordination between the lead agencies appointed by UNHCR. At field level, an operational concept of coordination was lacking; thus each lead agency operated under self-devised structures. Thus, coordination translated into three distinct models corresponding to practices in the North East, Coastal and North West of Kenya that each came under a different lead agency.

At camp level, the level of coordination was determined by the perception of the NGOs about each other, the interpretation of the lead agency's definition of coordination by the subcontracted agencies, the relationship between international and local NGOs, and the relationship between the large and small NGOs. Support for coordination initiatives was sometimes hindered by the preoccupation of agencies with institutional survival.

Legal and policy frameworks propounded by the government and UNHCR were often unclear, though clarity in this regard began to improve with the appointment of focal points within the government, NGOs and the UN agencies through which to promote regular dialogue. Supplementary to these were some useful informal interpersonal links within the refugee sector as well as more formal sectoral and geographical networks, though links between such networks was limited. Where they were encouraged and supported, such efforts considerably improved coordination.

It was apparent that the proliferation of humanitarian aid agencies did create a coordination problem for the Kenyan Government. The capacity of Kenya, like most 'Third World' nations, to absorb and manage inputs of assistance was limited and the failure to coordinate the activities of the actors inevitably led to different coordination models on the ground (*Loescher, 1993*).

Finally, the integration of development principles into relief work was lacking throughout most of the emergency period. Although there was an effort to redirect rehabilitation efforts towards development, many of the projects were not within the National Development Plan. This was perhaps a reflection of poor coordination between humanitarian aid and any national planning strategy and may have contributed towards misunderstandings and suspicions between government and NGOs. Like so many similar emergencies, humanitarian aid work can easily become little more than disbursing money and materials (*Allan, 1988*).

Above all, the period from 1992 onwards witnessed a growing concern for closer information sharing and programme collaboration. A climate for coordination was slowly developing as NGOs moved from their traditional insularity towards an acceptance of collective representation on issues of common interest.

ACRONYMS AND ABBREVIATIONS

AMREF	African Medical Research Foundation
CARE	Co-operative of American Relief Everywhere
DMT	Disaster Management Team
HRW	Human Rights Watch
IDS	Institute of Development Studies
IFRC	International Federation of the Red Cross and Crescent Societies
IMF	International Monetary Fund
IRC	International Rescue Committee
IRRES	International Relief and Rehabilitation Services
JRS	Jesuit Refugee Services
KANU	Kenya African National Union
KENGO	Kenya Energy and Environmental Non-Governmental Organisations
KNCNGOs	Kenya National Council of NGOs
KNCSS	Kenya National Council of Social Services
KRCs	Kenya Red Cross societies
KREP	Kenya Rural Enterprise Programme
LWF	Lutheran World Federation
MCSS	Ministry of Culture and Social Services
MSF	Médecins Sans Frontières
NCCK	National Christian Council of Kenya
NRPC	National Relief Coordination Programme
OAU	Organisation for African Unity
ORAP	Rural Associations for Progress
PVOs	Private Voluntary Organisations
RSAK	Religious Superiors Association of Kenya
UNHCR	United Nations High Commissioner for Refugees
UNICEF	United Nations Children's Fund
USCR	United States Committee for Refugees
VADA	Voluntary Agencies Development Assistance
WFP	World Food Programme

REFERENCES

Anderson, M B and Woodrow, P J (1989) *An Approach to Integrating Development and Relief Programming: An Analytical Framework* Cambridge University Press, Cambridge

Allen, T (1988) 'Coming Home: The International Agencies and the Returnees in West Nile' *Journal of Refugees Studies*, vol 1, no 2, pp 166–175

Chepkwony, A (1988) *The Role of Non-Governmental Organisations in Development: A Study of the National Christian Council of Churches (NCCK) 1963–1978* Arkitiktkopia, Uppsala

Collins, C (1992) 'An Overview of the Refugee Camps in Kenya, February 1991–February 1992.' SCF: Nairobi

DANIDA (1991) *Case Study of 11 Agencies in Kenya, Nepal, Sudan and Thailand: Effectiveness of Multilateral Agencies at Country Level* Ministry of Foreign Affairs, Copenhagen

Daley, P (1994) 'The Situation of Refugees in East Africa' paper for the 4th International Research Advisory Panel Conference, Oxford

Duell, C B and Dutcher L A (1987) *Working Together: NGO Cooperation in Seven African Countries* InterAction, New York

Fowler, A (1988) 'Non-governmental Organisations in Africa: Achieving Comparative Advantage in Micro-Development' *Discussion Paper 249*, University of Sussex, Institute of Development Studies, Brighton

Fowler, A (1991) 'Submission to the NGO meeting in February 1991' *Weekly Review*, 22 February

Harrell-Bond, B E (1986) *Imposing Aid*, Oxford University Press, Oxford

Harrell-Bond, B E and Voutira, E (1992) 'In Search of the Locus of Trust: The Social World of the Refugee Camp'. The Refugee Studies Programme, Oxford

Headly, W R (1988) 'A Hard Look and a Fresh Start: Local Responses to the Refugees in Kenya and Implications for African Refugee Services' Urban Refugee Project, paper presented to the Silver Jubilee of the Africa Studies Association (UK), 14–16 September, Refugee Studies Programme, Oxford, p27

HRW (1991) *Kenya: Taking Liberties* An Africa Watch Report, London

Kanyinga, K (1990) 'The Role of NGOs in Development' MA Thesis, University of Nairobi

Kanyinga, K (1991) *Non-Governmental Organisations Coordination Act, 1990. A Report of the Proceedings of the IDS/NGOs Workshop* held in February 1991, IDS, University of Nairobi

Kenya Gazette (1990) Supplement No 77 Bills (No 17) Bills, 1990. Bill for Introduction: The Non-Governmental Organisations Bill, 1990; 9 November, in Kenya Gazette, Government Press, Nairobi

KNCNGOs (1993) *Bulletin No 1* KNCNGOs, Nairobi

KNCSS, (1990) 'Recommendations to the Government Of Kenya on Supportive Policy and Legislation for Voluntary, Non-Profit, Non-Governmental Organisations, Development and Welfare Activities', KNCSS, Nairobi

Loescher, G (1993) *Beyond Charity: International Cooperation and the Global Refugee Crisis* Oxford University Press, Oxford, p175

Mbogori, E (1992) Extract of a petition to the Attorney General expressing the insufficiency of the Amendments to the 1990 NGO Act

Muktaza, J (1991) 'Discussion Notes on the NGO Coordination Act 1990

(No.19 of 1990, Laws of Kenya)' in *Kanyinga* Autumn 1990, Nairobi, Kenya

Nicholds, J B (1988) *The Uneasy Alliance: Religion, Refugee Work and US Foreign Policy*, Oxford University Press, Oxford

Nicholds, N and Borton, J (1994) 'The Changing Role of NGOs in the Provision of Relief and Rehabilitation Assistance: Case Study 1– Afghanistan/Pakistan' *Working Paper 74*, Overseas Development Institute, London

OAU (1969) *Convention Governing Specific Aspects of Refugee Problems in Africa* OAU, Addis Ababa

UN (1993) *United Nations 1993 Consolidated Inter-Agency Appeal: Kenya*, Special Emergency Programme For the Horn of Africa (SEPHA), Geneva, p6

UNHCR (1992) *Information Bulletin*, June, UNHCR, Nairobi

UNHCR (1992) *Information Bulletin: Kenya Refugee Emergency*, July, November, UNHCR, Nairobi

UNHCR (1993) *Information Bulletin: UNHCR Cross-Border Operation. Kenya–Somali* February, UNHCR, Nairobi

UNHCR (1993) *Information Bulletin: Kenya*, June, UNHCR, Nairobi

UNHCR (1993) *Information Bulletin*, July, UNHCR, Nairobi

UNHCR (1993) *Appeal for Repatriation to Somalia*, (Link with the Consolidated DHA Appeals), September, UNHCR, Nairobi

UNHCR (1993) *Information Bulletin: Somali Cross-Border Operation*, October, UNHCR, Nairobi

UNHCR (1993) *Refugee Women Victims of Violence: A Special Project*, UNHCR, Nairobi

USCR (1993) *World Refugee Survey*, US Committee for Refugees, Washington

Weekly Review (1990), 23 November, Nairobi

Weekly Review (1991a), 1 February, Nairobi

Weekly Review (1991b), 15 February, Nairobi, p26

Weekly Reviews (1991c), 22 February, Nairobi

Wellard, K and Copestake, J G (eds) (1993) *Non-Governmental Organisations and the State in Africa: Rethinking Roles in Sustainable Agricultural Development* Routledge, London

Williams, A (1991) 'Kenya NGO Bill World Bank/Donor Assessment of the Government Effort', submission to the NGO meeting, Nairobi

AGENCY REPORTS AND DOCUMENTS

Crescent of Hope, (1992) Memoranda of Operation Draft Donor Statement on the NGO Act

JRS, (1991) Directory: Refugee Service Agencies. JRS: Nairobi

Kituo Cha Sheria, (1993) Haki Mali, Vol 1, No 1, April. KCS: Nairobi

Kituo Cha Sherio, (1993) Haki Mali, Vol 1, No 2, August. KCS: Nairobi

KRCS Mombasa, 'Camp Site Profile' and ' Refugee camp Reports Marafa, Utange and Hatimy'

International Save the Children Fund, 'The International Response to Emergencies'

IRRES, (1993) Newsletter Vol 1. IRRES: Nairobi

Proceedings of the NGO meetings on the NGO Coordination Act of 1990 (1st, 2nd, 3rd, 4th, 5th and 6th)

UNICEF 1992–1993 Monthly Water and Sanitation Reports

6

LEBANON:
THE LEBANESE NGO FORUM AND THE RECONSTRUCTION OF CIVIL SOCIETY 1989–93

Jon Bennett

The People: Population: 2.9 million. Ethnically homogeneous, mostly Arab with a small number of Armenians and Europeans. Also a large group of Palestinian refugees.

Religion: Although often contended, approximately 65 per cent are Muslim. The traditionally powerful Sunni are now being challenged by the more militant Shiites. There is also a large Druze population. 35 per cent are Christian, mostly Maronites with a smaller group of Catholics and Orthodox Christian

The Government: Led by Prime Minister Rafiq Hariri, the government is beginning, after years of war, to command support among the population, although the Maronite Christian factions oppose his leadership. The continuing presence of Syrian forces is an important factor in maintaining order. Southern Lebanon remains under the occupation of Israel as a buffer security zone.

Development Aid: US$134 million (1990); US$50 per capita.

After 17 years of bitter civil war and external interference, Lebanon is slowly on the path to recovery. Throughout the war, Lebanese NGOs proved themselves capable of holding together a fragile welfare system at a time when international aid declined and the civilian population was torn apart by factionalism.

By the early 1990s, the Lebanese NGO Forum, the largest coalition of NGOs, was at the forefront of the debate over what constitutes an appropriate NGO profile in civil society; their close ties with the major confessional groups, though controversial, were arguably their enduring strength. In the wake of the new Middle East peace initiative, the Forum demonstrates interesting ways of operating and organising coordination in complex emergencies where political consensus is as important as the simple delivery of aid.

BACKGROUND

On 23 October 1989, under the auspices of the Arab League, the Taef accords were signed in Saudi Arabia, putting an end to 17 years of war in Lebanon. Precariously poised between Syria and Israel, this small country had been torn apart, since the 1973 Arab–Israeli war, by religious and political factionalism, fuelled by external interests. With the Taef agreement, the Lebanese people were able to take the first tentative steps towards reconciliation and peace.

Lebanon was in ruins. Apart from huge loss of human life and destruction of property during the war, the country's productive capacity had been severely reduced, resulting in the deterioration of capital stock and the emigration of thousands of skilled Lebanese.[1] Internal displacement was estimated at 750,000, causing immense social and economic suffering as well as disrupting the regional balance of the country's multi-confessional society.[2] Lebanon's law is based on the existence of the different confessional groups, eg Muslim, Orthodox, Catholic, Druze etc.

Although a semblance of normality has returned to Lebanon, the focus of continuing dispute has been the southern part of the country bordering Israel. In February 1991, the government requested the UN to extend its mandate to the peace-keeping forces in the south – United Nations Interim Force in Lebanon (UNIFIL) (see, for example, *LeRoy, 1991*). Now that the army had disarmed the militias operating in the borderline territories, the government also demanded the withdrawal of Israeli forces from these areas (*Instituto del Tercer Mundo, 1992*).

The Israelis did not accede to the demands, despite the fact that in July 1991 the Lebanese army forced the Palestine Liberation

---

1. The United Nations Development Programme (UNDP) office in Lebanon has often stated that the return of emigrants – representing mostly those with skills and capital – is one of the most important factors which would lead to recovery of the country's economy in the medium term. Between 600,000 and 650,000 fled over the war years, adding to a total of some five million in the Lebanese diaspora as a whole (*Mardelli-Assaf, 1988*).

2. The precise number of displaced persons is unknown. Estimates vary between 500,000 and 900,000 (*Tag-Eldeen, 1992*).

Organisation (PLO) out of its main operating base east of Sidon. The confrontation in the security zone has resulted in the mass exodus of nearly 100,000 Shiites from the borderline towns, exacerbating Lebanon's already chronic problem of internal displacement.

Israeli incursions out of the security zone continued. In February 1992, in the lead up to the Middle East peace talks, an agreement was reached between guerrilla leaders of the Hezbollah, the Amal movement and the representatives of the Syrian forces that allowed for a temporary truce with Israel. It was not to last. Fighting again flared up in April 1992 and several Shiite villages were bombed by the Israeli airforce in the Bekaa Valley. The Lebanese government, taking its cue from the lifting of the US arms embargo (in place since 1984), began purchasing military hardware.

In July 1993, there were massive Israeli airforce, army and navy attacks on southern Lebanon. Their intention, as before, was to force an end to Syrian (and, allegedly, Lebanese) support for the Hezbollah, accused of attacks against Israeli positions. The air strikes on Lebanon destroyed an estimated 1500 dwellings and displaced approximately 250,000 people. To date, the future of the security zone is still unresolved.

Recovery short-lived

Before the war, Lebanon enjoyed a long period of rapid economic growth and financial stability as the traditional haven for Arab oil capital. With the onset of hostilities in 1975, the country suffered a rapidly growing budget deficit caused by lack of tax revenue and increasing pressure to augment public services. The 'dollarization' of the economy was coupled with runaway inflation throughout the war years. In addition, more than US$12 billion of Lebanese capital was transferred and invested abroad.

With the breakdown of central government authority, illegal economic activities flourished, notably drug cultivation and processing, arms trafficking and substantial external funding of political parties. At their peak, these represented an additional US$500 million to the country's total income.[3]

In 1991 the first signs of recovery encouraged a sense of optimism. Various UN reports applauded the government's active monetary stabilisation policy (*UN General Assembly, 1991*). Central authority was resumed over ports, public buildings and utilities, and subsidies for bread and fuel were removed.

Soon, however, central and regional political tensions were again heightened by prolonged delays of promised international assistance

---

3. As the government begins to clamp down on these activities, the immediate victims have tended to be those most vulnerable to economic pressure; for instance, the thousands of poor farmers in the Bekaa who are dependent on opium and cannabis crops for their survival.

and the linking of this aid to Lebanon's involvement in the Middle East peace process. This was demonstrated by the failure to mobilise assistance through the International Fund for the Assistance of Lebanon (IFAL), a provision of the Taef accords.

By early 1992, inflation and economic collapse reached alarming levels. Almost 27 per cent of the national budget was absorbed in servicing foreign loans, while a further 25 per cent was used for defence. With most remaining public funds being spent on reconstruction, there was precious little left for social programmes. The value of the Lebanese pound had plummeted, leaving low income and vulnerable groups, such as the displaced, in dire straits. A study conducted by the National Labour Union in January 1992 showed the minimum monthly subsistence cost for a family of five to be US$438. The actual minimum wage was a mere US$85 (*LNF, 1992a*).

In April and May 1992, the National Labour Union called for a general strike. Opposition centred upon the government's economic policy, its alleged corruption and its clampdown on public freedom. Violent public demonstrations followed, causing the resignation of prime minister Karame's pro-Syrian government. The president designated Rashid Al Sohl, a moderate Sunni, as the new head of government. His cabinet of 24, half Christian and half Muslim, was to continue to campaign for the liberation of southern Lebanon. Strategic areas of defence and internal security continued to be dominated by Syrian interests.

By 1993, there were again signs of slow, if uneven, recovery on the streets of Beirut and elsewhere. A marked increase in building investment and trading, particularly in the more prosperous areas of the country, reflected a cautious optimism, witnessed by the gradual return of middle class emigrants.

NGOs in Lebanon

The history of voluntary social service organisations in Lebanon can be traced to the second half of the 19th century, when local and foreign religious missions stimulated, by example, the formation of national benevolent organisations. Intermittent wars and non-democratic regimes aside, the country has been able to sustain a flourishing private social sector ever since. Often, governmental services originated first as initiatives by private citizens; indeed, the distinction can still be confusing, with a plethora of NGOs sponsored by serving politicians coming into existence in the 1980s when it was easier to attract foreign funding through non-governmental sources.

The lack of homogeneity in the country is reflected in its institutions which have tended to be formed by ethnic, religious or political groups; these institutions are also witness to the country's dedication to a pluralistic society. Historically, there were 17 communities that made up the modern Lebanese state. There was no state religion. By law, individuals were registered with one or another confessional community and marriage, divorce, etc were arranged through that community. Today, as in the past, special interest groups guard jealously their right to form their own associations. The result is a mosaic of services reflecting different cultural orientations under various public and private arrangements.

NGOs today

There is no accurate register of the number of voluntary associations operating in Lebanon today. Indeed, the legislation governing social service organisations dates back to 1909 and was promulgated under the Ottoman Turkish regime. The law requires that the establishment of an association be made known to the authorities ('notification'). The origin of this requirement relates to the desire by the state to criminalise the existence of secret societies only. Few checks are made on the independence, financial viability or managerial strength of the supplicant. Social service organisations continue to exist within this deficient legal framework; indeed, some more active organisations encountered in this study have yet to be registered and do not see this as an impediment to their operations.

Various surveys and directories of NGOs have been published since independence in 1941. An official estimate in 1964 put the figure at 405, representing an increase of 41 per cent between 1945 and 1959.[4] In 1980, a joint Lebanese government and UNICEF study showed this to have risen to 1,587 registered organisations, though it is not clear how many of these were active (*UNDP, 1990*).

When the author asked how many NGOs were operational in Lebanon, his respondents' replies ranged from 4,000 to 13,000.[5] The confusion was in part due to definition. A full classification of NGOs in Lebanon would include private voluntary organisations (PVOs), cooperatives, labour unions, development education and advocacy agencies, women's associations, youth associations and cultural and media associations. Except for the first, most of these categories could be given a generic classification – community based organisations (CBOs). Many of these CBOs are partners and recipients of assistance channelled through the PVOs.

For our purposes here we shall assume a universal definition of NGO as PVO, a not-for-profit body 'established and governed by a group of private citizens for a stated philanthropic purpose, and sup-

4. This was the figure presented to the former Ministry of General Planning. Of some 658 licensed organisations, 405 were deemed to be 'active' (*UNDP, 1990*).
5. Other written estimates of the number of NGOs in Lebanon include: 4000 (*Mardelli-Assaf, 1988*) and 1500 (*Mohanna, K 1991b*).

ported, at least in part, by voluntary individual contributions' (*OECD, 1988*).

Given this more restrictive definition, it is likely that the number of operational NGOs in Lebanon is not more than 1,600, of which fewer than 50 have a truly national scope and capacity. It is the coordination of these national NGOs that forms the main focus of this study.

Lebanese NGOs, within this definition, can be categorised further with reference to their allegiances and identity under a number of headings:

Religious charitable welfare institutions
Both Christian and Muslim, and of various sub-denominations, these are often long-established (pre-independence) 'traditional' NGOs. They hold considerable influence within their communities and may have institutions throughout the country. Their political outreach may also be considerable. Although some efforts are being made towards modernising management structures and image, their welfare activities have tended to concentrate on education, orphans, medical services, the elderly, etc

Confessional NGOs
During the war, in the absence of central services, confessional groups came under pressure to provide assistance in the form of relief, medical care, schools and shelter to distressed and displaced families. Many so-formed NGOs continue their work today.

Local and specialised NGOs
Their activities usually involve one or two specific programmes within a defined geographical area.

Major national NGOs
With the decline of public social services during the war, many larger NGOs dealing with health, disability, relief, vocational training, child welfare, etc, sprang up, particularly when foreign sources of funds became available. Some are now well established, backed by support committees and state funding; others, with the decline in foreign funding, have collapsed.

International NGOs
Many foreign NGOs, particularly during the war, established offices in Lebanon and either became operational themselves or served as funding channels to indigenous NGOs. In some cases the agency became ostensibly 'localised', ie run entirely by national staff and occasionally registered as a national entity. However, primary funding and direction continued from their headquarters abroad; for this reason, they remain within the 'international NGO' category. In other cases – for instance,

Caritas-Lebanon – although part of a worldwide federation, they are wholly independent and thus categorised as a local NGO.

CHANNELS OF ASSISTANCE

It is notoriously difficult to assess accurately the amount of money channelled through Lebanese and international NGOs. The former tend jealously to guard their sources for fear of competition; in some cases their sources are irregular contributions from benefactors abroad, rarely featuring in any official annual statements. By contrast, funds passed through international NGOs may be accounted for twice – once through the NGO and again either through the multilateral or bilateral programme of the donor countries in question.

These qualifications aside, the UNDP states that the total external assistance to Lebanon in 1991 was US$161 million (*UNDP, 1991a*). Of this, 72.6 per cent was from bilateral sources (notably Saudi Arabia and the USA) 16.3 per cent was from multilateral sources and 11.1 per cent was from international NGOs. Again, it should be stressed that this final figure does not represent the total funds available to NGOs; NGOs were also the preferred channels of implementation of resources disbursed by bilateral and multilateral donors. The US$30 million from United States Agency for International Development (USAID), for example, was mostly humanitarian assistance channelled through NGOs.

Almost all external assistance in 1991 was, in broad terms, for the social sector. Approximately 29.2 per cent (US$46 million) of this total was for emergency and relief assistance. Major NGO recipients, from bilateral, multilateral and private sources, included the Save the Children Fund (US$19.4 million), Caritas (US$9.2 million), YMCA (US$4.1 million), the International Committee of the Red Cross/Crescent (ICRC) (US$ 2.1 million) and World Vision (US$1.2 million) (*UNDP, 1991a*).

Faced with figures of this size, it would be easy to designate local NGOs as the 'poor cousins' of the international NGOs. This is not necessarily the case. Although it receives scant attention, external assistance from unofficial sources is certainly substantial.[6] Perhaps surprisingly, we find that aid dispensed by the Lebanese diaspora – estimated at around US$60 million per month at its height in 1988 – is greater than the sum of all other external funds (*Mardelli-Assaf, 1988*). For the most part, this money is passed from family to family; thus there was no institutional manner in which it

---

6. The UNDP states that 'external resource flows other than ODA' [official development assistance] were marginal...important efforts were made to provide financing from domestic private sources, including NGOs. The most important contribution was by the Hariri Foundation, reportedly on average tens of millions of US Dollars in each of the past few years. (*UNDP, 1991a*).

can be accounted for.[7] Some funds, however, are passed through Lebanese associations abroad to local religious welfare associations, NGOs, church groups, etc.

Domestic private sources can also be substantial, particularly if one allows for funds raised through community-based organisations, churches, mosques and through the Muslim *zakat*. The Lebanese NGO Forum, for example, lists the programme expenditure of its ten members in 1992 as US$39.7 million.[8] Most of this will have been raised in its Muslim, Druze, Maronite, Greek Orthodox and Greek Catholic constituencies.

Local NGOs often complain that their humanitarian fundraising and distributions are, at best, marginalised or, at worst, totally ignored by official aid literature. This is hardly surprising. Administrative overheads for producing exhaustive activity reports are not usually available to local NGOs. If they were, how different the total picture in Lebanon might be! Yet, who would be the audience for such reports? As already noted, donors invariably prefer their own international NGOs as implementors, applaud them for greater 'accountability' and thus close a rather restrictive circle of information.

CHANGES IN THE NGO COMMUNITY

The quantity of international assistance to Lebanon dropped considerably between 1988 and 1991. There were various reasons for this:

- NGO and UN expatriate staff pulling out due to perceived insecurity;
- the linkage of foreign aid to the release of hostages and to desired changes in the priorities pursued by the Lebanese government;
- the closure, or reduction, of programmes carried out by foreign NGOs on the ground;
- with inflation almost out of control, the prohibitive expense of running programmes in Lebanon; and
- the profound changes taking place in the former Soviet Union and Eastern Europe and the consequent shift of donor interests.

In consequence, Lebanese NGOs found themselves virtually alone in tackling the overwhelming needs of the population. In response to priorities identified by the nascent government, the UN's rather limited programme was almost entirely in support of infrastructural development. The government's public sector programme, as far as it existed, was run very much with a top-down approach, making extremely limited use of community-based participation. Collective NGO initiatives

---

7. An exception is the Office for Social Solidarity (OSS) – 'Muassassat al Tadamon al Ijtimai' – which, in the mid-1980s, launched a vast twinning operation between emigrant families and needy resident families. Through bank transfers from person to person, this programme assisted in excess of 50,000 families (*Mardelli-Assaf, 1988*)
8. Figures provided by the LNF to the author, 1993.

were, consequently, launched against a background of general alarm at the decline of external aid desperately needed for social programmes. They felt a sense of betrayal by the international community:

> 'Lebanese NGOs feel increasingly isolated and lacking in material and other forms of support from the international community. NGOs throughout Lebanon insist on the need to correct the image of the country commonly projected by the western media whose main focus is on such issues as armed conflicts, the kidnapping of foreign citizens, and inter-communal problems that caused, and are maintaining, indifference abroad to the problems facing the people of Lebanon.'
> (*UNDP, 1991b*).

That NGOs provided a safety valve during the war for a dislocated society is unquestionable. Some analysts have gone further by suggesting that the NGO community, as the antithesis of the existing divisions created by the war, had in fact helped to preserve a unique unity and continuity. This was soon to foster a general belief in the central role of NGOs as guardians of democratic civil society (*Mohanna, 1991b*).

Some interesting changes took place as the war drew to a close. Many traditional Lebanese NGOs had been illequipped to manage large-scale external assistance when it became available during the war. Bolstered by external assistance and management control, certain internationally accredited confessional organisations and a small group of local NGOs – favoured by donors as 'reliable' channels – came to the fore. These 'privileged NGOs' contrast starkly with the more traditional sector, whose resources were severely depleted.

Among those that flourished was a small number of Lebanese NGOs which belonged to international networks of agencies such as church bodies or the Red Cross. Thus, Caritas-Lebanon attracted substantial funds from abroad, as did the YMCA Lebanon. The Middle East Council of Churches (MECC) was also prominent, especially through its Emergency Relief and Rehabilitation Programme created in 1975.[9] Similarly, the Maronite Social Fund and *Al Maqassed Al Islamiyya* were able to continue important, albeit localised, programmes with foreign backing.

There was also an interesting 'third group': secular, specialised NGOs emerging as a result of the voluntary efforts of energetic individuals. In part, they were motivated by a desire to break with the more formal institutional mentality of traditional welfare associations. *Arc en Ciel*, for example, set up training institutes for the disabled and

---

9. This huge programme continues countrywide, even though the MECC Secretariat moved to Cyprus in 1983.

a programme of reintegration into the labour market, very different from the more prevalent 'homes for the disabled'. Mardelli cites this as an example of an agency that is 'raising the curtain of foreign aid' previously monopolised by a handful of local NGOs sustained by the de facto or deliberate policy of European or American donors (*Mardelli-Assaf, 1988*). We shall see how this new breed of NGO was to become a yardstick for those advocating the de-linkage of aid from politics and/or confessionalism in Lebanon.

NGO COORDINATION

Foreign NGO coordination

Various *ad hoc* coordination initiatives have taken place since the 1960s, most originating in the desire to quantify and, where possible, regulate NGO activities at a sectoral level. Most have foundered as government departments find themselves severely underfunded and understaffed. It remains to be seen whether the Ministry of Social Affairs will again take up the mantle in overseeing national coordination of NGO activities. In the meantime, such initiatives lie solely in the hands of the NGOs themselves.

With the intensification of the war in the 1980s, foreign NGOs were disinclined to form any permanent structure for coordination in-country; rather, their efforts were concentrated on consortia originating abroad for specific purposes.

One such initiative was launched in 1989 through the Vatican. An *ad hoc* committee of 15 NGOs was drawn together under the general direction of Caritas which comprised the largest church-based agencies in Lebanon. By 1991, only four agencies remained – Caritas, Catholic Relief Services (CRS), Pontifical Mission for Palestine and World Vision – who together formed the NGO Coordination Committee for Lebanon. In 1993, CRS closed its offices in Lebanon. The final three, with a collective budget of approximately US$20 million, now pool some US$2–3 million per year in equal shares through the Committee.

The Committee has a full-time secretariat in Byblos and meets monthly to process applications from local NGOs, community groups, etc. It has maintained strict criteria for the disbursement of funds, perhaps in part reflecting an equivocal attitude towards local applicants. It does not allow indigenous NGOs to administer funds and prefers to manage the projects with staff drawn from each of the three members. Two of its senior representatives reported being 'overwhelmed' by the number of local NGOs, the lack of criteria for their registration and the potential for mismanagement of funds.[10]

---

10. Interviews conducted with Issam Bishara, Field Director, Pontifical Mission for Palestine (Beirut, 28 May 1993) and Jean Bouchebi, Field Director, World Vision (Beirut, 25 May 1993).

For our purposes here, we shall look more closely at how Lebanese NGOs coordinate among themselves. Their experience is instructive for several reasons:

- they highlight the challenge of creating an effective democratic alternative to donor-driven consortia;
- they present lessons in institution building in the face of chronic emergency needs;
- and they reflect the political complexity of Lebanese society as a whole.

Coordination among Lebanese NGOs

Various workers' federations, unions, women's councils and specialist umbrella groups existed for many years before the war. These were more traditional institutional models relying upon a national network of members pursuing common interests in relatively stable political conditions. Some still exist, though few can claim to have a truly national remit and almost all have faced grave financial difficulties during the war.

The history of NGO coordination is complex, relying heavily upon the energies of dominant individuals, yet sometimes confounded by their mutual competitiveness. In each case, it would be difficult to divorce the collective dynamic from the dominance of several well-respected individuals whose 'political' prestige was as important as their managerial competence.

A significant early attempt at cross-sectoral coordination of NGOs as a distinct group was done by Mouvement Social Libanais (MSL), founded in the 1960s. Under the prominent leadership of Gregoire Haddad, MSL built up specialised coordination committees for dispensaries, summer camps, youth clubs and literacy centres. By the time war broke out, MSL was itself an implementing agency and Haddad had built up an impressive constituency of potential donors. This was due in part to the fact that MSL represented a secular option – attractive particularly to foreign donors – and was itself working with Palestinians in Lebanon, a focus of foreign support in the early 1980s.

In an attempt to capitalise on increasing international funds, MSL developed a project proposal in 1986 for a national coordination network, divided into sectors. This was sent to the headquarters of NGOs in Europe, including Christian Aid, Diakonia, Oxfam, CIMADE and Dutch Inter-Church Aid. The proposal, with a budget of US$200,000, was questioned because MSL, while claiming to represent a broad-based Lebanese NGO membership, had not fully consulted with them. The initiative received a lukewarm response, particularly in view of opposition from the MECC. With UN recognition and support, Haddad proceeded, but apart from funds raised for MSL's own programme, few funds were generated for its 'members' and the coordination attempt broke down.

Several *ad hoc* initiatives were launched in 1988. Following an International Council of Voluntary Agencies (ICVA) mission to Lebanon the previous year, Encounter was formed. As an *ad hoc* committee of the larger national NGOs, it also included Haddad's MSL. Although several key figures, including Haddad, were subsequently to leave, Encounter was seen as the prototype for the LNF, founded in 1989.

In another development, an Inter-NGO Forum was created in February 1986, following a conference arranged by ICVA and the United Nations Relief and Works Agency for Palestinian Refugees in the Near East (UNRWA). The primary motive for this sub-regional gathering of national and international NGOs was to develop medium-term strategic inter-agency initiatives for Palestinians, rather than single agency project approaches. While the ICVA/UNRWA decision was Palestinian-specific, the Inter-NGO Forum developed without a Palestinian focus. Several foreign NGOs, plus leading figures from the Lebanese collectives, attended these meetings in Cyprus.

There followed a period of confusion and shifting allegiances that, above all else, reflected the volatile situation in Lebanon as the war intensified. Some have laid charges of poor coordination at the doors of egotistical individuals. It should be remembered, however, that at this stage in the war Lebanese NGOs were virtually the only operational agencies on the ground; their offices and projects were subject to frequent bombardment and humanitarian demands were more intensive than ever. The handful of NGO leaders pushing for greater coordination was unable to promote a long-term strategy in the face of such pressing needs. Their efforts were tied primarily to the quest for emergency international aid. Expediency overrode systematic planning and coordination was never more than piecemeal.

Relations with the UN

In an atmosphere of mutual suspicion, it is difficult to see how any lasting tripartite dialogue could have been established between the UN, NGOs and government in the immediate aftermath of the war. This was undoubtedly due to the small UN presence and the rather low-key fundraising strategy it adopted after reopening its offices in 1990. In early 1993, an extensive study of 26 NGOs, the UN specialised agencies and multilateral agencies concluded that:

> 'cooperation between the government of Lebanon and NGOs is only partially developed. Work is conducted almost in isolation from each other. This situation also exists in the relationship between NGOs and the Inter-Governmental Organisations.' (*Mardelli-Assaf, 1993*).

Though it is difficult to separate individual shortcomings from structural faults, several observations are pertinent to our study here:

1. there was no formal structure for contact between the UN as a whole and the NGO community;
2. the UN was keen to endorse a framework for government–NGO relations that it could then support but no such framework was created;
3. since 1990, the UN had been requested by the government to emphasise institutional economic reconstruction rather than a social programme, thus obviating the need for close NGO relations;
4. lacking a clear sectoral policy, the government was unlikely to establish a *modus operandi* with NGOs; and
5. the UN felt that the legal process of NGO regulation needed to be improved before it could promote long-term partnerships.

A unique feature of the UN system in Lebanon was the Office of the UN Coordinator of Assistance for Reconstruction and Development of Lebanon (UNARDOL), which was established by the UN General Assembly in 1978. Its role was to promote and coordinate economic assistance for reconstruction and development of the country. Although UNARDOL was not operational itself, its coordinating role was supplemented by a Trust Fund for Reconstruction and Development (*UN Lebanon, 1992*). For emergency projects in Lebanon (funds mobilised through Office of the UN Disaster Relief Coordinator (UNDRO), now incorporated into DHA), the period 1982–1992 saw contributions of over US$420 million. On the development side, the UNDP managed a host of the UN specialised agencies not represented in Lebanon. Through its Indicative Planning Figure (IPF) funds, it anticipated a budget of some US$41 million from 1993–96 for development and technical assistance.

In 1992, a UNDP country programme was drawn up for the first time in seven years. Because of the government's emphasis on economic reconstruction, consultation with NGOs was minimal. The programme for the displaced, however, was to involve UN Volunteers (UNVs) placed within NGO programmes and this resulted in some debate on how appropriate this approach was. Prior use of UNVs had been for programmes administered and financed by government and/or inter-government agencies with NGOs as the implementing agencies. Many new NGO programmes for the displaced were entirely independent, requiring a more innovative approach to the sharing of staff and resources (*Mardelli-Assaf, 1993*).

The complex, often personalised, relationships between NGOs and the UN system are not central to our concerns here. The gradual normalisation of government, UN and private sector protocol by 1993, however, made it imperative to clear away the debris of the past and seek mutually more beneficial relationships. Coordination bodies were perhaps the only institutions capable of representation and dialogue with the UNDP and others on aspects of longer-term development planning for Lebanon. While NGOs clearly had the upper hand in outreach and experience, they were rarely able individually to engage in medium-term strategic planning. For most, the shortage of funds and continuing political uncertainties prevented them establishing sustainable programming. The 1992 UNDP Country Programme stated that:

> 'while the well developed private sector networks and the extraordinary efforts of non-governmental organisations (NGOs) provided emergency and humanitarian assistance in the social sectors during the war years, they could not maintain a social development programme.' (cited in *Mardelli-Assaf, 1993*).

The counter argument from NGOs would be that with very limited programme support from either the government or the UN, how could this be otherwise?

New initiatives

Two main NGO groupings emerged from 1987-1989 that were to become key players in the coming years: La Coordination des ONG en vue du Developpement au Liban (CDL-ONG), initially headed by Msgr Haddad, then from 1991 by Kemal Mohanna; and the LNF, headed by Ghassan Sayah (formerly Encounter, co-chaired by Mohammed Barakat). At face value the difference between the two was clear: the CDL-ONG presented a mix of foreign and local NGOs whereas the LNF had an exclusively local NGO membership.

At another level the differences were quite pronounced. Kemal Mohanna had quiescent political ambitions, maintained international contacts through the French Ministry of Humanitarian Affairs and ensured that the CDL-ONG achieved consistent media recognition and prominent mention in UN literature.[11] President of the Amel Association, a health care NGO, Mohanna was an ardent and respected advocate of NGOs in Lebanon. Yet his presentations, with their impressive contextual and conceptual analysis of how NGOs fitted into Lebanese society, belie the difficulty of identifying the precise operational capacity of CDL-ONG. From a list of 23 NGO members and associates given to the author, several were purely nominal members, expressing the view that it is better to be on a list than off it.[12]

The CDL-ONG was not, however, a purely paper exercise. From 1990 onwards, the monthly General Assembly, with its intermittent

---

11. For example, his presentations at UNESCO 'Peace Building and Development in Lebanon' meetings, Paris, 1991.
12. Interviews conducted in Beirut, May 1993. For reasons of confidentiality, no organisations can be named.

attendance, presented a useful focus of debate much missed during the war years. To his credit, Mohanna has consistently acknowledged other coordination efforts and invited collaboration wherever possible.[13]

THE LEBANESE NGO FORUM

The second coordination body in Lebanon is in several respects more interesting for our purposes here. The LNF was founded by a small group of the larger Lebanese NGOs. An influential member from the outset was Ghassan Sayah, Chief Executive Officer of the YMCA, one of the largest NGOs in Lebanon. As a field practitioner, Sayah could boast that his organisation, with its nationwide network of 124 licensed dispensaries, 23 regional hospitals and a relief programme reaching some 120 smaller NGOs, was better placed than most to harness support for a national rehabilitation programme (*YMCA Lebanon, 1993*).

In truth, the YMCA became not only the 'lead agency' of the LNF but Sayah himself was to invest a great deal of his time on the Forum. We might draw a more general observation from this: that the dynamics of coordination, in so far as it depends on the energies of a lead agency and individual, also depends upon that agency's management structure allowing its key personnel to spend time developing external interests. Paradoxically, Sayah's own agency, with its already well-established international funding links, stood to gain less from this initiative than other LNF members. The LNF has, nevertheless, provided him and his colleagues with a vehicle for pursuing a fairly radical ambition on behalf of Lebanese NGOs – that of bringing together various confessional groups to create a viable foundation for a reconstituted civil society.

LNF formation

One of the most intensive periods of fighting in the war was in 1985–87 when some 750,000 people were displaced, plunging the already overstretched NGO community into crisis. Previously, many local NGOs could raise money within their communities and were often entirely self-sufficient. Now the tables had turned; they needed desperately to attract international funds but few knew how best to go about it. For its part, the CDL-ONG was well prepared because its membership was dominated by the larger foreign NGOs. For reasons explained above, however, the CDL-ONG represented a 'constituency of need' rather than a membership base. As such, it was unable to promote a cross-sectoral, inter-NGO programme.

---

13. For example, Mohanna shared a platform with Ghassan Sayah at the Canada-Middle East Working Group meetings, Ottawa, June 1993. His papers, such as 'The role of NGOs in Lebanon: Experiences in war time', 1992, have always acknowledged LNF as the important 'other' NGO coordination body.

By contrast, the LNF could, by 1988, demonstrate a tenuous but growing membership base. The momentum was sustained through active support extended by ICVA through its Working Group on the Middle East. ICVA's value here was not in cash terms but in the linkage it provided to the international community and in the experience it could lend to the formation of the LNF as a viable institution.

In March and September 1988, the LNF participated in ICVA meetings in Rome and Geneva. These meetings, plus the inter-agency mission to Lebanon in January 1989, provided the LNF with much-needed international exposure. The diplomatic campaign culminated in an LNF meeting with the UN Secretary-General in Geneva in April 1989 where it pleaded for active UN initiatives to alleviate continuing suffering in Lebanon.

Sectarian versus non-sectarian

The one fundamental issue that continued to inhibit support for the LNF was its identification with confessional groups. Deeply embedded sectarian and ethnic divisions in the country were bound to be reflected in its institutions. The question for international donors was whether to accept and work within such divisions or to form partnerships, only with those few non-sectarian organisations which claimed to represent the 'new' Lebanon.

Several arguments were raised against providing support to separatist or confessional NGOs. By either deliberate or *de facto* discrimination, a separatist NGO might seriously deprive members of another – but locally weaker – minority. Moreover, a level of social control implicit in long-established confessional social services may not only advance the interests of a particular ethnic/religious group but may also inhibit innovative methods in how to deal with a particular social problem.

In 1988, the Swedish NGO, Diakonia, became the first international donor to LNF, with institutional support provided through ICVA. This was contentious. An ICVA meeting in Geneva in October 1988, attended by LNF, saw a clear division of opinion on the matter. Nederlandse Organisatie voor International Ontwikkelingssamenwerking (NOVIB) and Oxfam-UK were unhappy about ICVA's association with an inter-confessional group and advised against ICVA sending a mission to Lebanon at that time. With support from some 35 other agencies, however, the ICVA mission went ahead, though the ramifications of this disagreement are still being dealt with today.

The LNF membership by 1989 comprised 13 NGO umbrella agencies. Of these, two were Shiite, two were Sunnite, one was Druze, five were Christian (including one Maronite, two Greek Orthodox and one Catholic) and three were non-confessional. Since each member had a constituency of community-based organisations and smaller NGOs, the

LNF could claim a substantial national coverage of NGO interests. It could not, however, avoid being tarred with the confessional brush.

It is instructive to look at one of LNF's members as an example of how opinions were divided on this issue. The Social Welfare Institutions/Islamic Orphanages (SWI), a Sunnite NGO founded in 1917, provided residential care for over 4,500 orphans, physically and mentally handicapped and elderly persons in 15 homes throughout Lebanon. They were seen as rather Dickensian in the eyes of, for example, Save the Children Fund, for they presented a paternalistic, institutionalised approach to social care, very much at odds with the community integration approach of standard development textbooks.

Yet these institutions were a reflection and integral part of Lebanese Sunnite thinking for generations; though willing to consider innovation, the SWI could not change its approach overnight. Moreover, there was an established link between the organisation and its constituency that transcended a mere donor-recipient relationship. This was consolidated during the war, particularly in the face of opposition from the militia. At that time, Beirut was a mosaic of fiefdoms where the militia each represented a 'state within a state'. Although they maintained various social services themselves, these were for the most part a political tactic to enhance the status of the militia. Food and medicine may have been provided as a matter of necessity but meanwhile war was being prosecuted by the militia; they were persecutors as well as latter-day providers.

If power was in the hands of the militia, influence was still very much in the hands of traditional heads of communities and their welfare institutions. Indeed, the families of the militia themselves depended on these social services. In this important respect, there was a *modus vivendi* between militia and traditional-confessional NGOs which was to act as a constraint to further intercommunal violence. However, the overlap of personalities, politics, welfare and religion created an enviable, though almost impenetrable, cohesion that foreign NGOs and their satellite agencies were unlikely to replace.

Several international donors would not, as a matter of principle, support sectarian groups, no matter how impressive their community outreach. They argued that the institutionalisation of separatism, whether categorised in terms of income, class, colour or creed, was itself divisive, representing precisely the cause of Lebanon's ruin (see, for example, *Karam, 1991*).

A full treatment of confessionalism in the Lebanese context would require an operational definition of 'secular' NGOs. Few international donors troubled themselves in this respect. For example, Secours Populaire (SP), one of the larger NGOs in Lebanon, has been treated as a secular agency; but could a social action committee of a political party be considered a 'secular' NGO in the European sense? The SP is organically part of the Lebanese Communist Party. Similarly, the

Kamal Joumblatt Foundation relates to the Progressive Socialist Party. Interestingly, both these NGOs have been funded by donors who fought shy of 'confessionalism'.

The LNF has argued that confessionalism is not inherently conservative or exclusive. Indeed, as an inter-confessional umbrella group, it could be argued that it has done more than most to bring together otherwise exclusive communities. Working through the LNF had several advantages for donors and members alike:

- it could assure equal and unbiased distribution of resources to all members and their confessions;
- it 'absolved' donors of the responsibility of choosing between confessions; and
- the programmes it promoted allowed difficult moral dilemmas within the confessional communities to be deflected in favour of the 'common good'.

For these reasons, the LNF argued that it was a fundamentally progressive association.

Consolidation of the LNF

By 1988, there had developed a general climate of dissatisfaction among certain Lebanese NGOs towards international donors. This was in part because only a handful of Lebanese organisations had reaped the benefit of substantial funds over the years. In the exceptional circumstances of war, a small 'NGO elite' had emerged which had become subject to priorities and operational methods not of their own making.

When Ghassan Sayah of the YMCA began lobbying for the formation of the LNF, he was an outspoken critic of foreign NGOs. He claimed that no initiatives were introduced by foreign NGOs that were not already in place via local NGOs. Yet rather than identify the institutional needs of existing NGOs, these foreign 'experts' pronounced on the needs of the country as a whole and mobilised funds for a preferred coterie of NGOs of their choosing. Although the YMCA was perhaps closer than most to foreign thinking and methods, it had no structure for lobbying on behalf of local NGOs – 'the field was ours, the international scene was theirs'.[14]

In contrast to CDL-ONG, the LNF excluded foreign NGOs from its membership from the outset. Its international 'link' was through ICVA. Membership criteria were based on size and geographical scope, denomination and the commitment and influence of the NGO's representative. The 13 members who eventually comprised LNF could

---

14. Interview with Ghassan Sayah, 25 May 1993. The UNDP *did* draft a programme of institutional support to indigenous NGOs but, to the author's knowledge, by 1993 this had still to be implemented.

boast a sizeable output of services on a national scale. By 1992 their combined budgets were more than US$40 million.[15]

Gradually the LNF became an important political lobby. In February 1991, it organised a national conference on Lebanon's social needs that was attended by senior government officials, the UN and several international and national NGOs. Following meetings with the president and prime minister in the same year, the LNF developed a national programme for Lebanon's displaced population and went on to form a joint committee with the Council for Development and Reconstruction (CDR), the government's planning body. In October 1991, a further conference was called – 'The Government's Role and the Role of NGOs in Building the Modern State' – in which the government was challenged to coordinate more closely with the organisations of civic society (*LNF, 1992a*).

Political sensitivities precluded the LNF from working through an independent administration in the early years. The members preferred to lend staff time to basic chores and where representation was required, this was done by the Chief Executive Officers of the various members. Administrative and legal affairs were initially the responsibility of the YMCA. The General Assembly of 13 members met at least four times a year and the Board of Directors comprised six member representatives meeting once a month.

By 1992, the number of LNF activities had grown sufficiently for it to need a full-time secretariat. The membership dues covered core costs while project costs (including administration overheads) were met by several international donors including Diakonia, Danish Refugee Council, CIMADE, UN High Commissioner for Refugees (UNHCR), Canadians for Education, Development and Reconstruction (CEDRI) and Norwegian Human Rights Fund. The two years budget for 1991–92 was US$898,180.[16] The LNF found separate office accommodation and took on three full-time staff but by mid-1993 was still looking for an Executive Director.

Relations with the government

The peculiar nature of the Lebanese state that imparts a high degree of legal and social autonomy to the various religious confessions has ensured that the government's role has been curbed in all areas except the management of public utilities and major infrastructural services including education and internal security. The war years were characterised by a gradual erosion of government authority. Bolstered by the 1990 Taef agreement, the new government began by concentrating mainly on major reconstruction programmes.

---

15. This is the combined budget of ten of the 13 LNF members. The other three budgets were not made available to the author
16. The bulk of this was for the LNF's Reconstruction and Rehabilitation project line (*LNF, 1992c*).

At the end of the war, the only social programme actively under government consideration was the problem of the displaced and the need for a resettlement plan. In 1991, a new Ministry of the Displaced was created. It set about forming a nationwide pyramid structure of committees from village up to national level.

The National Council of the Displaced, the final level, held its first conference in June 1992 to which the LNF, CDL-ONG and several national NGOs were invited. Although some US$12 million were raised through the NGOs, most government officials were worried about using the larger NGOs as implementors. They pointed to inter-NGO rivalries, poor coordination and the low absorption capacity of most NGOs; often local NGOs (ie community-based organisations) were the government's preferred channels for this programme. To the extent that national NGOs were to be used, the new Ministry highlighted the necessity for appropriate training of their personnel and a greater degree of sectoral coordination.[17]

In August 1991, the LNF began developing a pilot project for the return of the displaced to six villages in various parts of Lebanon. The LNF's government counterpart was changed, however, which due to political changes (the creation of a National Council for the Displaced in early 1992 and of the Ministry for the Affairs of the Displaced in late 1992), explains, in part, delays in the project's implementation. It was still incomplete by 1993.

Most government officials demonstrated their willingness to develop joint programmes with NGOs, yet tensions were never far beneath the surface. This was partly due to a perceived relationship between NGOs and the militia during the war that the government now wished to supplant. It was also a recognition that government must compete with NGOs for meagre international resources. The instruments of potential 'control' – registration, government coordination committees – were, in turn, regarded with deep suspicion by the NGO community.

The LNF programme

Since 1991, the LNF's work has concentrated on three main themes:

1. Rehabilitation of members' institutional capacities;
2. A migration project incorporating refugee/displaced services and legal aid; and
3. A training and public information campaign around designated issues.

In 1989/90, the Swedish funding agency, Diakonia, channelled grants totalling US$620,000 through LNF for an emergency assistance pro-

---

17. Interview with Kemal Feghali, Advisor to the Ministry of Social Affairs and the Ministry of the Displaced, 28 May 1993.

gramme carried out by 15 Lebanese NGOs. The money was primarily to help 1400 families, children and infants displaced by the war (*LNF, 1990*).

Again in 1991, Diakonia provided a further US$709,690 to LNF for an integrated emergency assistance programme. This was later supplemented by smaller grants from other foreign donors (the combined grants from six other international donors totalled US$87,741 and membership dues amounted to US$61,228).[18] The programme activities were divided as follows:

Institutional rehabilitation
LNF member NGOs were selected for assistance according to the degree to which their operational centres were damaged during the war. The LNF executive committee reviewed plans presented by the members and assigned sub-grants accordingly. The money was used for a wide range of repairs to hospital equipment, offices, residential camps, schools and orphanages. Often, the NGO in question would also receive additional grants from other donors (*LNF, 1992b*). Besides the obvious material benefits of the programme, it was an important test of unity for the LNF membership and an exercise in equitable distribution of funds across confessional lines.

Training seminars and conferences
National conferences with high attendance from government, UN and NGO officials have attracted prestige and funding for the LNF and helped it to establish an agenda for future action as a coordinating body. In collaboration with the International Management and Training Institute (IMTI), the LNF in 1992 organised a conference and two seminars around the issue of NGO training (*LNF, 1992b*). In the same year, it also undertook a survey of NGO salaries in Lebanon.

In November 1992, the LNF, in collaboration with ICVA, organised a unique Children's Conference. It brought together more than 200 children aged between 10 and 18 from all confessions and backgrounds, facilitated a free expression of their wishes and set priorities with respect to the children's place within the post-war country. It was arguably one of the LNF's most successful events to date in terms of participation, output and public relations (*LNF, 1992d*).

Migration Unit Project (MUP)
This ambitious project was launched in 1990 and, with start-up funds from the Danish Refugee Council, began in 1991. The MUP was 'a framework for developing, implementing and evaluating' (*LNF, 1991*) projects related to refugees, displaced, undocumented and stateless persons in Lebanon. It rested on four main elements:

1. a legal advice and aid scheme, especially for stateless and undocu-

---

18. Information provided to the author by LNF's accountant, June 1993.

mented persons;
2. a series of refugee-specific emergency and development projects;
3. assessment of individual cases of persons seeking asylum abroad; and
4. an information and documentation scheme.

The autonomy of each module made it possible to seek funding and carry out the various projects separately. The LNF was initially disconcerted by poor funding and inconsistent levels of interest by its partners abroad (*LNF, 1992b*). In 1991, the Danish Refugee Council, Diakonia, Norwegian Human Rights Fund and UNHCR began funding the MUP. These were later joined by the European Community (through CIMADE) and the Church of Sweden in 1992. The first year's budget was for US$244,000, of which only about 50 per cent was received (*LNF, 1991*).

Achievements of the MUP

What was achieved, however, was an interesting interplay between the LNF as field-based 'agitators for change' on the one hand and the Government of Lebanon, international governments and foreign NGOs on the other. In a highly charged political atmosphere, the issue of Lebanon's 750,000 displaced people – and the propensity of many to leave the country, though the fighting had stopped – had become a *cause célèbre* for a handful of NGOs pressing for action. The Lebanese government was preoccupied with political and security issues at a time when the mechanisms for regulating emigration had completely broken down. Similarly, the breakdown of procedures regarding the integration of refugees from ethnic and religious minorities in the hinterland left tens of thousands of undocumented and stateless persons with no alternative but to seek asylum abroad. Finally, international governments themselves were repatriating some asylum seekers without full knowledge of the situation in Lebanon and without a thorough assessment procedure.

The LNF tackled the issue in several ways. At an international level, it established links with NGOs in countries of asylum and attempted, case by case, to bring local conditions to the attention of immigration authorities. It also established an important linkage between local NGOs, their constituencies, UNHCR and IOM, and countries of asylum. This module of the MUP has been slow, complex and dependent on skilled staff that, by the end of 1992, the LNF was still seeking.

The information and documentation module of the MUP has been more successful, particularly with the partnership established between LNF and UNHCR. In January 1992 the LNF was commissioned by UNHCR to conduct a survey and put forward recommendations for Lebanon's 114,000 persons who lack protection because they have no official residential status. The survey (followed by a series of open conferences) has fed into the government's 'Draft Law on Nationality'. The LNF continued to promote this and other programmes through an information system that included a database and a regularly produced magazine, *Ebb and Flow*, distributed locally and abroad.

The Legal Aid module of the MUP has also been an opportunity for the LNF to explore closer collaboration with UNHCR. Thousands of people displaced by the war have returned to find themselves stripped of their own legal status and their rights to evacuated property. There is a great need for legal assistance in submitting applications to the courts and other authorities. Many poorer families can afford neither the legal representation nor the ubiquitous bribery. In 1992, the LNF established a relationship with the Beirut Bar Association with a view to creating a Public Defender Service and Legal Aid Fund to be used by those (particularly the stateless) unprotected by existing laws. The strategy was to develop a transitional or *de facto* recognised status that guaranteed social, economic and cultural rights to the vulnerable groups.

With encouragement and funding from UNHCR, the LNF had, by 1993, established itself as the only organisation in Lebanon dealing with these matters consistently. The Legal Aid programme had several positive repercussions. As the first project ever carried out by the Bar Association in cooperation with NGOs, it showed the important role the latter could play in reinstalling democratic institutions in the country and in raising the profile of human rights issues. At a time when Lebanon had yet to ratify the 1951 Refugee Convention and its 1967 Protocol, it also presented a public forum in which the government could be challenged to live up to the spirit of these international instruments of protection.

Approximately 80 per cent of Lebanon's displaced people are Christian. To avoid future conflict, their return, the LNF insisted, should be promoted by an intercommunal body in which human rights and the instruments of law are common property. The LNF consensual approach would also avoid opposition to 'western' legal systems; in turn, the process would lead towards the depolarisation of society through a specific programme of action.[19]

The Israeli attack of July 1993

From 25–31 July 1993, an unexpectedly fierce Israeli attack on Southern Lebanon caused widespread destruction of property, an estimated 128 persons killed, 470 wounded and approximately 250,000 displaced (*Carragher, 1993*). Population displacement was, in fact, an acknowledged political strategy and military tactic by Israel in this well planned exercise. The results were widely publicised in the international media.

---

19. Interview with Attorney Georges Assaf, President of the Beirut Bar Association Legal Aid Commission and Advisor to the LNF, 29 May 1993.

The rapidity of events and the necessity for immediate response challenged all agencies' (government, multilateral and NGO) commitment to and capacity for coordinated action. The government's High Relief Committee invited the Lebanese Red Cross, LNF, Caritas-Lebanon, the Middle East Council of Churches, CDL-ONG and Mouvement Social to coordinate their emergency activities through the committee. The LNF was elected to take the lead-agency role in developing and carrying out an inter-NGO emergency relief programme for 40,000 children under two years of age who were displaced or found in zones of conflict. In addition, the LNF with SP began an immediate field survey to identify temporary shelter centres. By 2 August, distribution of relief items began to 1300 children. In the same week the LNF launched an international appeal for US$3.6 million to support their programme for three months. Simultaneous appeals were coordinated through the High Relief Committee and the United Nations.

A three-day visit in August by the UN's Under-Secretary-General for Humanitarian Affairs, Mr Jan Eliasson, was concluded with the launch of a UN inter-agency appeal for US$29 million. In several meetings in Beirut, Eliasson stressed the pivotal role played by the NGOs in responding quickly to the disaster. That the LNF was entrusted with coordinating part of the general relief strategy was noted (*LNF, 1993*).

CONCLUSION

The Lebanese NGO community is undergoing a gradual shift towards modernity as it seeks more inventive ways of achieving financial stability. Its central position in civil society has tended to intensify debates with a still weak government; the type and nature of NGO relations with a stable government have yet to be worked out. Meanwhile, growth of the NGO sector will be increasingly contingent upon a fundraising base within the population. Principal NGOs are no longer simply 'client' agencies of foreign donors; they have, especially in the last three years, reasserted their strength as key actors in the country's development. In pitting themselves against what they perceive as the cynicism of foreign donors, they have refused to become hostage to the fluctuating fortunes of external benefactors.

In the socially and politically charged atmosphere during and immediately after the war, there was a high degree of 'impression management' by NGO leaders, rarely backed by achievements on the ground. The lack of government supervision left the field open for big talkers. Some emperors outlived their empires; as former sectarian community leaders or aspiring politicians, they could hide behind an NGO mask while watching the political fallout of the post-war years.

A clearer picture will emerge once Lebanese NGOs accept greater transparency and accountability, to a large extent a product of upgrading professional staff. Some smaller secular agencies have been ahead of the field in this respect but their approaches are unsystematised. It has fallen to the coordinating bodies to develop systematic training programmes for their members. The LNF has undoubtedly been the most useful forum in this respect, with a well-established conference programme and links with multilateral and government bodies.

The LNF has not, however, entirely overcome the 'talk shop' mentality of some of its members. There are several structural weaknesses in its development:

- It has no specific structures for sectoral coordination or for developing joint guidelines in health, education, etc;
- In so far as it is a loose cross-confessional alliance, it has no mechanism for establishing standards of development practice as such;
- Cooperation with the government, UN and others has rested on personal contact and individual projects;
- There have been few formal structures demanded; and
- The quest for consensus and unity of its membership has led to the avoidance of some issues that might have been tackled by a more progressive alliance.[20]

To its credit, the LNF has concentrated on developing political and humanitarian 'space' for NGOs by highlighting specific problems in high-profile fora such as national and international conferences. In doing so, it has broken through the confessional impasse that has created so much divided opinion both at home and abroad. The LNF has become an attractive option, an acceptable intermediary. Its success is still, however, closely tied to political developments in the country as a whole. The Taef agreement was essentially an international contract designed to serve regional interests. As a transitional mechanism, it has not addressed the fundamental sectarian nature of national politics.

The challenge for the LNF is to assemble a sufficiently large cross-section of civil society to create a useful lobby for social policy based on participation and equal opportunity. The challenge is not purely at a governmental level; after 17 years of bloodshed, very few institutions are capable of laying the foundations of national reconciliation. With a foot in many confessional camps, the LNF has begun to break down some barriers.

---

20. The Forum is not, for instance, in a position to tackle the issue of integration of Palestinians in Lebanon – which would undoubtedly be opposed by most of its members. With regard to those Palestinians who arrived after 1949, Lebanon considers that it is the international community, or their original country of asylum (Jordan, Syria, Egypt & Occupied Territories) that has the primary responsibility to protect them. For its part, the Forum upholds the right of return, which is the Arab and PLO political position within the on-going peace process. Palestinians are, for instance, included in the Legal Aid programme.

As 'survivors' of the conflict, Lebanese NGOs are uniquely placed to speak for a disengaged polity. At a time of confessional conflict and internecine warfare it was the NGOs alone that provided continuity and a degree of common bonding among communities otherwise torn apart. It remains to be seen whether the LNF can build on this reputation and help forge a social contract from the principles of humanitarianism while establishing the pivotal role of NGOs in the country as a whole.

ACRONYMS AND ABBREVIATIONS

CBOs	Community Based Organisations
CEDRI	Canadians for Education, Development and Reconstruction
CDL-ONG	La Coordinator des ONG en Vue du Developpment au Liban
CDR	Council for Development and Reconstruction
CRS	Catholic Relief Services
ICRC	International Committee of the Red Cross/Crescent
ICVA	International Council of Voluntary Agencies
IFAL	International Fund for the Assistance of Lebanon
IMTI	International Management and Training Institute
IPF	Indicative Planning Figure
LNF	Lebanese NGO Forum
MECC	Middle East Council of Churches
MSL	Mouvement Social Libanais
MUP	Migration Unit Project
NOVIB	Nederlandse Organisatie voor Internationale Ontwikkelingssamenwerking
OSS	Office for Social Solidarity
PLO	Palestine Liberation Organisation
PVOs	Private Voluntary Organisations
SP	Secours Populaire
SWI	Social Welfare Institutions/Islamic Orphanages
UNARDOL	United Nations Coordinator of Assistance for Reconstruction and Development of Lebanon
UNDP	United Nations Development Programme
UNDRO	Office of the United Nations Disaster Relief Coordinator
UNIFIL	United Nations Interim Force in Lebanon
UNRWA	United Nations Relief and Works Agency for Palestinian Refugees in the Near East
USAID	United States Agency for International Development
YMCA	Young Men's Christian Association

REFERENCES

Carragher, D (1993) 'Humanitarian Issue Brief', report to donors, unpublished, Beirut

Instituto del Tercer Mundo (1992) *Third World Guide, 93/94* ITEM, Colombia

Karam, A (1991) *A Comprehensive Report on NGOs in Lebanon*, UNDP, Beirut

LeRoy, Bennett (1991), *International Organizations* Prentice-Hall, New Jersey

LNF (1990), 'Final Statement of Income, June 30, 1990', auditor's report; LNF, Beirut

LNF (1991) 'Migration Unit Project', proposal circulated in 1991,LNF, Beirut

LNF (1992b), *Report on the Lebanese NGO Forum's Achievements During 1991* LNF, Beirut

LNF (1992) 'Emergency Assistance Program – Lebanon 1991/92', submitted to Diakonia by the LNF, unpublished

LNF (1992b) 'LNF Proposed Plan for 1992', LNF, Beirut

LNF (1992d) 'Lebanon Children's Conference, Final Report', LNF, Beirut

LNF (1993) 'Migration Unit Situation Report No 2', 11–17 August 1993

Mardelli-Assaf, M (1988) 'Economic and Social Cost of the War in Lebanon', Beirut, unpublished

Mardelli-Assaf, M (1993) 'On the Way to the Right to Development', commissioned report for UNDP, Beirut

Mohanna, K (1991a) 'The Role of NGOs in Lebanon, Experiences in Wartime', occasional paper, Beirut, unpublished

Mohanna K (1991b) 'Non-Governmental Organisations in Lebanon', Beirut, unpublished

OECD (1988), *Lebanon*,OECD, Paris

Tag-Eldeen, M (1992) 'Management and Resettlement of Internally Displaced in Lebanon', UNDP/OPS mission report, Beirut

UNDP (1990) 'A Comprehensive Report on Non-Governmental Organisations in Lebanon', UNDP, Beirut

UNDP (1991a) 'Lebanon, 1991 Report', UNDP, Beirut

UNDP (1991b) 'Institutional Development of Non-Governmental Organizations', Project Proposal LEB/90/002, UNDP, Beirut

UN General Assembly (1991) *Assistance for the reconstruction and development of Lebanon* Report of the Secretary-General, UN, New York

UN Lebanon (1992) *The United Nations System in Lebanon* UN, Beirut

YMCA Lebanon (1993) 'Medical Assistance Program, 1992–1993', YMCA, Beirut

7

CENTRAL AMERICA: NGO COORDINATION IN EL SALVADOR AND GUATEMALA 1980–94

Alun Burge

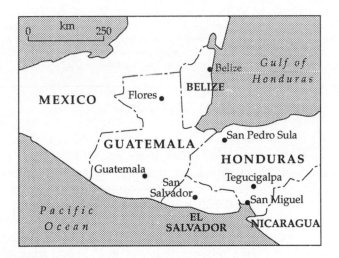

El Salvador

The People: Population: five million. Almost 90 per cent of the population are mixed descendants of American natives and Spanish colonizers. The remainder are indigenous and European.

The Government: Alfredo Cristiani, president since 1989, leads the nationalist Republican Alliance (ARENA)

Development Aid: US$446 million (1989); US$87 per capita; 7.6 per cent of GNP.

Guatemala

The People: Population: nine million. Approximately 70 per cent are of Mayan descent, the remainder being of European origin.

The Government: José Serrano Elías elected President in 1991.

Development Aid: US$256 million (1989); US$29 per capita; 3.1 per cent of GNP.

Central America has suffered a series of crises for the last 15 years. Conflicts arising from injustice have resulted in nearly 1.3 million refugees and 1.5 million internally displaced in the region as a whole. Each country has been affected in different ways. NGO experience also varies considerably according to the different historical, cultural and political contexts. In El Salvador, for instance, NGO coordination has generally worked well, both between organisations and in relation to the churches and organisations of the uprooted population. A positive dialogue and collaboration developed between national and international networks, such as ICVA. Various attitudinal and internal organisational factors ensured the success of such endeavours.

In Guatemala, collaboration between the uprooted population and NGOs is more recent. COINDE, a national coordination body, was established in 1976. To facilitate returnees from Mexico and other neighbouring countries, a new body, Coordination of NGOs and Cooperatives Accompanying the Population Affected by the Internal Armed Conflict (COORDINACION), was formed in 1992. At a regional level, ARMIF (Regional Association of NGOs Working on Forced Migrations), formed in 1990, ensures a forum for dialogue between these and other countries and has become the regional NGO voice with UNHCR and governments. Through this and its local variants, NGOs have developed from being simple executors of projects to being important lobbying platforms and instigators of national policy development.

BACKGROUND

At the end of the 1970s and throughout the 1980s the countries of Central America experienced severe internal conflicts. These conflicts were rooted in 'social injustice, political intolerance, repression, authoritarian practices and the exhaustion of the economic model...' (*Homero Mendez Angel, 1992*). Central America became one of the regions in the world that suffered most from forced migrations as a result of scorched earth, low intensity and counter insurgency warfare. All eight countries between Panama and Mexico were affected, though each in a different way. Approximately 1.5 million people became internally displaced and a further 1.3 million became refugees, only about 100,000 of whom were officially recognised as such (*Homero Mendez Angel, 1992*). Most of the officially recognised refugees left *en masse* in relatively short periods and were concentrated in camps (*Sergio Aguayo Quezada, forthcoming*).

The majority of the 2.8 million uprooted people were from El Salvador, Guatemala and Nicaragua, which between them had a combined population of around 15 million. A major 1991 study of forced migrations in Central America found that Mexico, Costa Rica and Honduras were the most important recipients, although all countries, including those expelling people, accepted refugee populations (*Pacheco & Sarti, 1991a*).

For over a decade humanitarian organisations have been responding to these national and regional crises. Churches, national and international NGOs have been working with the uprooted populations. Responses have varied in relation to each country's experience. Here, I shall look primarily at El Salvador where, by 1994, the emer-

146

gency phase was essentially completed and where the organisations' work was regarded as successful. I shall also look at Guatemala where organisational collaboration on behalf of the uprooted populations was, in 1994, still relatively new. In so doing, I shall contrast organisational experiences in countries where the uprooted populations were largest. I shall also review aspects of regional coordination. Even with such small neighbouring countries, each experience was unique, so I make no claim to have covered the whole of the Central American experience.

One issue that will not be addressed is the role played by political organisations and their relations with NGOs. In El Salvador there were regular assertions that NGOs were aligned to the Farabundo Martí Front for National Liberation (FMLN), a charge that may have had considerable implications for their work. With such a heavily polarised situation, both during and after the civil war, it is unrealistic to expect NGOs to have maintained complete independence. However, in the still extremely politicised atmosphere of El Salvador, a rigorous discussion of such issues is not possible here.

By contrast, NGOs in Guatemala were not politically aligned in any way; indeed, they have rigorously maintained the principle that humanitarian work should be undertaken without interference. Even so, NGO workers have had to contend with difficult political conditions which, in some cases, remain a potential threat to their personal security.[1]

I shall examine some aspects of NGO coordination in El Salvador and Guatemala while taking into account the various roles of government, UN High Commissioner for Refugees (UNHCR), grassroots organisations and churches.

EL SALVADOR

Throughout the 1980s a civil war was waged in El Salvador. The violence uprooted more than a million people, which represented 25–29 per cent of the population, particularly from the countryside (*Sergio Aguayo Quezada, forthcoming*). The worst affected areas were those where the FMLN was strongest and which were subjected to all-out assault by the army. The military sought to de-populate much of the countryside by invasion or bombing. Many massacres took place. About 50,000 people became internally displaced and neighbouring countries received hundreds of thousand of refugees, the vast majority of whom were not documented. The uprooted peoples, who later repatriated, can be divided into four categories (*after Schrading, 1990*):

---

1. For instance, internationally respected NGO workers, such as Myrna Mack of AVANCSO, have been killed simply for researching the plight of the uprooted population.

1. Those who dispersed and were atomised, unorganised and often went to urban areas;
2. The displaced who went to internal refuges run by the churches;
3. Refugees who went mainly to camps in Honduras (to these should be added those who went to other neighbouring countries such as Panama and Nicaragua); and
4. Those people who remained permanently displaced, moving from one location to another.

People fleeing army raids in the countryside took refuge in churches, sometimes for an entire year, with the army surrounding their refuges. The few civilians who remained in conflict zones lived in very precarious conditions. It was in such circumstances that the uprooted populations began to organise themselves.

The response: organisation, resettlement and return

The hardship visited upon the uprooted population also severely disrupted those social organisations which might otherwise have been expected to support them. Only the Church and related organisations felt capable of assuming a role of support and protection, often themselves having to suffer for the consequences. NGOs were unable to work openly, since the scope for humanitarian work (also referred to as 'humanitarian space') did not exist.[2] Many went into exile and continued their support from Mexico or elsewhere.

The churches insisted on the right to be involved. They set up refuges, provided protection and interceded with the Government. Significantly, the churches already had experience of working together. Schrading (*1990*) pays eloquent testimony to the work of both Catholic and Protestant churches. In 1983, a national ecumenical grouping called Diaconía was formed, and much of the work over the next five years was carried out under its aegis. Through its channels, resources from donor agencies were distributed to implementing organisations. It was this work that opened the strategically important first humanitarian space.

By the mid-1980s, some of those who stayed in the country had formed organisations such as the Christian Committee for the Displaced of El Salvador (CRIPDES) and the National Repopulation Coordination (CNR). CRIPDES attended to the general problems of the uprooted, while the CNR concentrated on the right to return to places of origin, resettlement and the reception of those returning. Strong refugee organisations also emerged in neighbouring countries.

From 1985, the internally displaced civilian population started to return to its places of origin. In some regions of the country, such as

---

2. The concept of 'humanitarian space' was a much-used term in Central America and has been explored in detail elsewhere (see, for example, *Eguizabal et al, 1993*).

northern Morazán, it was done quietly and in small numbers, while in Chalatenango and Guazapa such movements were openly organised, had a high profile and involved large numbers of people (*Schrading, 1990*). The army did not want them in the conflict zones, claiming that they were the social base of the guerrillas. By 1986, however, the civilian population had resisted army attempts to dislodge it and had asserted its right to live there. The army continued to harass them for years, including regularly destroying their crops.

The return of the internally displaced played an important role in reopening the conflict zones. It established the right of the civilian uprooted population to live in their places of origin. The international recognition gained was as important as the aid they also received. The resettlements also helped create the conditions for the return of larger groups of refugees from outside the country which began in 1987.

Returning refugees faced considerable difficulties, particularly delaying tactics from the Government and hostility and aggression from the army. The Government used bureaucratic red tape to make life more difficult for the returnees – for example, by withholding permissions to enter the country. The army stepped up its confrontation, denying access by blocking roads, arresting refugees and harassing returning communities by shooting at them as a part of its counter-insurgency strategy. As more returns took place, relations with the army became increasingly acrimonious.

A fundamental principle for the refugee organisations was that the returns should be collective and undertaken in large numbers. They were to be accompanied by national and international observers to guarantee their security. This sparked serious differences between government and refugees. The government applied pressure to try and make the refugees repatriate individually or gradually in small numbers. The refugees successfully rebuffed such pressures and over several years around 20,000 people returned on their own conditions, mainly from Honduras, and from other countries of the region.

A number of important factors helped the returns. A solid base of organisation and support was provided for the returning refugees by the prior return of internally displaced people. Fluid communication existed between the refugees, the displaced, the returnees and the churches. Moreover, large tracts of land were unoccupied in the return zones as a result of the conflict. They provided opportunity for the prompt subsistence of the returnees.

Regional accords

The return of the refugees was also facilitated by regional accords, a turning point for the uprooted populations. The 1987 *Esquipulas II* regional peace agreement recognised the refugees' right to return. The subsequent International Conference on Refugees, Displaced and Repatriates of Central America (CIREFCA) and the ensuing process provided an international forum for analysing, discussing and looking for solutions to the problems of forced migration. Through CIREFCA, UNHCR, governments, international donors and subsequently NGOs and organisations of the uprooted themselves were brought together.

CIREFCA's commitment to attending to refugee and displaced populations led to the development of principles and criteria for refugee returns. It also allowed the monitoring of changes in the circumstances of those who were uprooted. It further provided the context within which the work of the coming years would take place, both in El Salvador and elsewhere in the region. A political space was created for NGOs and refugees which helped them become independent actors, organised and able to negotiate with governments. Whereas earlier it was difficult to bring pressure on the government within the country because of the problems of repression, now CIREF-CA provided an international forum (*Homero Mendez Angel, 1992; interview Andres Gregori, February 1994*).

New NGOs

As a result of CIREFCA, a number of national NGOs were formed specifically to support the process of return to places of origin across the country. The new NGOs knew that they would have to fight for freedom of association as well as access to resources. The civilian population in the conflict zones was usually prepared to work with them as these organisations were considered co-participants not associated with counter-insurgency. The NGOs also brought important new extra organisational capacity to supplement that of the church and displaced and refugee groups.

Despite an initial tendency to compete for 'profile', NGOs soon began to work more closely together. Diaconía invited these new NGOs to meet and a new forum, the *Concertacion*, was established which coordinated the work of the six NGOs working with different groups of the uprooted population. The forum's collective role was essentially political, related closely to the country's changing circumstances. Members undertook to support one another – for instance, in pressuring the army to stop hindering their work.

The *Concertacion* quickly gained an international profile. Central to its success was its avoidance of negotiating finances jointly for the first years of its operation. The NGOs realised that haggling over money would prove divisive, so they determined to accentuate that which unified them.[3]

---

3. Not until 1992, as a part of the process of transition from a war society, did they sit down collectively and negotiate funding with the European Community (EC) – until then each had done it separately. With that experience and sufficient mutual trust, a number of joint financial negotiations subsequently took place with government and large aid organisations.

From the mid-1980s onwards, the EC funded the return and rein-tegration of the refugees. First through Diaconía and later through the new NGOs, many millions of dollars have been allocated to regenerate agriculture and social services. The Segundo Montes community, for instance, was anxious to use the skills accumulated while in Colomoncagua refugee camp in Honduras to break out of the cycle of subsistence agriculture and a number of small production units and workshops were established in a novel experiment. Significantly, nei-ther these populations, nor the NGOs with which they worked, would have a relationship with the US Agency for International Development (USAID), which they considered to be a part of the US/El Salvador Governments' counter insurgency strategy.[4]

The contribution of international agencies

Throughout the 1980s, there was close collaboration between a small group of international agencies. Within the country they were known as 'ICVA' (International Council of Voluntary Agencies), although ICVA affiliation was not a precondition of participation. These agen-cies included the Project Counselling Service for Refugees, Oxfam, the Jesuit Refugee Service, Catholic Relief Services, Lutheran World Federation and the Mennonites. For the first population return, joint planning took place with nationals and internationals sitting together planning the return, including budgets, reporting and organising accompaniment via delegations. After the first return, the work was less integrated with national organisations assuming greater responsi-bility for the return, and international agencies focusing on the dissemination of information, accompaniment and advocacy. International NGOs also supported projects with the uprooted popu-lations as well as the strengthening of indigenous organisations.

These levels of participation were only possible because of the deep respect and trust that existed between national and international representatives in grassroots organisations, churches and NGOs. All shared a clear perspective and knew how to relate to one another in a complementary manner. International agencies did not seek to occupy roles beyond those acceptable to national organisations, nor to replace national organisations. A fluid and effective relationship developed, which was to last for several years.

International NGOs had workers who had already gained valuable experience working with the Salvadoran refugee camps in Honduras. This gave them a continuity of experience when working inside El Salvador, in addition to a high level of understanding and commitment. They were able to relate effectively to UNHCR, and to apply pressure when necessary through the experience of providing protection in the

---

4. Since the 1992 national peace accords, most organisations have been prepared to consider collaborating with USAID.

refugee camps. For example, UNHCR originally wanted national organisations to work with the government on the returns. Diaconía did not agree, international NGOs supported them and their position prevailed.

Beyond the region, representatives of agencies in Europe visited the refugee camps, represented the interests of the displaced, etc, at international fora and were usually prepared to respond to needs as they arose. The joint agency information project referred to above, along with complementary work by the church and other networks, greatly facilitated the flow of information to Europe, North America and beyond. With the increasing return of refugees, international attention, accompaniment and funding increased, helping ward off the increased hostility from the army and the government. On many occasions the government or army had to ease their pressure on uprooted organisations, NGOs and agencies because of international attention.

The displaced and the refugees now accept that they asked a lot of the churches and international agencies up to the late 1980s when the new generation of NGOs began to provide support. Indeed, refugee and displaced organisations themselves were very adept at working through churches and NGOs and using them to gain greater 'space' for their freedom of action. The coherence of action by grassroots organisations, churches and NGOs can be attributed first to a shared perspective and tradition and, second, to a high quality of leadership.

UNHCR

The performance and perception of UNHCR changed considerably after the signing of the regional accords. Before then, it was regarded with some mistrust, particularly because of its inaction over internally displaced persons who were thus left entirely in the hands of NGOs and churches. UNHCR's mandate restricted its role, yet it changed considerably its stance and attitude towards the refugees when the *Esquipulas II* and CIREFCA processes gave it a basis and principles on which to act. UNHCR pressed the government and the army to allow the returns to take place. The more the army resisted and harassed the returning refugees, the more UNHCR lobbied. Within the government the uprooted population was not treated as a humanitarian issue, but as a matter of state security; UNHCR had to discuss refugees with the Ministry of the Interior.

Gradually, confidence in the UNHCR grew, not least because the agency agreed to accompany returnees all the way back to their destinations in El Salvador and not leave them at the frontier where their mandate ended. NGOs and refugees probably appreciated in retrospect that they demanded too much of UNHCR...'at the time with the anxiety, there was not the time to reflect that there is now. And we always asked more of ourselves than we did of them' (*Lorena Martinez interview, CRIPDES, February 1994*).

Over time, cooperation became close, and the relationship developed into one of trust including pooling information with the NGOs. UNHCR played a crucial role in facilitating the return of refugees with the government while working through NGOs as operational partners. Before the peace accords were signed, and within the CIREFCA process, UNHCR brought the government and NGOs together and coordinated a debate through the medium of technical proposals. As a representative of the *Concertacion* reflects: 'We sat down to negotiate with the Government before the FMLN did' (*Andres Gregori interview, February 1994*). After the event, it was often stated that the unique partnership that existed between NGOs, the population at risk and UNHCR should have been more closely evaluated and important lessons drawn from it.

A pronounced success

Overall, the coordination between all those engaged in humanitarian work in El Salvador was extremely good, in spite of adverse circumstances including increasingly intense opposition from the government and army. Much hard work was required to bring about the factors allowing for such close coordination. The conduct of the displaced and refugees themselves provided an enormous and continuing boost to the humanitarian endeavour (*Schrading, 1990*). The resettlement and return processes were always linked to the general situation in the country and the quality of the national organisations which supported these processes was high.

The role played by the church in supporting the population and keeping the 'humanitarian space' open despite considerable repression was vital, as was the maturity of the new NGOs in quickly consolidating themselves operationally and in gaining considerable political credibility. They quickly gained the trust of the displaced and refugees, helped by a shared political perspective. As both churches and NGOs were sophisticated in their international links they were also able to extract the maximum advantage from such links.

The Salvadoran NGOs perhaps made more of the opportunities available to them than any other NGOs in the region. The organisations showed a remarkable capacity to take advantage of the peace process and the end of the Cold War. In 1992, after the signing of the country's peace accords, proposals for presentation to the forthcoming CIREFCA follow-up conference were worked out jointly by the government and NGOs, something remarkable for a country which had been so divided.[5] The importance of such achievements was not lost on other countries.

---

5. Andres Gregori, head of FASTRAS, said '(the proposals) were more from the nation than the government' (interview, February 1994).

Conclusions

Humanitarian activity came to have profound political consequences in El Salvador. Activities among the returning displaced and refugee populations transformed the lives of those involved and helped shift the balance of Salvadoran society towards a more inclusive civil society that emerged after the war. As the emergency passed, with the signing of the 1992 Peace Accords, the experience gained by NGOs has set the foundations for the post-war transition and a new focus on reconstruction. Although the NGOs handled millions of dollars in the context of the war and emergency, they now face the much more complex task of planning and administering long term projects within the context of peace and development.

GUATEMALA

The demographic composition of Guatemala is starkly different from the other countries of Central America. The majority of the population is indigenous, with 22 distinct Mayan groups, each with its own language. It is this indigenous population which has been most subject to state violence. It has been estimated that the repression of the early 1980s caused around 75,000 deaths and disappearances, the destruction of 400 villages and the uprooting of more than one million people from the countryside. Of these, more than 200,000 became refugees including 46,000 officially recognised in camps. Between 1987 and 1992, approximately 8000 refugees returned under the government programme of individual repatriation. In 1992, the government estimated the figure for internally displaced to be 150,000 (*COINDE & COORDINACION, 1992; ICVA, 1993*).

In the late 1980s and early 1990s, the uprooted population inside and outside of Guatemala began to organise themselves. Officially recognised refugees in UNHCR camps in Chiapas, Campeche and Quintana Roo in Mexico formed the Permanent Commissions (PCs) in 1988. The dispersed non-recognised refugees in Mexico were brought together by ARDIGUA (the Association of Dispersed Refugees of Guatemala), which announced its existence in 1992. ARDIGUA faced a difficult task. It had 5000 families as members, perhaps 10 per cent of the total non-recognised population. Likewise, the national NGO, CONDEG (National Council of Displaced People), sought to organise the displaced inside Guatemala. Finally, in the more remote areas of northern Guatemala, organised communities of displaced people, called the Communities of Population in Resistance (CPR) existed in the most marginal conditions for over a decade. They refused to be incorporated into the army's counter-insurgency-inspired model hamlets, with their close controls and obligatory participation in the civil defence patrols (PACs). The CPRs made their existence known in 1991 and were aware that returning refugees and other displaced groups might create an opportunity for some form of social reintegration for themselves at a later stage.

The returns: problems and some responses

Both the PCs and ARDIGUA planned the return of people from their respective areas to places of origin where possible. In October 1992, the PCs signed an agreement with the government to allow a secure and dignified return. It was particularly significant because it was the first time that refugees had negotiated with their government directly and without intermediaries to facilitate a repatriation programme, culminating in a signed accord (*ICVA, 1993*). The agreement covered eight points including:

- the right to a collective and organised return;
- the right to free association, organisation and movement within the country;
- the right to national and international accompaniment;
- the right of access to land; and
- the establishment of a verification agency.

Returns under ARDIGUA were to take place within this agreement and be coordinated operationally with the PCs.

The PCs organised the first return in January 1993 when approximately 2500 people went to Poligono 14, which the refugees renamed 'Victory 20 January', in the Ixcan, Quiche. Others have happened subsequently and 20 more returns were in the pipeline in 1994. There were more than 20,000 refugees ready to return immediately, although this was likely to increase dramatically depending on the outcome of the return process.

The army was antagonistic towards the returns, seeking to agitate amongst the local population against the returning refugees. Indeed, in many of the communities there existed counter-insurgency-inspired and hostile PACs. Unlike El Salvador, there was almost no supportive and organised civilian population already awaiting the refugees. The PCs formally expressed their dissatisfaction over the government's failure to agree on the location of military bases, the formation of civil defence committees and the naming of military commissioners around the return sites.

The situation was further complicated by the lack of unoccupied tracts of land to which to return in Guatemala, in spite of signed agreements to the contrary. Even those refugees who owned lands before they had fled now found their lands occupied by others, often at the army's behest. Each resettlement thus involved a complex negotiation over land. Refugee land commissions visited Guatemala to try to ensure adequate land was available before each return took place.

Sectors of civil society were very badly affected by the repression of the early 1980s and remained weak in the 1990s. Eguizabal et al *(1993)*, say that only the churches (and the army) had maintained the capacity to organise social groups. While the situation eased somewhat by 1994, Guatemalan society remained comparatively closed with little opportunity for social organisation.

The depth of the repression in the early 1980s, reinforcing the experience of 500 years, caused the indigenous victims of violence to cling to survival by avoiding expressing their innermost feelings, except to those they trust most closely. This prevents an easy understanding of the issues pertinent to the people. The church – Catholic and Protestant – was probably better placed than most to deal with this level of communication and to assist where it could. The church played an important role in preparing for the returning population, raising general awareness in the population, accompanying returnees, collaborating in arranging documentation and providing legal and human rights support.

In contrast, most NGOs had no previous experience of working in the conflict zones or with the various displaced and refugee communities. Army hostility was such that working with the organisations of the displaced or other victims of the violence had been perceived as virtually impossible. Many NGOs were formed long before work with the refugees or displaced was contemplated *(AVANCSO-IDESAC, 1990)*; yet their work has been mostly in community development where their role was confined largely to that of intermediaries with grassroots communities which were not victims of violence. They were certainly not used to working with groups as well organised as the refugee and displaced organisations which had such a clear agenda. Nor were they accustomed to working in such a politicised arena.

Developing cooperation

A new organisation – Coordination of NGOs and Cooperatives Accompanying the Population Affected by the Internal Armed Conflict (COORDINACION) – of around two dozen organisations was established in 1992 to support the uprooted populations and in particular to prepare for the returns. It set up programmes in four areas relating to the return:

1. information, research and dissemination to keep national and international organisations up to date;
2. legal assistance and human rights programmes to train affiliates and the affected population to handle problems which they may confront;
3. public relations and lobbying; and
4. reinsertion and reintegration.

COORDINACION grew out of a national NGO coordination initiative,

COINDE, which was established in 1976. All members of COINDE were in COORDINACION, along with over a dozen others. COINDE had three areas of work: community development, foreign relations and refugees, displaced and returnees.

There was apparently considerable euphoria among the NGOs at the prospect of all working together to support the uprooted population. NGOs were to support the phases of settlement and reintegration and COORDINACION started with great expectations. Shared concerns around refugees and the displaced brought the various member organisations closer together.

However, the large numbers of NGOs involved and their heterogeneity made it hard to find common styles of work. Without a history of coordination, it would take time to develop cohesion and a collective identity. A study published in 1992 refers to institutional jealousies, with each NGO interested in maintaining the expansion of its programme, funding and geographical operations (*AVANCSO, 1992*). There was also some overlap in activities between the work of COINDE and COORDINACIO, with COINDE maintaining its own work on the uprooted, even though each member NGO was also a part of COORDINACION.

Undertaking humanitarian work had extremely serious implications in Guatemala. A series of death threats were made against organisations and individuals involved in the coordination of such work. This was not something to be taken lightly in a country where NGOs suffered assassinations and kidnapping in the 1980s and early 1990s. Mutual protection of the members of COORDINACION was, therefore, an essential part of the coordination and such menaces have helped bring the NGOs closer together. In this respect they also developed cooperation with the churches and with others under threat, such as journalists.

Relationships

Between refugees and NGOs
Relations between NGOs and refugee organisations in Guatemala were not straightforward. Refugee and internally displaced organisations working at grassroots level were overwhelmingly indigenous, while the NGOs attending them at intermediary levels were predominantly non-indigenous. Their linguistic and cultural differences – and the lack of shared traditions, religious or political – made links hard to establish. Even the rhythm – the perceptions of time – of the indigenous population was different from that of UNHCR, the international agencies and NGOs. Refugees in the camps in Mexico were isolated and contacts with NGOs and international workers were restricted by UNHCR and the Mexican government. This lack of knowledge and understanding of one another was further complicated by the organisation of the PCs into three *vertientes* – north, northwest and south –

157

each relating to one of the three geographical areas to which the refugees returned. While the PCs collectively attended to matters such as negotiations with the government, each *vertiente* dealt with its respective population to implement the returns. As the *vertientes* developed their own priorities and policies, the number of necessary relations to be handled by the NGOs multiplied.

Differences between the PCs and NGOs over work styles, approaches and interpretations soon came to the fore. An editorial in *Reencuentro*, the journal of COORDINACION, just after the first refugee return, reflected on the differences and called for a frank and open dialogue in March 1993. One issue was the balance in the relationship between NGOs and the refugee organisations. Should the relationship be horizontal or vertical? If vertical, who should be on top? How much independent scope should NGOs have to organise accompaniment as they see necessary, or to what degree should the refugee organisations determine its nature? Another key difference was the refugees' perception of the NGOs' wish to remain neutral and to provide support that was primarily technical. In general, the refugees demanded a greater commitment to their cause than that.

How the refugee organisations and NGOs would cooperate in the future was likely to vary depending on local circumstances. The lack of an overall operational agreement did not easily facilitate technical support. NGO coordination structures were modified to reflect better the specific support requested by the refugees. Those NGOs supporting a return to a particular geographical area worked in *ad hoc* groups. The local support group for preparation for the return to Nenton, for instance, included sections of the Catholic and Protestant churches, four NGOs affiliated to COORDINACION, plus the French agency, Médecins Sans Frontières.

COORDINACION did not aspire to a central coordination of NGO operations in the country as a whole. Instead, it focused on lobbying, dissemination of information and organising public fora. In the process, various practices were refined or changed as relationships between NGOs improved. The common commitment to work for the betterment of the uprooted populations ensured a continuing level of cooperation, though the process of building necessary bridges was slow.

Between international agencies and governments
Generally, contact between the uprooted populations and their international supporters was somewhat diffuse. The isolation of refugee camps in Mexico contributed to this, and it was reinforced by the comparative cultural and linguistic inaccessibility. The situation was further complicated by the geographical divisions within the PCs as each developed its own international contacts. The national NGOs which could have been expected to act as intermediaries were still developing their own

relationship with the uprooted organisations. More time was required for the development of understanding of what each could expect of the other and to allow the build-up of trust which was a pre-condition for effective relationships. Only then could international networks be fully mobilised. Such mobilisation was, however, undermined by the diminished capacity for lobbying that existed in the countries of the North. Events in Guatemala in 1994 were against a regional and world backdrop completely different from the late 1980s, and attention had undoubtedly moved away from Central America.

The CIREFCA process in Guatemala proved generally positive. NGOs participated in a four-way forum with the UNHCR and the governments of Guatemala and Mexico (something which was not achieved by their counterparts in El Salvador). Through an International Group to Consult on the Returns (GRICAR), four embassies and two international bodies supported the refugees and government as they discussed preparations for the returns. ICVA, as a member of GRICAR, played an important role in Guatemala, including the sending of a delegation in 1993.

Relations with the Guatemalan government were not good. In the first meeting of CIREFCA in 1989, the Guatemalan government sought the exclusion of the Guatemalan NGOs and argued against their legitimacy. In 1992, the refugees and the Guatemalan government signed an agreement covering the return. After the governmental changes of 1993 (when the former human rights ombudsman became President), the situation improved considerably for the refugees, although the Government remained hostile towards organisations of the displaced. The refugees were now able to have a useful dialogue with some government agencies, including the Special Commission for Attention to Repatriates (CEAR). The returns were being coordinated with CEAR and, in 1994, appeared to be going comparatively smoothly. Relations with UNHCR were generally good, with less criticism being expressed than was the case in El Salvador. COORDINACION was taken into account by both the UNHCR and government in workshops and analysis.

Conclusions

In 1994, the process of social reintegration was still new. Much had been learned since 1991 and considerable progress was recorded, not least because grassroots refugee organisations had become more sophisticated and had organised a number of successful collective and accompanied returns. NGOs accompanying returnees had also made significant improvements in their performances. For its part, COORDINACION made an impact internationally through lobbying, producing an effective journal and undertaking useful studies. The NGOs were now a more important voice in the country and were more willing to assume a higher profile in contributing towards the building of civil society in Guatemala than they were in the past. Perhaps this was their most substantial contribution to date, rather than their direct support to the returns. The coming together of churches, NGOs and grassroots organisations to address the social problems of Guatemala was an important development.

Despite important improvements, the persistence of many of the factors outlined above resulted in a less than optimum overview. The situation confronting Guatemalans was much more complex than in neighbouring countries. Moreover, until substantial advances in the national peace negotiations were made, the scope for more generalised change was likely to remain limited.

CENTRAL AMERICAN REGION

Until the late 1980s, the various national experiences had no regional expression or coherence. Polarisation within and between countries generally deterred inter-country contacts by grassroots organisations or NGOs as they aroused suspicion and invited repression. To some extent this vacuum was filled by international NGOs.

The agencies take the lead

From the early 1980s, international agencies had been concerned at the levels of suffering in Central America. Against the backdrop of counter-insurgency wars and the manipulation of displaced populations by the military, they began working with organisations in each country to develop a policy response to the needs of the region's displaced and refugee populations.

In 1983, a key conference in Switzerland, convened by ICVA, successfully pressed the UNHCR not to relocate the Salvadoran refugee camps in Honduras from their frontier locations. At the time, there was concern that UNHCR, in supporting such a move, might be submitting to the counter-insurgency plans of the US and Salvadoran governments. In the event, ICVA provided an important counterweight to the governments of El Salvador and the USA. It may also have helped UNHCR to acquire greater independence, be stronger in its relations with governments and more able to resist their pressure. Henceforth, ICVA had the respect of UNHCR and was thus treated more seriously.

Within the region, the ICVA sub-group on refugees played a strategic role in bringing together people from the various countries. Organisations which did not know one another, including many which were in exile, were able to meet. These meetings provided a unique opportunity to share experiences, come to common positions and then to lobby the UNHCR and donors. Without this forum, cross-country and regional collaboration would have been much more difficult. For nearly five years, until the late 1980s, the initiative on policy development and lobbying lay with international NGOs.

The balance shifts towards the NGOs

The signing of the *Esquipulas II* accords and the CIREFCA process changed the balance within the region. A flurry of activity followed nationally and regionally. New NGOs, new national coordinations and a regional coordination quickly emerged to work with the uprooted populations. The resulting 'humanitarian space' enabled NGOs to seize the initiative.

In March 1989, the move to set up a regional body was taken by a handful of national NGOs from across the region, an impetus provided by the First International NGO Conference on Central American Refugees, Displaced and Returnees in Mexico. NGO representatives determined that they should have the right to shape regional events, not just be invited to participate in them.

Two months later, in May 1989, three key NGO representatives in the region – Edwin Zablah of Fundacion Augusto César Sandino (FACS) in Nicaragua, Dimas Vanegas of Diaconía in El Salvador and a Guatemalan counterpart – went to the first CIREFCA meeting in Guatemala and set up a parallel office in an hotel to lobby for support. With Nordic backing, they persuaded CIREFCA to pass a resolution recognising the role of local NGOs working with the refugee organisations.

A regional network was set up which would later become ARMIF. With its formation, the initiative passed from international to local NGOs. ARMIF was formally constituted in February 1990. It then grew to include eight national coordination bodies from Mexico to Panama with around 90 NGO members. ARMIF's objective was to strengthen and coordinate NGO members that work with populations affected by the wars in the region. Its remit included:

- recognised and non-recognised refugees;
- the displaced;
- the demobilised;
- the disabled and economic migrants; as well as
- those who were able to return.

ARMIF sought to find solutions to the problems of these groups by working with them in organisation, education and training around development alternatives, self management, social justice and human rights. ARMIF's General Assembly met two to three times per year and the Executive, comprising four members elected by the Assembly, met three times per year.

National coordination mechanisms in Central America came from somewhat different backgrounds. Of the two highlighted here, *Concertacion* in El Salvador comprised a small number of organisations set up specifically to work with the uprooted populations while the COORDINACION in Guatemala was formed by a much larger number of NGOs and cooperatives already in existence. Models elsewhere included, for example, the Federation of NGOs in Nicaragua. *Concertacion* and the Federation were both national bodies belonging to ARMIF while, somewhat confusingly, for historical reasons COINDE in Guatemala, although being a member of COORDINACION was, in fact, itself the national arm of ARMIF. As COINDE also worked independently with refugees and the displaced, lines of communication were not always clear.

ARMIF was an important forum for interaction and a source of national and regional analysis. Its most far-reaching regional study was undertaken in 1991 accompanied by a regional action plan (*Pacheco & Sarti, 1991a and b*). More recently, an analysis of the UNHCR Rapid Impact Projects (PIR) was carried out by cross-regional working parties. ARMIF also provided a valuable forum for dialogue and inter-relationship between countries and for countries to discuss their shared problems and learn from one another. With international NGOs, it has helped both Guatemalan NGOs and refugee population leaders to exchange experiences with their Salvadoran counterparts. Costa Rican and Nicaraguan members of ARMIF soon began collaborating over the problem of the new wave of Nicaraguan economic refugees reaching Costa Rica. ARMIF tried to ensure that the issue of adequate attention to the internally displaced stayed on the international agenda.

Criticisms of ARMIF by its members included the charge that, like the international NGOs, it tended to focus too much on 'hot spots' – countries currently in the news – while neighbouring countries were given comparatively little attention. Thus, the focus was first Nicaragua, then El Salvador, then Guatemala. Interestingly, though, complainants often felt that ARMIF was more regionally focused when it was their own country assuming the leadership! Perhaps such complaints were inevitable given the decision to avoid creating a separate bureaucratic structure and instead bestow the leadership responsibility on one individual country at a time – often the one that has been the regional 'hot spot'. This pattern was ended in March 1994 when the Presidency was assumed by Nicaragua and the other officer posts passed to Costa Rica, Honduras and Belize.

ARMIF became important regionally as the voice of the Central American organisations in relation to the UN, the EU and the presidents of Central America and international governments. It, and its national bodies, became strong advocates on behalf of the affected populations. ARMIF's voice was also heard within the regional body of Central American NGOs, the *Concertacion Centroamericana de Organismos de Desarrollo*, to which it was affiliated.

Regional dynamics would change, but even when the CIREFCA process was to end, ARMIF and its national components were likely to retain their importance. By 1994, the scope of their work was already widening. Besides responding to the victims of violence in Guatemala and attending to the demands of reconstruction in El Salvador, the definition of the uprooted was now being extended to include ex-combatants. Furthermore, hundreds of thousands of Nicaraguan economic refugees were expected in Costa Rica as Nicaragua's dramatic economic deterioration continued. Having learned to respond to war-based emergencies, NGOs now had to respond to a 'permanent crisis'. The challenge for ARMIF was how to continue providing cross-regional support at a time when national agendas appeared to be more divergent than in the 1980s (*Gabriella Rodriguez interview, February 1994*).

UNHCR

The role of UNHCR regionally up to 1990 has already been studied in detail (*Pacheco and Sarti, 1991a*). UNHCR varied by country depending on the personalities of its functionaries and their appreciation of political processes underway. Across the region, UNHCR was generally regarded as having made a positive contribution. The CIREFCA process provided a unique political context which helped UNHCR build up relationships with NGOs and governments. Before CIREFCA, UNHCR seemed less approachable, but it soon was regarded as the UN agency to which grassroots groups and NGOs felt most able to relate. It was perceived as being not as close to governments as other branches of the UN system and there was common concern that as UNDP replaced UNHCR in the region, relations would deteriorate.

In El Salvador, UNHCR's image improved considerably over time as its dialogue with NGOs and grassroots organisations crystallised into positive action. The meeting of representatives of the Salvadoran and Guatemalan uprooted organisations with the High Commissioner for Refugees at the CIREFCA follow-up meeting in New York in 1990 was a significant breakthrough. However, tensions continued in 1994 as NGOs relating to UNHCR over PIR were less happy with the balance in the relationship. UNHCR, the NGOs claimed, tended to equate partnership with NGOs as simply a subcontracting agreement for school construction and the like. The achievements of NGOs over the years highlighted the necessity to include them in all levels policy and planning in recognition of their unique place in Central American society.

UNHCR was yet to address the issue of protection for the internally displaced and support for the non-recognised refugees. These were the groups which probably suffered most throughout the crisis and considerably outnumbered officially recognised refugees. They lived in more marginal conditions, were more difficult to organise and often still suffered direct violence. They received little support compared with recognised refugees, gaining neither aid nor protection from international organisations. The lifeline for the displaced, if one existed, was the national organisations such as the church or NGOs, although continuing physical harassment often limited what could be done. Even when they were allowed to return, they received much less support than returning refugees. Non-recognised refugees without legal documentation were a particularly vulnerable group.

Conclusion

Refugee and displaced populations in Central America, while badly affected, have not all remained victims. Through being effectively organised, many have succeeded in contributing to shaping, and in some cases determining, their own futures. For their part, NGOs have developed an important and legitimate way of networking in the region by sharing experience, disseminating information and lobbying. Throughout the 1980s and into the 1990s, NGOs and their partners established a prominent profile and humanitarian space that facilitated a just resolution of the problems of the uprooted and, perhaps, contributed towards the democratisation of their respective societies.

By 1994, the fighting had stopped in most countries of the region but the underlying causes of conflict were yet to be addressed. The need for fundamental structural change was widely recognised; without this, the manifestations of a broader crisis would continue across the region.

ACRONYMS AND ABBREVIATIONS

ARDIGUA	Association of Dispersed Refugees of Guatemala
ARMIF	Regional Association of NGOs Working on Forced Migrations
CAR	National Repopulation Co-ordination
CEAR	Special Commission for Attention to Repatriates
CIREFCA	International Conference on Refugees, Displaced and Repatriates of Central America
CONDEG	National Council of Displaced People
COORDINACION	Coordination of NGOs and Cooperatives Accompanying the Population Affected by Internal Armed Conflict
CPR	Communities of Population in Resistance
CRIPDES	Christian Committee for the Displaced of El Salvador
EC	European Community
FACS	Fundacion Augusto César Sandino (Augusto César Sandino Foundation)
FMLM	Farabundo Martí Front for National Liberation
GRICAR	International Group to Consult on Returns
ICVA	International Council of Voluntary Agencies
PAC	Civil Defence Patrol
PCs	Permanent Commissions
PIR	Rapid Impact Projects (of UNHCR)
UNHCR	United Nations High Commissioner for Refugees
USAID	United States Agency for International Development

REFERENCES[6]

AVANCSO (1992) *Donde Está El Futuro? Procesos de Reintegracion en comunidades de retornados*, Cuadernos de Investigacion no 8, AVANCSO, Guatemala

AVANCSO-IDESAC (1992) *ONGs, Sociedad Civil y Estado en Guatemala elementos para el debate*, AVANCSO-IDESAC, Guatemala

COINDE and COORDINACION (1992) *Assistance Programmes for the Uprooted Population and Refugee Return in Guatemala*, COINDE and COORDINA-CION, Guatemala City, September

COINDE and COORDINACION, *Reencuentro*, COINDE and COORDINA-CION, Guatemala, nos 1-16

Eguizabal, C, Lewis, D, Minear, L, Sollis, P and Weiss, T G (1993), 'Humanitarian Challenges in Central America: Learning the Lessons of Recent Armed Conflicts', *Occasional Paper no 14*, Thomas J Watson Jr Institute for International Studies, Brown University, Providence, R I, USA

ICVA (1993) 'ICVA Mission to Mexico and Guatemala', *Humanitarian Affairs Series no 3*, ICVA, Geneva

Angel, H M (1992) *Discurso de la Asociacion Regional para Las Migraciones Forzadas*, paper delivered to the second follow-up meeting of CIREFCA, April 1992

Pacheco, G O and Sarti C C (1991a) *Las Migraciones Forzadas en Centroamerica: Una Vision Regional*, San Jose

Pacheco, G O and Sarti C C (1991b) *Plan de Accion Regional* Asociacion Regional de Coordinaciones Nacionales que Trabajan Con Refugiados, Despalzados y Retornados, Nicaragua

Quezada, S A (forthcoming) *International Aid in the Case of Central American Refugees and Displaced Persons*

Schrading, R (1990) *The Repopulation Movement in El Salvador*, The Project Counselling Service for Latin American Refugees, Costa Rica

---

6. Much of the information and analysis in this chapter came from interviews or conversations with the following:
Gabriella Rodriguez, El Productor, Costa Rica; Lorena Martinez, CRIPDES; Gloria Nuñez, Nueva Esperanza; Juan Jose Rodriguez, Fundacion Segundo Montes; Andres Gregori, FASTRAS; Oscar Perez, CORDES; Dimas Vanegas, Diaconía, El Salvador; Representatives of the Permanent Commissions of Refugees; Edgar Cabnal, Rachel Garst and Byron Garoz, COINDE; Carlos Gomez, Marco Tulio Gutierrez, and Adolfo Herrera, Nueva Amanecer; Marcel Arevalo, Coordination of NGOs and Cooperatives; Arturo Echevarría, ARMIF, Guatemala; Gilberto Aguirre, Armando Gutierrez and other members of the directorate of CEPAD; Evaristo Garcia, Edwin Zablah FACS; Nicaragua; Agencies: Martha Thomson, Patti Ardon, Pauline Martin, Oxfam; Gordon Hutchinson, Ana Eugenia Marin and Juanita Camposeco, PCS; Beate Thorensen, ICVA Leila Lima, UNHCR/ONUSAL. I also used documents and publications of ARMIF,COINDE, COORDINACION and The Nicaraguan Federation of NGOs as well as those specifically named in the references.

8

Cambodia:
NGO Cooperation in a Changing Aid Context, 1979–94

Jon Bennett and Charlotte Benson

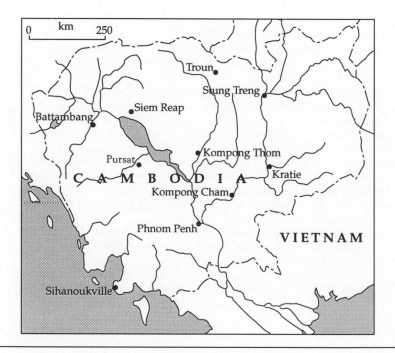

The People: Population: 8.1 million (1990). The Khmers are culturally homogenous, inhabiting an area that extends beyond the present borders of Cambodia. There are also Vietnamese and Chinese minorities.

The Government: From October 1991 until May 1993 a UN-supervised interim government prepared for democratic elections following many years of civil war and Vietnamese incursions. The royalist FUNCINPEC party and the left-wing People's Revolutionary Party (PRP) formed a coalition after the May 1993 elections and drafted a new constitution which created a democratic monarchy with Prince Sihanouk as the reigning King and head of state. The Khmer Rouge continues to provoke violence in the countryside.

Development Aid: US$25 million (1989), though now increasing as international isolation is lifted

Cambodia is today slowly recovering from more than 20 years of warfare and internal upheaval, the scars from which will be felt for many years to come. Most memorable in the catalogue of horrors was 1975–1979 when the country underwent a period of incalculable repression during which time an estimated two million people were either executed or died of starvation, disease and hard labour. The 1980s saw almost a decade of isolation from any external assistance other than that of a handful of eastern bloc countries and a few NGOs. The withdrawal of Vietnamese troops in 1989 gave way to a transitional government and the UN Transitional Administration in Cambodia (UNTAC) monitored a ceasefire and a peaceful election in May 1993.

A large increase in the number of NGOs and the scope of their work after the Paris peace agreement of 1991 required greater coordination and planning for longer-term reconstruction. In anticipation of this development, the Cooperation Committee for Cambodia (CCC) was formed in 1990. It borrowed heavily from the longer established and highly regarded Committee for Coordination to Displaced Persons in Thailand (CCSDPT), the coordination body for NGOs working with displaced persons in Thailand. The CCC faced the familiar challenge of convincing NGOs of the need to move beyond simple information exchange and into policy development and advocacy. Hitherto close relations between NGOs and government became more formalised by 1993. In the aftermath of UNTAC, UN roles were more conventionally assigned and the CCC was well placed to strengthen and encourage greater cooperation among NGOs and with government, the UN and bilateral donors.

BACKGROUND

The exceptional horror of Cambodia in the 1970s has yet to be fully recorded and perhaps will never be entirely understood. A handful of writers have left us with an enduring image of Khmer Rouge rule, that of unprecedented violence and the tragic consequences of ideology out of control (*Pilger, 1986*, for example). It took the world almost a decade to wake up to this horror; it will take the Cambodians a great deal longer to heal the wounds. Against this background of national trauma, the level of cooperation among aid agencies provides pointers to future stability in the fledgling 'civil society' of Cambodia as the country begins to emerge from a long period of darkness.

The politics behind the crisis

Cambodia was one of the 'sideshows' of the Vietnam war. When, after several years of social and political chaos, the Khmer Rouge marched into Phnom Penh in 1975, they were initially greeted as liberators. Very soon, however, the people were subjected to an extreme agrarian programme which forcibly resettled almost the entire population in rural areas, separating families and causing immense upheaval. From 1975 to 1979, the country underwent a period of incalculable repression during which time an estimated two million people were either executed or died of starvation, disease and hard labour (*Shawcross, 1984*). In a bid to rebuild the old Angkorean Empire, part of which straddled the Cambodia–Vietnam border, the Khmer Rouge also launched a number of attacks against Vietnam. Retaliation came in 1978 when Vietnam invaded. In January 1979, Pol Pot was overthrown and replaced by the Vietnamese-backed Heng Samrin government.

In spite of ancient animosity between Cambodia and Vietnam, the new 'liberators' were again welcomed by an exhausted population. The Khmer Rouge retreated to bases along the Thai border from where they conducted guerilla warfare that has yet to be abated. In a turn-around viewed alternately as pragmatic and cynical, the Khmer Rouge were covertly supported by the US and Chinese governments. In 1982, they formed a coalition with two new groups, the Kampuchean People's National Liberation Front (KPNLF) and the National United Front for an Independent, Neutral, Peaceful and Cooperative Cambodia (FUNCINPEC) (Sihanoukists).

This new coalition – the Coalition Government of Democratic Kampuchea (CGDK) – with its headquarters in the refugee camps along the Thai border, was to gain increasing international recognition, though the civil war continued for a further 11 years. Protracted peace negotiations began in 1987, Vietnamese troops withdrew from Cambodia in 1989 and, finally, US military support to the insurgents stopped. A peace agreement was signed in Paris on 23 October 1991. Under this settlement, a Supreme National Council (SNC) under the presidency of Prince Sihanouk, acted as interim government until the 1993 elections. UNTAC was also created to enforce a ceasefire and disarmament, to arrange the repatriation of displaced persons from the border camps, and to arrange free and fair elections that eventually took place in June 1993.

EVOLUTION OF THE ROLE OF NGOS

The Vietnamese occupation of Cambodia in 1979 was viewed by most members of the UN as an invasion by a foreign power and as such was condemned. The UN therefore voted to allow the Khmer Rouge government in exile to maintain its seat at the UN and permitted only the provision of emergency aid to Cambodia. The complexity of political factors on the Thai–Cambodian border and within Cambodia itself was therefore to influence significantly the evolution of the relief effort as well as the longer-term rehabilitation work. (see also Box 8.1)

The Vietnamese-backed Heng Samrin government's basic position was that assistance should only be provided through Phnom Penh. It was opposed to the Khmer Rouge's seat at the UN and was distrustful of the non-Communist donor community. Conversely, the Khmer Rouge considered that since it alone was the UN-recognised Government of Cambodia, all assistance should be delivered via the Thai–Cambodian border.

The history of NGO experience inside Cambodia can be broadly

Box 8.1
THE REFUGEE EXODUS

The Royal Thai government is not a signatory to either the 1951 Convention Relating to the Status of Refugees or the 1967 Protocol on Refugees. Thus persons entering the country are classified as illegal immigrants or displaced persons. The government's response to events on the border from 1979 onwards was primarily motivated by its concern for national security. Although temporary asylum was granted in 1979, all camps were located near the Cambodian border. These were closed camps, strengthening the buffer by leaving the citizens accessible as a support base to the Khmer military factions rather than permitting them to move to a more neutral environment further into Thailand (*Reynell, 1989*). A secondary concern of the government was to maintain conditions in the camps at such a level as to prevent the large-scale attraction of Cambodians to the border. In doing so, they intended to hold down the cost of the relief operation and to maintain it as a clearly international, rather than Thai, effort (*Rabe, 1990*).

The first movement of Cambodians displaced to the Thai border began in 1970–75 when some 34,000 Cambodians, mostly well-educated and relatively affluent, fled to Thailand. A further 20,000 arrived during the Pol Pot years. Between 1970 and 1979, some 470,000 persons also fled southwards to Vietnam. The renewed fighting between the Vietnamese and Khmer Rouge forces in 1979 led to a new movement to the Thai border of Khmer Rouge forces and displaced Cambodians. By the end of 1979, there were up to 700,000 Cambodians gathered at the border.

Thai policy towards the first mass flow of refugees in 1979 was inconsistent, allowing some to stay and sending others back. In April 1979, some 30,000 Cambodians were forced back across the border and many thousands were reportedly killed by mines and Thai gunfire during border skirmishes. Finally, in October 1979, an asylum agreement was reached. A condition, however, was that a border relief operation would also continue to support the resistance movements against the Vietnamese and so provide a buffer between Thailand and Vietnam and Vietnam's (ex-) communist allies.

The border remained open until January 1980, during which time an estimated 180,000 to 200,000 Cambodian asylum seekers crossed the border into UNHCR holding camps. The majority were granted refugee status and were resettled to third countries. Thus the operation split into two – the UNHCR holding centres and the border camps administered over time by the various Cambodian resistance factions. Until 1982, there was continual fighting between the border camps as each of the three military resistance factions fought for control of them and their populations, causing constant movements of camps. This ceased in 1982 when the three main factions formed the CGDK. However, even after this, the camps were subject to dry season offensives from the Vietnamese.

There was thus a constant splitting and reforming of camps in the early 1980s.

Camp security finally stabilised in 1984, but the existing 21 border camps were forced into Thailand in 1985 by a major Vietnamese offensive. The 'civilian' and 'military' populations were then separated by the Thai authorities, with the civilian population placed in nine 'displaced persons' camps (later reduced to six). The military camps also included women and children, though they had virtually no access to them by relief workers.[1]

summarised within three distinct phases since 1979 (*after Charny, 1992 and UNDP, 1990*).

The emergency period 1979–82

From early 1979, the deplorable conditions inside Cambodia, where there had been no foreign aid presence since 1975, began to emerge. A relief effort was launched by the Joint Mission, comprising the International Committee of the Red Cross (ICRC) and the United Nations Children's Fund (UNICEF). Neither agency was constrained by mandate to operate in countries whose governments were not internationally recognised. Later joined by the UN High Commissioner for Refugees (UNHCR), the UN's Food and Agriculture Organisation (FAO) and the World Food Programme (WFP), the Joint Mission provided US$366 million throughout the emergency period, though development assistance was prohibited (*Mysliwiec, 1988*). Some bilateral western assistance was also received, channelled through the multilateral organisations and, to a lesser extent, NGOs. Cambodia also received well over US$450 million assistance from Eastern bloc countries, principally the USSR, during the same period.

Between September 1979 and mid-1981, total NGO expenditure in Cambodia amounted to some US$110 million. About 40 per cent of this was accounted for by the 35-member NGO Consortium led by Oxfam-UK. Oxfam-UK itself pioneered a sea-going route for delivering aid to the country.[2] American church groups also formed a consortium and a number of Catholic church organisations collaborated under Coopération Internationale pour le Développement et la Solidarité (CIDSE). Meanwhile, a few NGOs – such as the American Friends Service Committee (AFSC) and World Vision – chose to act independently of the various consortia. By the end of the emergency period, 13 NGOs were working in the country.

---

1. For a detailed explanation of the different types of camps, see *Benson, 1993*.
2. An extraordinary series of events followed as the Cambodian government played one agency off against another, resulting in Oxfam for a while ending all cooperation with the UN and ICRC and the latter halting assistance through the Thai border areas. Though finally resolved, it remains one of the more interesting episodes in aid history (see, for example, *Shawcross, 1984*, and *Black, 1992*).

Isolation 1982–87

At the beginning of 1982, the UN declared the emergency period over, resulting in the withdrawal of most multilateral agencies and a substantial decline in western assistance. Between 1982 and 1988, bilateral and multilateral organisations provided a total of only US$ 150 million. A trade embargo and a general ban on development aid were also imposed on the country by the UN and the West, although Cambodia continued to receive substantial flows of assistance from the Eastern bloc countries. The OECD estimates that Cambodia received around US$700 million from 1982–88 (*OECD, various dates*).

Meanwhile, atrocities committed by the Khmer Rouge from 1975–79 had come to light. As a consequence of subsequent international pressure, the Khmer Rouge's seat at the UN was taken over in 1982 by the CGDK. The Khmer Rouge, however, controlled Foreign Affairs in the coalition, so effectively were still represented at the UN. Vietnam's occupation of the country encouraged a veto of assistance to the country for seven years.

For their part, NGOs worked in a highly polarized context both in Cambodia and at the border for much of the 1980s. The government formalised its dealings with NGOs and, initially at least, was very suspicious of their activities. For instance, it prevented NGOs from involvement in training and technical assistance to Cambodians for ideological reasons. Programmes demanding substantial material inputs from abroad began to founder as most bilateral support for NGOs was halted. Throughout the isolation period, total NGO funding probably amounted to less than US$60 million. However, as a percentage of western assistance, this was still significant. In fact in per capita terms, total western assistance to Cambodia was a mere US$4 per annum, compared to receipts on the Thai border of some US$327.

Throughout this period some NGOs also began campaigning for an end to the embargo on humanitarian assistance. They realised that only a joint effort by the NGO community would begin to mobilise the public pressure needed to force a change in western governments' attitudes towards the embargo. In 1986, some 20 European, Australian and North American NGOs joined together in an unprecedented international initiative to form the NGO Forum on Kampuchea. The focus of the campaign was to challenge the reasons commonly used for continuing to deny humanitarian and development assistance to Cambodia – namely that:

- the Cambodian government was a puppet government controlled by Vietnam;
- the Vietnamese were imposing extremely harsh laws on Cambodia;
- aid which the country was receiving was not being distributed;

and

- NGOs were not being allowed to monitor and supervise their assistance programmes.

As part of their campaign, in 1988 the NGOs agreed to support a joint publication, *Punishing the Poor* (*Mysliwiec, 1988*), to increase international awareness of the plight of Cambodia. Some NGOs claimed the Forum was uncritically biased in favour of a government with a doubtful human rights record, though several Forum NGOs had, in fact, supported Amnesty International's failed attempts to send a mission to Cambodia.[3]

Given the sheer scale of the requirements of the country, from the post-emergency phase until the late 1980s, NGOs were forced to attempt to fill the void created by the virtual absence of multilateral and bilateral donors, other than Eastern bloc countries, working on large-scale projects. They adopted a role more akin to larger donors, working at national or provincial, rather than district or grassroots, level and fitted into the workings of a centrally-planned economy. The government had little experience in dealing with humanitarian assistance and so was largely unaware of the distinctions between multilateral, bilateral and NGO agencies. This led to NGOs being given an unusual status with occasional direct access to high ranking officials. As government officials became more open from the mid-1980s, this gave NGOs unprecedented influence as the main source of information and 'opinion leaders' of the international community.

Transition and liberalisation after 1988

In December 1987, Prince Norodom Sihanouk and Prime Minister Hun Sen began a period of negotiations that led to the signing of the 'Agreement on a Comprehensive Political Settlement of the Cambodian Conflict' in October 1991. The period leading up to the Paris Agreement was characterised by a liberalisation inside the country which enhanced the overall effectiveness of NGO work. Very little direct bilateral or multilateral aid was expected until after the 1993 elections because of the continued ban on development aid by the UN and western donors until this time. NGOs, therefore, became increasingly important alternative channels through which donors, still reluctant to work directly with government structures, could channel resources.

By 1991, estimated NGO assistance had risen from US$20 million to US$40 million in two years. After the Paris Agreement, some NGOs were almost 100 per cent funded by bilateral donors. However, others,

---

3. In November 1989, Oxfam's public advocacy campaigns on behalf of Cambodia and elsewhere were investigated by the UK Charity Commissioners. The Commissioners concluded that the campaign was conducted 'with too much vigour' and *Punishing the Poor* exceeded the guidelines in its political tone.

particularly the older ones, were less willing to accept such funding, fearing that they would effectively become implementors of bilateral government programmes. Cambodia had, by 1990, stopped receiving large-scale assistance from the Eastern bloc, particularly the USSR. Although western assistance simultaneously increased, it failed to balance the negative impact of the loss of this important source of revenue for Cambodia.

The UNDP fielded the first UN mission to assess Cambodia's infrastructural needs in early 1990, closely followed by international financial institutions and a plethora of new NGOs. In view of the anticipated inflow of substantial new aid, longer serving NGOs began to question their continued provision of financial and technical support of large-scale enterprises, preferring now to redirect assistance to more community-based work. The handover of such programmes to the more traditional international financial institutions was not to take place until after the 1993 elections and even then some NGOs preferred to retain a national perspective to their portfolio of projects.

The post-1988 liberalisation enabled NGOs to place staff in the provinces, to train Cambodian counterparts and to engage in community development activities at village level. By August 1989, some 25 of the total 163 expatriates in Cambodia were based at the provincial level, including 16 Red Cross medical workers. The number of expatriates in the country rose steeply in the next three years to about 500 by 1994.

COORDINATION OF AID ACTIVITIES: CONSORTIA

During much of the 1980s, formal NGO coordination at a national level was not an issue simply because informal contacts were so frequent among the handful of operational agencies based in Phnom Penh. Cambodia's isolation from the West, the government's own lack of experience or capacity to coordinate aid agencies, difficult operating conditions and limited NGO resources relative to the requirements of reconstruction and rehabilitation, provided NGOs with a strong impetus to meet regularly. Sectoral working groups, formed under the leadership of the Joint Mission to coordinate foreign aid and share information, had ceased to function after 1982. They were re-established in 1988.[4] Nevertheless, weekly information meetings continued to be held by western aid agencies, including the multilateral organisations. Relationships between the NGOs and the UN organisations at this time were fairly informal and far closer than is normally the case. Of the UN agencies, only UNICEF, UNHCR and WFP were present in

---

4. The Sectoral Working Groups were re-established under the encouragement of the NGO Forum which was to produce a development planning report (*Cheriyan & Fitzgerald, 1989*).

173

Box 8.2
CCSDPT

The Committee for Coordination of Services to Displaced Persons in Thailand (CCSDPT) was founded in 1975 by a group of 17 NGOs in response both to a perceived need by NGOs to coordinate their activities and to the Royal Thai government's desire to register NGOs working on the borders. A medical sub-committee was formed in early 1976, reflecting the increased involvement of members in this area. In late 1979, following the massive increase in NGO relief activities as a result of the influx of Cambodians across the border, a full-time Executive Secretary position was created. Crucially, though, an effective coordination mechanism was already in place prior to the emergency period and proved invaluable during what was potentially a chaotic period.

The CCSDPT's objectives included facilitating contact between, and organising regular meetings of, member organisations, the Royal Thai government, international organisations, embassies and other interested parties. To help facilitate coordination, it compiled data on displaced persons in Thailand and operated at two levels: (i) technical and legal dealings with the government; (ii) membership activities. Although it had no separate voice, it represented NGOs' joint interests to the government, UN and donors. It also played an important role in maintaining a high profile for refugees and displaced persons in Thailand by organising, with the Ministry of Information, annual conferences in 1977 and 1979.

Thereafter, there was a shift of focus towards the UN Border Relief Operation (UNBRO), an important funder and coordinator of NGO activities from 1982 to 1991. Both government and donors recognised the coordinating role of UNBRO which provided most of the funds for NGO activities. The UNBRO-NGO mechanism ensured careful adherence to medical protocols, training programmes and security procedures and is often cited as one of the best relief operations ever coordinated by the UN. Throughout the 1980s, however, the CCSDPT continued to provide a useful focal point for NGOs and, indeed, for UNBRO.

The CCSDPT was particularly useful as a channel for setting up similar coordination groups elsewhere in the country. For example, Burmese refugees in Thailand are technically 'illegal immigrants' without refugee status. The Royal Thai government did, however, allow 'temporary' humanitarian assistance to be channelled through CCSDPT agencies working under the CCSDPT Burma Sub-Committee. In 1984, the Burmese Border Consortium (BBC) was formed and, due to increased refugee arrivals over the years, this became a permanent structure with a staff of three full-time persons. It had a 1994 membership of six NGOs and provided around 95 per cent of all food and relief items supplied to the border. It could not, however, have been set up without the pre-existence of CCSDPT through which it was registered *(BBC, 1994)*.

Membership of the CCSDPT was open to all NGOs approved by the Royal Thai government to provide services to refugees. Probably at one point in time over 90 per cent of eligible NGOs have been members. Throughout most of the 1980s, its membership was about 50 NGOs. In support of a staff of four persons and related costs, its 1992–93 budget stood at US$78,850 *(CCSDPT, 1993)*. Membership fell to fewer than 20 by mid-1993 with the winding down of the Thai–Cambodian operations. However, activities of the BBC and continuing unrest along the Cambodia border postponed the decision to close the CCSDPT for the time being.

the country until 1990. By the mid-1980s, UNICEF had either direct or indirect cooperative programmes with almost all of the 13 NGOs then working in Cambodia. In addition, it provided logistical and administrative support for a number of NGOs with no permanent base in the country.

As the number of NGOs increased in the late 1980s, however, weekly meetings became unfeasible. As a result, monthly sectoral meetings were set up in 1989, with nine such working groups in operation by August 1990. As with the weekly meetings, these groups also provided a forum for sharing information and problems. In addition, each group had unilateral relations with the relevant government departments, with government representatives increasingly being asked to participate directly in the meetings *(Charny, 1992)*.

An interesting feature of the NGO sector in Cambodia was the variety of consortia developed in both the emergency and rehabilitation phases. The Oxfam-NGO Consortium, which operated from October 1979 to mid-1981, was the largest, being composed of 35 NGOs and providing 40 per cent of the assistance provided by the NGO sector during the emergency period. American church groups also formed a consortium, Agricultural Relief and Rehabilitation in Kampuchea (ARRK), which was disbanded in 1980. Catholic NGOs collaborated under CIDSE, a network that already existed in other countries. CIDSE's first delegation visited Cambodia in 1979 and over the next ten years provided some US$11.3 million of assistance to Cambodia.

Further consortia have operated at various times in Cambodia. These include Partnership for Development in Kampuchia (PADEK), formed in 1982 by a number of NGOs previously associated with the Oxfam–NGO Consortium:

- the Joint Australian NGO Office (JANGOO), operating from 1986 until 1992 and providing administrative and coordinating services to participating NGOs; and
- the Cambodia Canada Development Programme (CCDP), created in 1991 and comprising 16 Canadian NGOs through which Canadian bilateral assistance was channelled.

Several factors appear to have encouraged the formation of consortia:

- They provided reduced administrative costs and greater coordination at a time when resources were limited;
- Staff could be pooled when the government restricted the number of western expatriates in the country;
- The difficult operating conditions and dearth of knowledge of the country discouraged NGOs from setting up programmes immediately on their own.

Raising donations in the NGO's respective countries could be enhanced by joint campaigning.

Particularly in the emergency period, the Heng Samrin government also viewed consortia as a particularly attractive form of NGO assistance. Given the government's suspicion, dealing with a single consortium was preferable to dealing with ten or even 20 NGOs each with their own programme. The sheer size of the Oxfam–NGO Consortium in particular, as measured in spending capacity, its numbers of members and its heterogeneity, increased its credibility and influence with the Cambodian government as well as with the world press (*Charny & Short, 1986*).

With the relaxation of government attitudes towards NGOs and the dramatic increase in the number of NGOs operating in the country from 1988, the motives for member NGOs to maintain such consortia weakened and the majority began to operate independently. The context in which they worked had also changed. There was a perceptible shift in power relations taking place inside and outside government, particularly as a result of the 'opening up' of Cambodian society and the sudden influx of new business, investment and aid. NGOs wrestled with the potential for massive amounts of aid and limited absorptive capacity, the growing inequalities between rural and urban areas and between rich and poor, and the emergence of new social problems related to rapid urbanisation. The 'development' phase had clearly begun and NGOs were likely, in the next few years, to assume a more traditional role *vis-à-vis* government and the larger international financial institutions and development agencies.

With this in mind, many NGOs felt that by 1990 it was time to develop a more formal NGO coordination process at a national level, particularly as the government itself had no coordination body or even a plan for humanitarian aid. In April 1990, NGOs thus founded the Cooperation Committee for Cambodia (CCC).

THE CCC

Foundation and mandate

The CCC was born of an idea shared by a small handful of international NGOs in Phnom Penh. They had watched the remarkable success of the CCSDPT, the NGO coordination body for NGOs working on the Thai border (see Box 8.2). A handful of international NGOs drew up the first charter for the CCC in early 1990 based very closely on the CCSDPT model. This was approved on 12 June 1990 by an initial membership of 25 NGOs. In August, the first five-person/organisation Executive Committee was elected. With initial funding from members, an Executive Secretary (expatriate) was appointed in April 1991 with one Cambodian Assistant. Accreditation to open an office was received in the same month and the Secretariat formally opened offices in May 1991. The first year's expenditure was about US$60,000 with funds received from members, Australian International Development Assistance Bureau (AIDAB) (Australia), Britain's Overseas Development Administration (ODA), Cebemo, Christopher Reynolds Foundation, Diakonia (Sweden) and International Coordination Committee for Development Projects (ICCO). In the second year, the Canada Fund and Novib also contributed.

From the outset the CCC was at pains to stress that it was not a coordination body. Rather, as the 'Cooperation' Committee, its primary role was to facilitate information exchange and liaison between NGOs and the various government and inter-governmental bodies in Cambodia. There already existed several aid coordination mechanisms – the sectoral Working Groups and those organised under UNTAC – for which CCC would provide NGO representation. The CCC secretariat was a focal point for information exchange and, in some cases, provided meeting facilities.

Inevitably, the CCC's first year was taken up with practical issues of setting up an office, registration with the Cambodian Government, recruiting staff and building up regular contact with its founding membership of 25 agencies. By August 1992, the membership had risen to 47 and the international aid community increasingly looked to the CCC as a convenient access point for information exchange. The organisation was beginning to build up a resource centre of its own. In October 1992, it employed an expatriate Resource Librarian (an Australian Overseas Service Bureau volunteer) and a Cambodian counterpart, bringing the Secretariat staff to five persons in total. CCC 'output' included a regular newsletter, *CCC News*, and the publication of a handbook outlining the activities of NGOs and multilateral agencies (*CCC, 1992*).

The CCC Charter and By-Laws (fully revised in January 1994) allowed for a three-fold classification of members: full member, associate member and observer. Full membership was required of those who were non-profit, non-governmental organisations, while others (inter-governmental, multilateral and ICRC, for instance) could be associate members without voting rights but allowed to participate on the various sub-committees of CCC. Observer status was usually for those NGOs whose application was pending. CCC required that its members should have had accreditation with the Cambodian authorities for at least three months prior to becoming a member.

The application procedure – including submitting information on objectives and programme, and a written pledge to uphold the CCC principles – was carefully vetted by the CCC Membership Committee. A two-thirds majority balloted vote of all members at a General Meeting was the final step in application. Interestingly, if a 'no' vote was registered, reasons alluding to eligibility criteria had to be cited in writing by the NGO member raising the objection. Thus personal differences, inter-agency jealousy or competition were kept to a minimum during the process (CCC, 1994).

The CCC structure comprised a General Meeting (monthly), an elected Executive Committee of seven persons and the Secretariat. Three Standing Committees dealing with Secretariat personnel issues, finances and membership applications operated alongside the Executive Committee and comprised at least one member of the Executive. In addition, *ad hoc* sub-committees dealt with particular matters as they arose.[5]

Sectoral meetings

The NGO sectoral meetings continued to run parallel to CCC activities, though not administered by the CCC. Many existed prior to CCC and participants felt that these structures were sufficient for their needs. Within the health sector, for example, Medicam was established. As agencies became more convinced of the need to build dialogue with the Ministry of Health and other related strutures, a Coordinating Committee (CoCom) for health issues was established, chaired by the Ministry of Health with participants from both NGOs and intergovernmental agencies. This committee specifically looked at coordination and planning. The three elected NGO representatives then reported back to the larger group of health agencies at the monthly inter-agency Medicam meeting. Medicam was sufficiently well-supported to consider setting up its own small secretariat in 1994.[6]

The NGOs sectoral meetings in total comprised 35 sub-groups under 11 independent sectors by 1994. Most meetings were held in

---

5. In March 1994, four such sub-committees existed: aid coordination, CCC Charter review, Local Initiative Group (LIG), and security.
6. In March 1994 it was suggested that Medicam's secretariat be placed under the same roof as the CCC, though independent from it.

Phnom Penh with some beginning their own sub-groups in the provinces. A few were also attended by government representatives and hosted by the UN, ICRC and various government ministries. It was at these meetings that day-to-day NGO coordination took place and although the CCC Secretariat had access to the meetings and passed on minutes, it was not itself directly involved as a facilitator of these activities.

Local NGOs

By 1992, there were more than 70 international NGOs registered in Cambodia with expatriates present in most provinces of the country. With the arrival of UNTAC the previous year, resources and trained personnel were very much concentrated in foreign hands.[7] Only at the end of 1990 had it become possible for NGOs to hire Cambodian staff and, with government employees being poorly paid and badly resourced, many were easily tempted to work for international NGOs, even while still officially retaining their government posts.[8] Returning Cambodians from abroad and from the Thai refugee camps took many of the key posts in aid agencies and in the newly burgeoning private sector.

Cambodian NGOs only began emerging after the 'opening up' of government and the consequent freedom of association. The lead up to national elections created the prospect of a Cambodian 'civil society' and the release of funds from foreign donors for local institution building. Inevitably, the capacity of the resulting new batch of local NGOs was poor. As so-called 'local initiative groups' (LIGs), they were assisted by several of the more established NGOs and UN agencies. The US agency, Private Agencies Collaborating Together (PACT) had registered some 103 LIGs by early 1994, 70 of which were also listed in the CCC's directory. A 'postbox' was established within the CCC to encourage contacts between LIGs and the wider aid community.

At this stage in their development, LIGs could not fully utilise the services of the CCC. Only two were members of the CCC by 1994. The breadth of their activities and the common issue of NGO 'definition' was part of the reason for this; LIGs included human rights organisations, student groups, protest/lobby groups, women's associations,

---

7. The first local NGO to be recognised by the government in October 1990 was the Cambodian Development Resource Institute (CDRI), though this was headed by expatriates. KHEMARA was arguably the first wholly Cambodian NGO to be recognised by the government in August 1991. It was initially funded by four international NGOs.

8. NGOs in the early 1990s often had to deal with the dilemma of whether or not to provide 'incentives' for government officials – ie supplement their salaries to encourage them to remain within government service and/or to train people in rural areas. An alternative to financial incentive was provision of transport and materials. Most NGOs endorsed the practice, seeing it as a temporary measure prior to the establishment of a stronger and better resourced government.

etc. More important, almost all LIGs needed very basic training, resources, staff and registration with the government.[9]

The only umbrella organisation for local NGOs was Ponleu Khmer, an organisation claiming 35 'members' (though no clear criteria were available by 1994). It was formed during the drawing up of the Constitution from May–December 1993 as a pressure group to enable social and gender issues to be discussed in the process. By 1994, it wished to evolve into a coordination body for national NGOs. PACT was assisting in the training of Ponleu Khmer staff for this purpose, though by early 1994 it was still very much perceived as a local NGO rather than an umbrella agency. Ponleu Khmer did, however, provide the Cambodian NGO input into the ICORC series of conferences.

Policy directives within the CCC

The integration of local NGOs into national programme planning and coordination was a much debated issue from 1993 onwards, yet the gap in capacities and ambitions between local and international NGOs was so large that it was unlikely that the CCC would be more than an 'access' point for Cambodian organisations for some years yet. Meanwhile, CCC members preoccupied themselves with defining a role for the CCC in strategic NGO planning in the 'new era' they now entered.

Since regional and sectoral coordination was essentially outside the realm of the CCC, its role was perhaps more difficult to define. While most NGOs had worked within sectoral meetings at some point or other, they still had no focal point for discussing wider policy issues. Neither did they have a joint representation towards the government or to the wider inter-governmental planning initiatives underway. Filling these gaps was a natural role for the CCC.[10] For example, the Donor Consultative Group (DCG) chaired by UNTAC included three NGO representatives selected by CCC. NGOs, through the CCC, were also invited to attend the Ministerial Planning Conference on the Rehabilitation and Reconstruction of Cambodia in Tokyo, Japan, 20–22 June, 1992 (*Charny, 1992*). It was here that an ultimately successful lobby was conducted to have the CCC represented at the forthcoming International Committee on the Reconstruction of Cambodia (ICORC) meetings. The ICORC meetings, involving donors, the UN, Cambodian

---

9. UNTAC and UN Development Fund for Women (UNIFEM) were initial funding sources for LIGs, many of which had been formed by foreign returnees concerned with issues of human rights in the lead up to elections. Paradoxically, some LIGs became 'competitors' to government ministries in getting funded for development projects.
10. A survey of 36 NGOs conducted by CCC prior to the August 1992 General Meeting indicated a need to strengthen the representational role of the body. The survey included a questionnaire on performance and expectations NGOs had of the CCC and represented a fairly thorough appraisal of the organisation's performance in the first year (CCC, 1992a).

Government and NGOs took place approximately every six months and were the main macro policy and planning tool for reconstruction and rehabilitation of the country.

By early 1994, CCC membership had risen to 58 full members and seven associates. The Secretariat staff was now nine persons and the projected 1994 budget was US$289,985. In the post-election period, substantial international assistance was likely to be released as socio-economic prospects for Cambodia improved. If they were to become effective partners in the process of building the country in the post-repatriation period, it was necessary for NGOs to develop an overview of trends and begin a collective dialogue on where their resources might best be spent. Large infrastructural programmes and foreign investment – already promised in the post-election euphoria – were unlikely to deal with the urgent needs of people in rural areas; it was here that NGOs could best be utilised.

The 'placement' of NGOs in Cambodia's overall development strategy involved a well-rehearsed argument over what an NGO is and is not. Given the government's previous reliance on international NGOs to assist even with large infrastructural programmes, it was unlikely that NGOs would easily be able to relinquish their somewhat artificial (and, arguably, inappropriate) role in the country. It was also true that some NGOs had neither the experience nor the desire to begin longer term developmental work.

A desire to combine collective NGO experience with longer-term strategic thinking led the CCC to begin looking for a senior Development Analyst to join the Secretariat in 1994 and upgrade the activities, the profile and, consequently, the prestige of the organisation.

CONCLUSION

From the outset, the CCC was characterised by a degree of caution over the extent of its mandate and the ambitions it set itself. Its emphasis was always on information exchange and 'cooperation' rather than coordination. In the interest of maintaining the widest possible consensus, it deferred coordination services to the self-managed sectoral working groups and advocacy issues to entirely separate organisations, such as the NGO Forum on Cambodia (formerly 'Kampuchea'). A strong lobby of CCC members wished to restrict its mandate to that of facilitating exchange of information and to representation on the various national and international aid committees.

Critics of the CCC would point to the familiar inertia of an organisation that sacrificed a leadership role for the lowest common denominator of consensus. Since the NGOs were so diverse, they claimed, the CCC could not be located within a clearly defined homogenous 'community' as such. Characteristic of the CCC's somewhat nervous approach was an organisational structure that invested little authority in the executive. Three standing committees dealt with personnel, fundraising and membership issues. Thus, even internal management of the Secretariat was deferred to voluntary committees already overstretched. One result was that the General Assembly spent a great deal of time debating internal structural issues – membership criteria, the limits of the constitution, staffing levels, salaries and the like – rather than initiating and distilling debate on NGO roles in Cambodia as a whole.

Conversely, the 'first generation' NGOs that had worked in the country during the long and difficult period of international isolation from 1979 to 1988 saw the CCC in a different light. During these years, some 12–14 NGOs with an expatriate staff of about 130 had been working and living in just two hotels in Phnom Penh. Regular contact and close sharing of resources meant that no formal NGO coordination structure was necessary. With only one international flight per week and no international telephone connections, information fed to increasingly influential advocacy groups abroad – in particular the NGO Forum – was sporadic, if comprehensive.

The situation changed dramatically in 1989. The number of expatriates rose to over 500, offices were opened throughout the town and, indeed, in the provinces. Bilateral and multilateral missions began arriving and the specific identity and accumulated knowledge of NGOs was in danger of being lost. The formation of the CCC in 1990 was not only to forestall the loss of continuity, it was also to provide a focus for the promotion of NGOs' views to the changing government and the newly-arrived intergovernmental agencies.

The rapid rise in membership of the CCC was encouraging, though the diversity of opinions and expectations within it curtailed some initial ambitions it may have had. Broadly speaking, sector-specific NGOs, small NGOs with perhaps only one project, and those with more pastoral concerns, were least likely to appreciate CCC's role as a facilitator of strategic planning and advocacy. For them, simple information exchange was the limit of CCC's required role. On the other hand, agencies with an international agenda and interest in furthering their strategic position *vis-a-vis* intergovernmental bodies in Cambodia and elsewhere, increasingly lobbied for CCC's role in this respect. The tension between the two schools of thought – and the resulting emphasis on internal debate – was further heightened by the desire for an inclusive rather than exclusive membership.

The potential stagnation of the CCC was soon recognised. The recruitment of a Development Analyst in 1994 was, in part, a response to this, for here was an opportunity to provide an expert and impartial stimulant to debate within the NGO community. A further crucial issue for the CCC was how rapidly it would be able to assimilate local NGO concerns and whether or not it could become a focus for training and harnessing local capacity. Meanwhile, the continuing – and increasing – presence of international NGOs was taken for granted. So, indeed, was the need for a viable collective NGO structure through which multilateral agencies and government could have a dialogue. The frustrating and often complex interplay between service provision, consensus and democratic representation was not unique to CCC. Neither was the fact that the CCC would have to be invented if it did not already exist.

ACRONYMS AND ABBREVIATIONS

AFSC	American Friends Service Committee
AIDAB	Australian International Development Assistance Bureau
ARRK	Agricultural Relief and Rehabilitation in Kampuchea
BBC	Burmese Border Consortium
CCC	Cooperation Committee for Cambodia
CCDP	Cambodia Canada Development Programme
CCSDPT	Committee for Coordination to Displaced Persons in Thailand
CDRI	Cambodian Development Research Institute
CGDK	Coalition Government of Democratic Kampuchea
CIDSE	Coopération Internationale pour le Développement et la Solidarité
DCG	Donor Consultative Groups
FAO	Food and Agriculture Organisation
FUNCINPEC	National United Front for an Independent, Neutral, Peaceful and Cooperative Cambodia
ICCO	International Coordination Committee for Development Projects
ICORC	International Committee on the Reconstruction of CambodiaICRC International Committee of the Red Cross/Crescent
JANGOO	Joint Australian NGO office
KPNLF	Kampuchean People's National Liberation Front
LIG	Local Initiative Group
ODA	Overseas Development Administration
PACT	Private Agencies Collaborating Together
PADEK	Partnership for Development in Kampuchea
PRP	People's Revolutionary Party
SNC	Supreme National Council
UNBRO	United Nations Border Relief Operations
UNHCR	United Nations High Commissioner for Refugees
UNICEF	United Nations Children's Fund
UNIFEM	United Nations Development Fund for Women
UNTAC	United Nations Transitional Administration in Cambodia
WFP	World Food Programme

REFERENCES

Benson, C (1993) *The Changing Role of NGOs in the Provision of Relief and Rehabilitation Assistance Case Study 2 – Cambodia/Thailand* Working Paper 75, Overseas Development Institute, London

Black, M (1992) *The History of Oxfam, 1942-1992* Oxford University Press, Oxford

BBC (1994) *Burmese Border Consortium: Refugee Relief Programme* BBC, Bangkok

CCC (1992) 'Cambodia – meet the challenge, make the change', *CCC Annual Meeting Minutes* plus 'CCC in Retrospect', results of the survey of CCC activities and List of Members, CCC, Phnom Penh, 4 August

CCC (1994) 'Charter By-Laws (proposed revision)', CCC, Phnom Penh, January 29

CCSDT (1993) *Review of CCSDPT Activities* CCSDPT, Bangkok, March

Charney, J R (1992) 'NGOs and the Rehabilitation and Reconstruction of Cambodia', Report prepared on behalf of the Cooperation Committee for Cambodia, the Advocacy Task Force of the NGO Development Workshop, the NGO Forum on Cambodia and the Japanese NGO Committee on Cambodia, Phnom Penh

Charney, J R and Short, J (1986) 'Voluntary aid inside Cambodia', in Levy, B S and Susott, D C (eds), *Responding to the Cambodian Refugee Crisis* Associated Faculty Press Inc, New York

Cheriyan, K C and Fitzgerald, E V K (1989) 'Development Planning in the State of Cambodia', Report of a Mission Organised by the NGO Forum on Cambodia, Phnom Penh

Mysliwiec, E (1988) *Punishing the Poor: The International Isolation of Kampuchea*, Oxfam-UK, Oxford

OECD (various years) *Development Cooperation Report* OECD, Paris

Pilger, J (1986) *Heroes*, Jonathan Cape Ltd, London

Reynell, J (1989) *Political Pawns: Refugees on the Thai-Kampuchean Border*, Refugee Studies Programme, Oxford

Rabe, P (1990) 'Background' in Standley, L (ed) *Back to a Future? Voluntary Repatriation of Indochinese Refugees and Displaced Persons from Thailand*, Committee for Coordination of Services to Displaced Persons in Thailand (CCSDIT), Bangkok

Shawcross, W (1985) *The Quality of Mercy* André Deutsch, London

UNDP (1990) 'NGO Assistance to Cambodia 1979–1990: Lessons for the United Nations Development System', Report of a UNDP mission to Cambodia, October

Index